FOREIGN POLICY
AND INTERDEPENDENCE
IN GAULLIST FRANCE

*Written under the auspices of
the Center of International Studies
Princeton University*

*A list of other Center publications
appears at the back of the book*

Edward L. Morse

Foreign Policy
and Interdependence
in Gaullist France

PRINCETON UNIVERSITY PRESS

PRINCETON, NEW JERSEY

Copyright © 1973 by Princeton University Press

LCC 72–5391
ISBN 0–691–05209–3

Library of Congress Cataloging
in Publication data will be found
on the last printed page of this book

Publication of this book has been aided
by a grant from The Andrew W. Mellon Foundation

This book has been composed in Electra
Printed in the United States of America
by Princeton University Press

In memory of
PETER V. WOODWARD

CONTENTS

PREFACE

FRENCH foreign policy during the 1960s has received a great deal of attention from both diplomats and scholars. De Gaulle's quest for global preeminence combined with a revitalization of French society made Gaullist politics a favorite subject of political controversy and of scholarly analysis. The sense of drama that enabled de Gaulle to appear to transcend the world in which he acted was frequently captured in the analysis of his foreign policy. Most of the writings on the subject stress particularistic and novel aspects of the external relations of the Fifth Republic. However, the more I studied French foreign policy during the Gaullist period, the more I felt that what was special about France was not what others had called unique. Rather, what has made French foreign policy in the 1960s so fascinating is the way a generalized condition of contemporary foreign policy was brought into sharp focus by the fact that the President of Fifth Republic France was so blatantly anachronistic.

In short, this endeavor to understand and to evaluate recent French foreign policy is one that stresses a universal rather than a particular set of conditions. The dilemmas of recent French foreign policy, especially the contradiction between the impulse to independence and the necessities of interdependence, are presented here as characteristic of the foreign policies of a more general set of states. What are so starkly apparent in Gaullist France are a set of contradictions that are present in the foreign policies of all highly modernized states and a set of dilemmas that seem to have developed from a central paradox of modernization. Objectively, modernization has brought about increased levels of interdependence among societies; subjectively, however, it seems to have tightened the psychological hold of the nation-state over the minds of men. Increasingly, the problems of foreign policy have required political organization at a level beyond that of the nation-state. Decreasingly, the nation-state has been able to serve as an adequate basis for political decision-making; yet nothing seems able to replace it.

The central problem of this study is to reconcile the particular experience of France with a general explanation. The theoretical analysis seems to necessitate a set of investigations beyond the scope of any single study. It bears upon the relations among modernized states as well as on the mechanics of foreign policy in each of them. Even when one looks into the foreign policies of a single state, a wide spectrum of investigations is required, for modernization has affected all three of the major components of foreign policies—their substantive contents, the processes by which they are formulated, and their effectiveness. This problem was resolved by selecting for analysis those aspects of foreign policy in France that are the most salient characteristics of foreign policies in modernized states. It seems that this is the best way to come to grips with the substantive problem that I have found most interesting.

The study is divided in two parts. The first is a theoretical exegesis of the conduct of foreign policy in any highly modernized society. Examples are drawn mainly, but not exclusively, from the French experience, so that the entire section also serves as an introduction to Part II. The second part, a more detailed case study of France during de Gaulle's Presidency, is designed to illustrate in concrete terms the more abstract and generalized theory of foreign policy. Thus, it centers upon several characteristics of French foreign policy that are also general characteristics of foreign policies in all modernized states. These are: (1) the breakdown in the distinction between foreign and domestic affairs; (2) the increased importance of foreign economic policy; (3) dilemmas of domestic control that have resulted from international interdependence; (4) the calling into question of governmental priorities for foreign affairs; and (5) the emergence of crisis management and crisis manipulation as part of the routine procedures of foreign policy control. A chapter is devoted to each of these aspects of French foreign policy in de Gaulle's Presidency.

Each problem is evaluated, as well as described, and explained in terms of the general theory. Too often, there is no touchstone or standard in foreign-policy analysis for formulating policy evaluations. Two factors alleviate this problem. First, the general explanation of foreign policies in modernized states presents a theoretical touchstone that serves as a standard for evaluating French foreign policy. Second, the general trend of politics in France and, especially, the resignation of de Gaulle enabled me to treat the de Gaulle years as a complete unit, one in which articulated objectives can be contrasted with the outcome of events.

Touching upon a host of additional issues, several of which could not be examined in more detail, could not be avoided. The emergence of bureaucratic or group politics in the formulation and execution of foreign policy has become significant in all highly modernized states; however, it was not possible to obtain sufficient data to include an analysis of politics within the Council of Ministers or any other body. Similarly, the growth of international investment and the consequent development of a transnational short-term capital market have restricted the autonomy in foreign and domestic political decision-making in every highly modernized economy, but a general analysis of the way these phenomena have restricted French foreign policy goals could not be included.

I had the great fortune to do the research and writing for this book in a scholarly environment that is remarkably open to innovative ideas. Richard Ullman, Nicholas Wahl, Harold Sprout, and Robert Gilpin were extremely helpful in encouraging me to develop the ideas embodied in it. They, together with Oran Young, Marion J. Levy, Jr., Joe A. Oppenheimer, and Norman Frohlich, were unremitting in both their criticisms and encouragements. Linda K. Morse was, as always, judicious and wise in the support and encouragement she gave me. She offered critical advice, when it mattered, without nudging. Ernst B. Haas, Stanley Hoffmann, Pierre Hassner, Linda Miller, Joseph S. Nye, Jr., and Charles Berry read parts of the manuscript and offered helpful suggestions. Cyril E. Black provided the use of the facilities of the Center of International Studies in carrying out the research and writing. Lewis Bateman and Sanford G. Thatcher of the Princeton University Press offered invaluable advice concerning organization of the book and prevented me from making serious errors. Virginia Anderson and Dorothy Dey were efficient and patient with me in typing the manuscript. I am highly indebted to all of these colleagues and friends. Needless to say, I remain responsible for any errors of fact or judgment that may be found in this study.

Princeton University
December 1972

I

MODERNIZATION
AND INTERNATIONAL POLITICS
A THEORETICAL ANALYSIS

INTRODUCTION

THERE are two basic perspectives that may be invoked for theories about contemporary international relations. One focuses upon the "rules of the game" and attempts to stipulate laws governing the politics between sovereign entities with the hope that these laws are sufficiently generalized to be applicable to a large sampling of international systems, past and present. The other argues that current problems of international politics are so different from those of the past that they must be applicable only to contemporary conditions and derivative from transformational changes in the way semiautonomous political systems adjust their mutually conflicting goals.

The perspective of this study is the latter. It is based on the following assumptions: that the foreign policy of Gaullist France, or of any highly modernized political system, is largely determined by a set of processes, the appearance of which is relatively recent, certainly no older than a century; that these processes did not become generalized to a set of societies until after World War II; that the appearance of these conditions has been and will continue to be destabilizing for the international system as a whole; and that the degree to which the political leadership of any one of these societies can act to maintain its environment is restricted to an extent that may be historically unprecedented. Only by viewing contemporary foreign policy in these terms can an observer or practitioner of international affairs appreciate the profundity of the transformation that has occurred in international politics during the course of this century.

The book is a theoretical case study designed to adduce evidence for the utility of these assumptions and to substantiate the hypotheses stipulated in Part I. The use of the case of Gaullist France for these purposes ought to be the most rigorous test for the hypotheses, since nowhere else in the modern world has the nationalist cause been so baldly articu-

3

lated. The dialectic between the will toward national autonomy and the exigencies of interstate interdependence was a sharp counterpoint in de Gaulle's foreign policy, especially after the termination of the Algerian War in 1962. If any modern industrialized state would contradict the generalizations of this study, it would be the Fifth Republic before de Gaulle's resignation in April 1969. However, it should be a significant confirmation of these generalizations that even France confronted the problems of foreign policy that arise from modernity.

A single theoretical case study will by no means, of course, provide a complete substantiation. But it can be justified on several grounds. First, the case of France is selected from a defined universe: relatively modernized societies where political systems are democratic. This universe is not so large as to weaken the force of the generalizations but covers a sufficient number of cases to make them widely applicable. Furthermore, and as noted above, the case selected is apparently unique, so that it should provide a plausible test of the stipulated hypotheses. A rigorous comparative study that would exhaust all available cases would, in any case, be beyond the organizational scope of a single study or the energies of an individual researcher. Without such inclusion, proof is dependent upon the achievement of a satisfactory level of confidence. It is hoped that this study will provide sufficient confidence in the generalizations to warrant their further examination. There is no doubt that every case within the universe is also characterized by unique traditions and objectives and that they must be compared if the generalizations are to be more fully supported. In the absence of that, confidence in the generalizations must be viewed as a function of the degree to which the case illustrates the more general model and of the internal consistency of the theoretical argument.

The general argument itself may be summarized in the following way.

Both the international and domestic settings in which foreign policies are elaborated and conducted have been transformed by the processes of modernization; these transformations, in turn, have brought about a situation in which foreign policies associated with modernized states differ on virtually all significant dimensions from those associated with non-modernized states.

Internationally, modernization has served to increase the levels and types of interdependencies among the various societies of the world, especially the more modern ones. Domestically, it has fostered greater centralization and a greater priority for domestic rather than external needs—notably, those needs of an economic nature. As a result of these changes, three general conditions have developed. First, the classical distinction between foreign and domestic affairs, which also lay at the heart of Gaullist foreign-policy ideals, has largely dissolved, even though the myths associated with sovereignty and the state have not. Second, the distinction between high policies and low policies has become less important as the latter have assumed an increasingly large role in the fate of citizens of any state.[1] Third, although there have

[1] The distinction between high politics and low politics belongs to the Saint-Simonian tradition of meliorism and was later adopted in the functionalist school of thought on supranational integration. High policies refer to a state's security and defense and has traditionally been conceived as having primary, or higher importance in statecraft. Low policies refer to relations between citizens in different states or to non-security intergovernmental relations and are usually identified with economic transactions.

Areas of low policy were assumed in the Saint-Simonian tradition as amenable to nonpolitical and technical manipulation by experts. When combined with the assumption that the growth and the survival of industrialized societies are dependent upon the international coordination of national politics related to these technical issues, this argument produced a powerful prescription for functional integration. Theorists who argued this position profoundly overestimated both the urgency of the task and the degree to which technical problems could remain out of politics. See Ernst Haas, "Technocracy, Pluralism and the New Europe," in Stephen R. Graubard, ed., *A New Europe* (Boston: American Academy of Arts and Sciences, 1964), pp. 62–88.

Stanley Hoffmann offers another argument on low policies and high

5

been significant developments in the instrumentalities of political control, the actual ability of statesmen to control events either internally or externally has decreased with the growth of interdependence and is likely to continue to decrease in the future.

---

policies in "Obstinate or Obsolete? The Fate of the Nation-State and the Case of Western Europe," *Daedalus*, xcv (1966): 862–915 and in International Regionalism, ed. Joseph S. Nye, Jr. (Boston: Little, Brown, 1968), pp. 177–230. Hoffmann feels that nuclear stalemate has served to reinforce the attributes of the nation-state by stabilizing the structure of postwar international society and that low policies do not generate the spillover expected of them by prophets of international integration. While Hoffmann is quite right that the integrationists overestimated the potential of economic exigencies for creating international integration, his denial of any effect of low policies is itself overstated.

ONE

THE TRANSFORMATION OF
FOREIGN POLICIES

THE notion that modernization has a revolutionary effect on foreign policy is not new. Comte and Spencer, for example, among other optimistic observers of industrialization in the nineteenth century, argued that war was irrational as an instrument of policy in the relations among highly developed economies. Others, including Hobson and Lenin, surveyed industrialization and linked it to the "new imperialism" of the late nineteenth century. They contended that what they understood as modernization would lead inevitably to conflict rather than cooperation among the same types of societies. While experience belies the specific predictions of both groups, it has reinforced their fundamental premise that foreign policy has been radically transformed in societies that have become highly industrialized. The difficulties that these observers found in tracing out the effects of various phases of the modernization process on foreign policy are still puzzling. However, there is evidence that indicates that once societies have reached a phase of high mass consumption or high modernization they confront a set of problems in all phases of foreign policy whose similarity is marked.

The hypothesis that underlies this study is that most of the significant features of the foreign policies of relatively modernized societies are similar and can be derived from the characteristics of modernity. The immediate implication of this hypothesis is that the principal set of determinants of foreign policy can be thought of as relating to domestic social structure rather than to any of the other sets of variables that theorists have suggested.[1] By and large, I have chosen to ignore

[1] These other variable clusters are neatly defined in James N. Rosenau, "Pre-Theories and Theories of Foreign Policy," in *Approaches*

7

these other clusters of variables because I feel that this one is compelling. The others are subsumed by those associated with either social structure in general or modernization in particular, or they can be invoked to explain variations from the model.

The argument of this chapter is divided into three parts. First, the general implications of high levels of modernization for foreign policy are outlined together with a definition of

---

to *Comparative and International Politics,* ed. R. Barry Farrell (Evanston, Ill.: Northwestern University Press, 1966), pp. 27–92. Rosenau suggests five sets of variables as follows: (1) "the idiosyncrasies of the decision-makers who determine and implement the foreign policies of the nation"; (2) "the external behavior of officials that is generated by the roles they occupy and that would be likely to occur irrespective of the idiosyncrasies of the role occupants"; (3) "governmental variables"; (4) "nongovernmental aspects of a society which influence its external behavior"; and (5) "any nonhuman aspects of a society's external environment or any actions occurring abroad that condition or otherwise influence the choices made by its officials" (p. 43).

Although Rosenau suggests that the importance of each cluster is yet to be determined and that all are necessary for a theory, each of these clusters has been used separately as an exclusive approach to the understanding of foreign policy; and each has been applied to the study of French foreign policy.

The first is the "great-man" approach that has been characteristic of some schools of diplomatic history. Writers in this school assume that foreign policy is determined by the great statesmen of an era. The genre that describes this kind of writing is generally biographical. In the case of France, examples are found in Wladyslaw W. Kulski, *De Gaulle and the World; The Foreign Policy of the Fifth French Republic* (Syracuse, N.Y.: Syracuse University Press, 1966); and Alfred Grosser, *French Foreign Policy Under de Gaulle,* trans. Lois Ames Pattison (Boston: Little, Brown, 1965).

The second approach has concentrated on institutional or decision-making foci. See Edgar Furniss, *The Office of the Premier in French Foreign Policy-Making: An Application of Decision-Making Analysis,* Foreign Policy Analysis Series, No. 5 (Princeton, N.J.: Center of International Studies, 1954); or John E. Howard, *Parliament and Foreign Policy in France* (London: Cresset, 1948).

According to the theory underlying the third approach, different

8

the universe of states whose foreign policies fit the model of analysis. The second section consists of an outline of the breakdown of the ideal distinctions between domestic and foreign affairs in Western thought. Finally, the transformations in foreign policy are elaborated with reference to its substantive dimensions, the processes associated with its formulation, and the instruments used to control its external and internal effects.

MODERNIZATION AND FOREIGN POLICY

The implications of modernization for foreign policy can be derived from many of the definitions of modernization that have been formulated. I have chosen to follow Levy's definition because of its power in isolating those societies in which I am interested. It is based on two variables: "the uses of inanimate sources of power and the use of tools to multiply the

---

governmental forms differ in their capacity to handle foreign policy. The comparison of monarchy and democracy in these respects in the case of France is the principal concern of the classical study of the foreign policy of the Third Republic: Joseph Barthélémy, *Démocratie et politique étrangère* (Paris: F. Alcan, 1917).

The fourth approach has been closely identified with geographic determinism. Perhaps the most famous such interpretation of French society is Jules Michelet, *History of France*, I, trans. Walter K. Kelley (London: Chapman and Hall, 1844): pp. 328–30. Also noteworthy are Jules Cambon, "France," in *The Foreign Policy of the Powers*, ed. Hamilton Fish Armstrong (New York: Harper and Bros., 1935), pp. 3ff.; and Jean Gottmann, *Geography of France* (New York: Henry Holt, 1954), pp. 245–56.

Finally, the fifth approach has been typical of systemic analysis, according to which the foreign policy of a society is determined by specified rules of the game that are requisites of survival. An interesting variation on this approach is found in Grosser's study of the Fourth Republic foreign policy. Grosser's thesis is that French foreign policy in the 1950s was imposed by two outside events: the split between communism and anticommunism, and the decolonization issue. See *La Quatrième République et sa politique extérieure* (Paris: Armand Colin, 1961).

9

effect of effort."[2] Each of these variables is conceived as a continuum, so that "a society will be considered more or less modernized to the extent that its members use inanimate sources of power and/or tools to multiply the effects of their efforts."[3] Accordingly, "among the members of relatively modernized societies, uses of inanimate sources of power not only predominate, but they predominate in such a way that it is almost impossible to envisage any considerable departure in the direction of the uses of animate sources of power without the most far-reaching changes of the entire system. The multiplication of effort by application of tools is high and the rate is probably increasing exponentially."[4]

Only a few such societies have existed in history, and they all reached high levels of modernization during the nineteenth or twentieth centuries. Those for which the generalizations in this essay are germane include the fourteen societies identified by Russett and others as "high mass-consumption" societies.[5] To these may be added some societies that are likely to become so characterized in the near future, and that are closely associated with these other societies via specialized international organizations.[6] They are all modern democracies. There is no logical reason to assume, however, that the foreign policies of nondemocratic modernized societies would not also be subsumed by these generalizations.

The general characteristics of modernized societies include

[2] Marion J. Levy, Jr., *Modernization and the Structure of Societies* (Princeton, N.J.: Princeton University Press, 1966), p. 11.

[3] Ibid.   [4] Ibid., p. 85.

[5] See Bruce M. Russett et al., *World Handbook of Political and Social Indicators* (New Haven: Yale University Press, 1964), p. 298. These fourteen societies are the Netherlands, West Germany, France, Denmark, Norway, the United Kingdom, Belgium, New Zealand, Australia, Sweden, Luxemburg, Switzerland, Canada, and the United States.

[6] For example, Italy and Japan are in the group of ten major reserve countries that became identified with the management and reform of the international monetary system in the 1960s.

the growth of knowledge about and control over the physical environment; increased political centralization, accompanied by the growth of specialized bureaucratic organizations and by the politicization of the masses; the production of economic surpluses and wealth generalized over an entire population; urbanization; and the psychological adjustment to change and the fleeting rather than acceptance of the static and permanent.[7]

It is obvious that each of these characteristics carries with it momentous implications for the ways foreign policies are conducted and controlled. For example, the intellectual revolution has expanded the spectrum of feasible goals that statesmen could hope to obtain in domestic or foreign affairs. Therefore it results in an emphasis on technological innovation in modern statecraft both for the purpose of achieving security and for the increased well-being of the members of society. The politicization of a large percentage of the population of modernized societies has infringed upon the reserved domain of state decision-makers in foreign policy and thereby restricted their freedom of action. The growth in political and economic instruments of control at the disposal of modern governments has similarly served to enhance as well as to restrict the decisional domain of governments in foreign and domestic affairs. Perhaps the most momentous product of modernization, however, has been the emergence of the nation-state framework as the most generalized form of political organization. The nation-state has provided the framework through which the physical and human environment has most generally been ordered and through which authority has been rationalized. A consequence of rationalization of authority, according to Huntington, is the "assertion of the external sovereignty of the nation-state against transnational influences and of the internal sovereignty of the national government

[7] These five characteristics are adopted from Cyril E. Black, *The Dynamics of Modernization: A Study in Comparative History* (New York: Harper and Row, 1967), pp. 9–34.

against local and regional powers. It means national integration and the centralization or accumulation of power in recognized national law-making institutions."[8]

The consolidation of the nation-state is also one of the central enigmas of contemporary politics, for modernization has
been accompanied not only by increased national development but also by transnational structures that cannot be subjected to the control of national political bodies individually.
The confrontation of the political structures developed along
the lines of the nation-state with these revolutionary transnational activities is one of the most significant features of contemporary international politics. Modernization has resulted
in the integration of individual societies under the political
control of individual governments. These governments, however, have been confronted by problems that can be solved
with decreasing reliability solely within the terms of the nation-state framework. In other words, modernization has
transformed not only the domestic setting in which foreign
policy is formulated; it has also transformed the general structures of international society by creating higher levels of interdependence among the diverse national societies, especially
among the more highly modernized ones.

The revolution in modernization has also served to bring
about new forms of diplomacy, especially those that lie on the
predominantly cooperative end of the spectrum,[9] including

[8] Samuel P. Huntington, "Political Modernization: America vs.
Europe," *World Politics*, xviii (1966): 378.

[9] Cyril E. Black has commented on this development as follows:
"The organization of peoples into relatively water-tight compartments
of modern states has meant that problems of organization involving
two or more states have had to be solved by other than conventional
political methods. The main method has been the development since
the seventeenth century of principles of international law and diplomacy
that make it possible for modern states to handle certain types of
problems without recourse to violence. A significant aspect of this development has been the establishment of international organizations
for the purpose of handling specialized functions affecting many states—
such as communications—and, more recently, worldwide organizations

the development and transformation of international law and organization and the creation of various types of regional and global integration. These developments, however, are only part of a more fundamental set of phenomena whereby domestic and foreign policies have been merged. The creation of interdependencies among societies, linked by the transnational forces of modernization, has resulted in the externalization of domestic policies and the internalization of foreign policies. The two are linked not only by the general characteristics of interdependence, whereby predominantly domestic policies have recognizable external and domestic effects, but also by the creation of policy instrumentalities that are used for the attainment of both domestic and foreign goals.

There are, of course, many different paths that a society may follow in the development of levels associated with high mass consumption; each path and each step of the way have manifold implications for foreign policies. Likewise, there are many ways in which a state can deal with interdependence. Once high mass consumption levels and high interdependence are reached, however, several common features appear that can be discussed in general terms and that pertain to democratic as well as nondemocratic forms of political institutions. It is to these features as exemplified in French foreign policy that the argument in this chapter is addressed.

Foreign and Domestic Policies

A fundamental distinction between foreign and domestic policies seems to break down under modernization. This distinction is much more characteristic of the foreign policies of governments in the premodern age in both ideal and actual terms than it is of modernized states. In modernized societies, the distinction is difficult to maintain because predominantly political and nonpolitical interactions take place across socie-

---

with a more general political function of preserving the peace" (*Dynamics of Modernization*, p. 16).

13

ties at high levels and because transnational phenomena are so significant that territorial, political, and jurisdictional boundaries are extremely difficult to define. The whole constellation of activities associated with modernization blurs the distinction in such a way that an observer has to analyze carefully any interaction in order to ascertain how it pertains to foreign and domestic affairs.

Foreign policies can be analytically distinguished from domestic policies. Foreign policies are, at a minimum, manifestly oriented to some aspect or objective external to a political system, i.e., to some sphere outside the jurisdiction or control of the polity. Domestic policies, on the contrary, are oriented predominantly to some sphere within the jurisdiction and control of the polity. Foreign policies may be addressed principally to some domestic interest group, but as long as they carry some minimum intention and recognition of an external orientation, they are considered foreign policies.

Classical distinctions between foreign and domestic policies are normatively based and break down once societies become modernized. Two sorts of classical distinctions exist. One, which underlies the Rankean tradition of the primacy of foreign policy, stresses the special significance foreign policies carry that other policies do not. This significance is the concern of foreign policy with the existence and security of a society: "The position of a state in the world depends on the degree of independence it has attained. It is obliged, therefore, to organize all its internal resources for the purpose of self-preservation. This is the supreme law of the state."[10]

The other emphasizes the primacy of domestic over foreign affairs. Unlike the Rankean tradition, associated originally with monarchic foreign policies and later with totalitarian ones, this tradition stresses the pacific nature of policy, its formulation by representative legislative groups, and the control of external events by open rather than closed-door

[10] Leopold von Ranke, "A Dialogue on Politics," in Theodore H. Von Laue, *Leopold Ranke: The Formative Years* (Princeton, N.J.: Princeton University Press, 1950), p. 168.

14

diplomacy. In this sense, democracies were thought to suffer severe disabilities in the conduct of foreign affairs.

In either case, there is an assumption that there exists an essential divorce between foreign and domestic affairs that carries with it in political analysis normative tendencies to stress one of the two while ignoring the other. Foreign policy has been thought to differ from domestic policy in its ends (the national interest as opposed to particular interests), its means (any means that can be invoked to achieve the ends, as opposed to domestically legitimate means), and its target of operation (a decentralized, anarchic milieu over which the state in question maintains little control, as opposed to a centralized domestic order in which the state has a monopoly of the instruments of social order).

Whether the substance of the distinction stresses domestic or foreign affairs, the separation of the two has a strong empirical foundation. Levels of interdependence among all non-modernized societies were generally so low that governments could take independent actions in either domestic or foreign affairs with little likelihood that there would be much spill-over between them. The instruments used to implement either domestic or foreign policies did not significantly alter policies in the other field.

This is not to say that domestic factors did not affect foreign policy at all, nor that the general international setting did not affect the substance of policies. What it does suggest is that the normative distinction between foreign and domestic activities was quite well matched by actual conditions. The degree to which the distinction did not coincide with reality led to debates about ways to improve the efficacy of separating foreign or domestic policies, or about their goals. But the extent of convergence was not so great as to call the distinction into question.

It was precisely this distinction between foreign and domestic affairs as implied by the principle of the primacy of foreign policy that was the key to the ideals of Gaullist foreign policy during the 1960s. The core of French foreign policy consisted in the pronounced contradiction between de Gaulle's desire to reassert French independence and the exigencies of interdependence and interpenetration characterizing France and the other societies of the West.[11] A policy of independence, smacking of traditional diplomacy and the separation of both high and low policies and of foreign and domestic affairs, confronted the contradictory realities of the contemporary modernized world. In the long run, the development of the new diplomacy, the politics of modern democratic society, the adumbration of high policies, and the merging of foreign and domestic affairs also meant that de Gaulle's implementation of his concept of international relations would be aborted.[12]

[11] Independence and sovereignty ought to be distinguished from autonomy. The former terms have psychological and juridical connotations while the latter can be measured objectively. For example, autonomy can be measured along a continuum, at one pole of which is autonomy and the other pole of which is dependence. Any individual or political community is said to be autonomous to the degree that an objective or set of objectives can be attained without the use of instrumentalities under the control of another individual or set of individuals. Autonomy, then, would be defined with reference to a particular goal or set of goals. Complete autonomy with respect to a specified set of goals would mean that any such objectives within the range of human attainment could be reached without recourse to other individuals or to the resources and/or cooperation of the authorities of another political community. Sovereignty, unlike autonomy, is a legal and normative rather than a behavioral concept.

[12] The contrast between ideal policies and actual policies as they are implemented is one of the oldest and most powerful distinctions in political analysis. It is a contrast between norms, or desired outcomes, and actual practices. It was this distinction that served so well in Walter Bagehot, *The English Constitution* (London: Longmans, 1915), where he distinguished the "dignified parts" of the British political system (Monarchy and Lords) with the "efficient parts." He called the latter, or actual structures, the "secret machinery" of British political decision-making.

A careful distinction between actual and ideal structures can be found in Levy, *Modernization of Societies*, pp. 26–30. Levy offers seven propositions about the relationship between ideal and actual structures that are germane to the present discussion.

The similarities between the Rankean position on the state and the Gaullist position cannot be overdrawn. Emphasizing the primacy of foreign policy over domestic policies, de Gaulle's entire conception of France was one based on French international stature. The famous first paragraph of his *Memoirs* is concerned with French international position and the French example for humanity.[13] The Constitution of the Fifth Republic, based on the principles outlined in the Bayeux speech of June 16, 1946, is one that was designed specifically with regard to foreign affairs. It was intended to prevent the recurrence of the situation that arose in June 1940 with the collapse of the Third Republic. The Constitution had to be one that recognized both the "rivalry of the parties in our country" and "the present state of the world" with its "opposed ideologies, behind which lurk the powerful states that surround us [and which] do not cease to inject in our own political struggle an element of passionate controversy."[14] Given the anarchic state of the world, France, for de Gaulle, needed a primacy of foreign over domestic affairs.

If the primacy of foreign policy was required by the state of international anarchy, it was also prescribed in de Gaulle's view by the requisites of greatness. The *telos* of France, as de Gaulle understood it, could be realized only if France were in the front-rank of states. Without the material resources for achieving first-rank status, de Gaulle felt that France could achieve stature only by being a mediator between any two concentric circles of conflict. Thus, de Gaulle's designs for the role of France consisted of a series of diplomatic triads, each of which centered on France. French political analyst Hassner has said:

> In her anti-American undertaking, France was conceived to be in competition with the United States in serving as

[13] See *The Complete War Memoirs of Charles de Gaulle*, trans. Jonathan Griffin and Richard Howard (New York: Simon and Schuster, 1964), p. 3 and pp. 716–70.

[14] Roy C. Macridis, ed., *De Gaulle: Implacable Ally* (New York: Harper and Row, 1966), p. 41.

the interlocutor of Germany and of Russia. In her conception of a desirable international balance, she wished
to serve as intermediary and arbitrator between Russia and
Germany in Europe and between Russia and the United
States in the world.[15]

And the position of arbitrator required complete independence and freedom of movement.[16]

Thus, independence was necessary for the fulfillment of
France's role. At the same time, the goal of independence was
supported by the Gaullist tactics of surprise, the use of negative policies to deny other states the achievement of their
goals, the manipulation of illusions that appeared to enhance
French power, the articulation of ambitious policies, the fostering of nationalism, and the consummate use of ambiguity
that permitted flexibility both at home and abroad.

The goal of independence and the instrument of the
primacy of foreign policy had similar corollaries in the separation of foreign and domestic affairs. Independence at the
national level was paralleled therefore by the independence of
the President from the turmoils of domestic politics as well
as by the ability of the President to mobilize the domestic
sphere for purposes of foreign policy.[17] Thus the constitutional arrangements of the Fifth Republic give the French President exceptional powers to control foreign affairs and to isolate foreign affairs from the domestic political situation.[18] In
fact, the 1958 Constitution stands as an exception to other

[15] Pierre Hassner, "La France aux Mains libres!" *Preuves*, No. 204
(February 1968), p. 55. This translation and subsequent ones unless
otherwise noted are mine.

[16] The general political initiatives for independence in ten years
of Gaullism are summarized in Paul Balta, "Dix Ans de politique
étrangère," *Revue de défense nationale*, xxiv (1968): 813–35.

[17] For a study of the Fifth Republic's Constitution and its doc-
trinal sources, see A. Nicholas Wahl, "The French Constitution of 1958
II: The Initial Draft and its Origins," *American Political Science
Review*, liii (1959): 358–82.

[18] See J. Chatelain, *La Nouvelle Constitution et le régime politique
de la France* (Paris: Berger-Levrault, 1959).

democratic constitutions drawn up during the past two centuries in that it "diminished parliamentary supervision [of foreign affairs] through the limitation of 'legislative' power."[19] It was the only democratic constitution written after World War II to "vest the supreme authority to conduct foreign relations in the Head of State again."[20] Articles 14, 15, 20, 21, and 49 defined the powers of the President and the advisory capacity of both the Prime Minister and the Foreign Affairs Minister with regard to foreign affairs. These powers were further enlarged by Article 5, declaring the President "protector of the independence of the nation," and by Article 16, giving him emergency powers whenever the independence of the nation is in danger.

The constitutional order of the Fifth Republic, with its emphasis on the ability of a President to conduct an independent foreign policy, falls into a hoary tradition in French political history known as the administrative tradition or, more precisely, the monarchic tradition of foreign policy. According to one interpretation of French history,

> there has developed . . . a coexistence of two primitive patterns of politics, the state-minded administrative pattern and the individual-oriented representative pattern. Unintegrated and unreformed, they remain competitive and mutually hostile because they are supported by hostile groups in society. . . . In brief, the principle of mixed government has not been realized in modern France.[21]

The primacy of foreign policy can only occur in the state-minded administrative tradition of a political order that has hierarchically defined the interests of the state, and is a com-

[19] Frans A. M. Alting von Geusau, *European Organizations and Foreign Relations of States: A Comparative Analysis of Decision-Making* (Leiden: A. W. Sythoff, 1964), p. 52.

[20] Ibid., p. 64.

[21] A. Nicholas Wahl, "The French Political System," in *Patterns of Government*, ed. Samuel Beer and Adam Ulam, 2d ed. (New York: Random House, 1962), p. 279. Also see Pierre Avril, *Politics in France*, trans. John Ross (Baltimore: Penguin Books, 1969), pp. 110ff.

plete divergence from the preceding representative tradition that was institutionalized in the Constitution of the Fourth Republic.

The ideal structures of French foreign policy during the 1960s thus represent the coincidence of the re-creation of the administrative tradition in French politics with de Gaulle's personal emphasis on a doctrine of political leadership based on maneuverability in politics just as in war.[22] An independent foreign policy required the freedom of action of the head of state, who would be able to take advantage of changes at the international level without the restraint imposed by domestic politics.

In developing a foreign-policy ideal, however, de Gaulle realized that under modernized conditions foreign and domestic affairs cannot be readily isolated. Given the primacy of foreign policy in his political thought, he concluded that all affairs of state, both domestic and foreign, had to be brought under his direction, so that the national interests abroad could be most effectively served. In ending the Algerian War in 1962, in taking advantage of the Sino-Soviet split and U.S. involvement in Vietnam, and in withdrawing from the military command of the North Atlantic Treaty Organization (NATO) in 1966, de Gaulle pursued a general policy of independence and neutrality. He clothed French foreign policy with a veil of illusion and hoped it would suggest the implementation of his highly normative vision of the place of France in the world. He thought he was creating a situation

[22] For a brilliant interpretation of the political elements in de Gaulle's doctrine of warfare, see Jean Lacouture, *De Gaulle*, trans. Francis K. Price, 2d ed. (New York: New American Library, 1968), pp. 47–87; and Lacouture's interpretation of C. de Gaulle, *The Edge of the Sword*, trans. Gerard Hopkins (New York: Criterion, 1960) and *Army of the Future*, trans. F. L. Dash (London: Hutchinson, 1940). These early books of de Gaulle emphasize the importance of morale and the regeneration of national *élan vital* as a basis of effective foreign policy. These concerns were central to Gaullist political thought throughout the General's career.

to which the great majority of Frenchmen would give passive if not active approval.

The whole of French foreign policy in the late 1960s as articulated by de Gaulle, together with the domestic programs incorporated to modernize the French economy for external objectives, the change of the planning process into a medium for achieving foreign goals, and the invoking of Article 38 of the Constitution after the election of 1967,[23] can be understood as preparation for a final phase of Gaullism. Fearing that domestic interest groups in their selfish private concerns would pursue particularistic policies that were contrary to the national interest as he perceived it, de Gaulle tried to mobilize domestic resources for external ends and to direct external policies in such a way as to assure their continuity after he completed his tenure as President. The development of this dual theme of French foreign policy in the late 1960s assumed an accelerated momentum after the presidential elections of December 1965. Assured of seven more years as President, de Gaulle then began to fulfill the *telos* of the Fifth Republic as he perceived it.

The failure of de Gaulle to achieve his foreign policy objectives was signaled by the social and economic crisis of 1968, the renewal of French cooperation in monetary and security affairs with other states of the West, and his own resignation in 1969, and should not have been difficult to predict, given the forms of interdependence between France and these other states, and the illusion of independence and autonomy interdependence gave. Similarly, the breakdown in

---

[23] The external aspects of these domestic programs were spelled out in de Gaulle's twelfth and fifteenth press conferences. In the twelfth press conference of September 9, 1965, he spoke of the Fifth Plan as a means of creating an independent economy suited for competition abroad. In the fifteenth press conference, he defended his use of special powers by invoking Article 38. See *Major Addresses, Statements and Press Conferences of General Charles de Gaulle, March 17, 1964–May 16, 1967* (New York: Ambassade de France, Service de Presse et d'Information, 1968), pp. 92–94, 173–76.

the ideal Gaullist view of the separation of foreign and domestic affairs should have been understood as representing a general foreign-policy failure, since de Gaulle found it more and more necessary to get involved in domestic affairs and to mobilize the domestic system in order to serve external objectives.

Regardless of how the distinction is made, the separation of foreign and domestic affairs and the primacy of foreign policy apparently breaks down once societies become relatively modernized. France was such a society by the mid-1960s. This does not mean, as Friedrich has suggested, that "foreign and domestic policy in developed Western systems constitutes today a seamless web."[24] Distinctions along the analytic lines, which were suggested above, still obtain, and governments still formulate foreign policies with a predominant external or internal orientation. But foreign and other policies formulated under modern conditions affect each other in ways that are not salient in nonmodernized or pre-modernized societies and that derive from both the domestic and international interdependence associated with modernization as well as from the increased scope of governmental activities under modern conditions. Before the Western societies became highly modernized, for example, the major part of government expenditures was devoted to three functions: defense, war debts (the cost of past wars), and governmental administration. Foreign affairs, in short, was the central concern of premodern governments. As the role of government in the economy and in domestic social life increases, concern for foreign affairs must decrease relative to the concern for domestic affairs. In addition, growing international interdependence means that domestic and foreign policies have more significant internal and external consequences, which may or may not be recognized, intended, or foreseen, and which become undesirable as was the case in the allocation of resources.

[24] Carl J. Friedrich, "International Politics and Foreign Policy in Developed (Western) Societies," in Farrell, *Approaches to Comparative and International Politics*, p. 97.

The Gaullist regime placed emphasis on conspicuous allocations of resources for external purposes, on nuclear weaponry and delivery systems, and on aid to former dependencies. The extreme visibility of these allocations served to increase domestic demands for welfare benefits and domestic services by creating the impression that those resources could be transferred to domestic ends.[25] The visibility of these symbols of grandeur is at least partially a function of modern communications networks and the increased levels of domestic or internal interdependence. Similarly, the goal of transforming the international monetary system and the presence of France in that system resulted in an emphasis on favorable balance of trade and an increase in the stockpiling of gold. A consequence of French international monetary policy and a requisite of it were the restraint of domestic economic growth and the maintenance of economic stability at home both to keep prices and wages at artificially low levels. At the same time, domestic growth is needed both for modernizing the economy so that an international position can be maintained and for satisfying increased domestic demands for greater wealth.

The growth of international interdependence and the transformation of domestic structures not only increase the likelihood of undesirable policy consequences but also serve to externalize domestic policies and internalize foreign policies;[26] that is, the internal aspects of predominantly externally oriented policies and the external aspects of predominantly internally oriented policies have become more significant. Domestic reforms, economic allocations, and external policies

[25] This was true even in the early stages of the development of a striking force. See the criticisms leveled by Raymond Aron, *The Great Debate*, trans. Ernst Pawel (Garden City, N.Y.: Doubleday, 1965), pp. 100–44, and in the party platforms of the socialists and independents in 1965 and 1967.

[26] Stanley Hoffmann has called this "internalized world politics," which, however, he feels comes not so much from interdependence as from the transformation of "policy stakes" with the impact of nuclear weapons. See *Gulliver's Troubles, or the Setting of American Foreign Policy* (New York: McGraw-Hill, 1968), p. 57.

are inextricable parts of one another. They are linked not
only by the externalities they generate (i.e., their unintended
consequences) but also by the fact that the instrumentalities
invoked to implement either sort of policy are frequently the
same and often lead to contradictory results, as is obvious in
the conflicting impulses toward domestic economic growth
and monetary stability discussed above. Such contradictions
become intractable insofar as economic and social policies,
which are the low policies, have become more significant relative to the traditional high-policy areas of defense and security under relatively modern conditions.

The linkages between domestic and foreign policies constitute the basic characteristic of the breakdown in the distinction between foreign and domestic affairs in the modernized,
interdependent international system. This proposition does
not imply that foreign and domestic policies are indistinguish-
able; for with regard to articulated goals and problems of
implementation, they remain separate. Rather, it suggests
ways that foreign policies are transformed by the processes
of modernization and the development of high levels of interdependence. These processes have put an end to the normative distinctions asserting the primacy of one over the other
and overshadow the empirical distinction according to which
foreign policies vary in type with the political institutions
through which they are formulated.

THE DYNAMICS OF FOREIGN POLICIES UNDER
MODERNIZED CONDITIONS

Modern governments devise foreign policies that cluster in
similar patterns and, like other policies, can be anlayzed in
terms of three basic dimensions.[27]

[27] For a general discussion of these dimensions coupled with an
analysis of the literature concerned with the examination of public
policies, see Austin Ranney, "The Study of Policy Content: A Framework for Choice," in *Political Science and Public Policy*, ed. A. Ranney (Chicago: Markham Public, 1968), pp. 3–21.

First, all policies have some content or substance, including the target toward which they are directed and the aspects of economic, political, or social life they stress as well as a set of instrumentalities used to attain them.[28]

Second, all policies are products of a policy process, the means by which leadership ultimately chooses one set of policy contents from many possible sets.

Finally, policies include an evaluative dimension usually called policy outcomes. Outcomes differ from content or output in that the latter have goals that are manifest, whereas outcomes are the consequences of policies and may or may not be intended or recognized by the authorities who formulate them.

Each of these three dimensions of foreign policies—the substantive, procedural, and evaluative—is transformed under the impact of modernization. This transformation has been all the more glaring inasmuch as the political institutions of the state have remained the basic structures through which foreign policies are articulated and implemented, although these structures have been substantively transformed themselves.

CONTENT OF FOREIGN POLICY

The Transformation of Policy Objectives

Preoccupation with high policies and traditional foreign-policy objectives and instrumentalities has drawn the attention of scholars away from the changes in policy goals that have accompanied modernization, and specifically from the increased salience of low policies and the separation of goals of power and goals of plenty.

---

[28] In the terminology of political systems analysis, policy contents are called outputs as opposed to outcomes, or results of policies. Even here, however, there is little analysis of outputs themselves, but a great deal of discussion of the "feedback" relationship between outputs and "demands" and "support." See David Easton, A *Systems Analysis of Political Life* (New York: John Wiley, 1965), pp. 343–63.

Most general discussions of foreign-policy objectives focus on the goals of high policies, which in the past were generally conceived as ultimate ends, and were transcendental. The classical goals of statecraft that Wolfers has defined as goals of self-extension or goals of self-preservation are transcendental. They describe the policies known as imperialism, security, prestige, and the ideal of postulated relationship between the state and the international system.[29] Primarily, the ideal goal of Gaullism was transcendental and was identified with a certain stature in the international system, or a fixed set of role premises. In this sense, Gaullist goals were typically transcendental.

Preoccupation with transcendental goals manifests itself in certain preferred instrumentalities.[30] Thus, discussions of high policies are usually oriented toward the military dimensions of statecraft. When these discussions pertain to relatively modernized states, they tend to center on technological innovations and nuclear weapons systems. This is done under the assumption that *plus ça change, plus c'est la même chose*, that neither military nor economic interdependence has grown in recent years, or that it has even diminished considerably.[31] In general, it is assumed that the development of

[29] Arnold Wolfers, *Discord and Collaboration: Essays on International Politics* (Baltimore: The Johns Hopkins Press, 1962), pp. 81–102. Wolfers adds a third category which fits a logical but not an empirical gap: self-abnegation. For a criticism of Wolfers' categories, see Ronald J. Yalem, "The 'Theory of Ends' of Arnold Wolfers," *Journal of Conflict Resolution*, IV (1960): 421–25.

[30] I do not wish to get involved in the ancient conundrum regarding means-ends relationships. In general, I take the position that since all ends are also means, save ultimate ends, the empirical goals described here pertain in a general way to means.

[31] The Gaullist argument, more persuasively stated in Pierre Gallois, *The Balance of Terror: Strategy for the Nuclear Age*, trans. Richard Howard (Boston: Houghton Mifflin Co., 1963) is also the argument in Robert E. Osgood and Robert W. Tucker, *Force, Order and Justice* (Baltimore: The Johns Hopkins Press, 1967). "The fashionable theme of state interdependence today often confuses fact with

nuclear weapons has a double, crosscutting effect. On the one hand, such weapons tend to result in the demise of the territorial state as a unit capable of providing defense and security by creating the first truly global international system linked together by the possibility of unacceptable levels of human destruction.[32] On the other hand, nuclear weapons are said to reaffirm the viability of the nation-state as a political unit, by providing its absolute defense by means of deterrence. Hoffmann has argued the following:

What tends to perpetuate the nation-states decisively in a system whose universality seems to sharpen rather than shrink their diversity is the new set of conditions that govern and restrict the rule of force: Damocles' sword has become a boomerang, the ideological legitimacy of the nation-state is protected by the relative and forced tameness of the world jungle.[33]

---

norm, reality with aspiration. And even when it avoids this confusion, it draws too optimistic conclusions from interdependence" (p. 325). Osgood and Tucker argue that interdependence has decreased in both economic and military terms since 1914. While they seem to me to be correct in indicating that increased interdependence would not lead to optimistic conclusions, I feel that they are quite wrong on the empirical question regarding the level of interdependence.

[32] This thesis, popularized by John H. Herz in "The Rise and Demise of the Territorial State," *World Politics*, ix (1957): 473–93, has been revised in his "The Territorial State Revisited: Reflections on the Future of the Nation-State," *Polity*, i (1968): 12–34. Herz's error was not in first assuming and then denying that territoriality ceased to be part of the traditional state entity. Rather, it was assuming that territory was the most fundamental basis of the state. Indeed, territory, as he now argues, has not lost its original function. Rather, the nonterritorial boundaries of the state, especially the barriers to communication, have been overcome by the transnational structures of modernization.

[33] Stanley Hoffmann, "Obstinate or Obsolete? The Fate of the Nation-State and the Case of Western Europe," in *Daedalus*, xcv (1966): 865; and in *International Regionalism*, ed. Joseph S. Nye, Jr. (Boston: Little, Brown, 1968), p. 181.

Whichever is the case—and, obviously, both aspects are relevant[34]—the possession of nuclear weapons is only one dimension of statecraft of modern states, albeit the most elucidated one. There is, therefore, great danger of error in selecting only that dimension for the purpose of examining the transformation of objectives. It is not only because nuclear proliferation has been rather slow that this study does not focus on it as the basis of foreign policies in modernized states but also because the costs of maintaining viable deterrence systems, even for the superwealthy, have been part of the increased salience of low policies.

Returning to the descriptive level, the most significant changes in foreign policy goals accompanying modernization come at two levels. In the first place, concerning transcendental goals, the classical goals of power and security have been expanded when not superseded by goals of wealth and welfare. Transcendental goals always have some empirical referent with which they are partially, but never wholly, identified, and what is interesting about these empirical referents is that "they change; new ones are created; old ones pass out of existence; and their relations . . . are shuffled."[35]

Though the transformation of policy goals that accompanied modernization is quite striking with reference to the ideal identification of power with territory and population, it is less apparent when power is identified with wealth, as it was in mercantilist doctrine, which underlies classical notions

---

[34] A highly balanced analysis of both schools of thought can be found in Pierre Hassner, "The Nation State in the Nuclear Age," *Survey*, No. 67 (1968), pp. 3–27. Hassner concludes that "nuclear weapons are the most powerful factor in favour of the twin nightmares of a tyrannical and of an anarchical world; by the same token, they are the most powerful incentive toward attempting to build a more tolerate and responsible one, in which nation-states would learn that cooperation is the pre-condition of independence and self-limitation the pre-condition of power" (p. 27).

[35] Marion J. Levy, Jr., "Rapid Social Change and Some Implications for Modernization," *International Conference on the Problems of Modernization in Asia, June 28–July 7, 1965, Report* (Seoul, Korea: Asiatic Research Center, 1965), p. 657.

of power politics.[36] The pursuit of both was thought to involve zero-sum conditions. Power, like wealth, was thought to be a universal constant. One state's gain meant another state's loss. Actual transformations associated with modernization and involving both domestic economic growth and international interdependence have changed these notions as well. The old ideals of diplomacy and the traditional sorts of goals depended on conditions that have radically changed but that, as Knorr has argued, "persisted throughout the nineteenth and the first part of the twentieth century."[37] These conditions, then, changed with rapid domestic economic growth, with the development of economic and other international interdependencies, and with the politicization of large groups in mass societies that were making increased demands upon governments.

Gaullist foreign policy, which was, in part, based on a position of weakness, sought to re-create the zero-sum conditions of mercantilism so that French power could be increased as the power of other states, principally the United States, diminished. Since the rules of the game had changed, the Gaullist efforts could have only short-term effect. Even here, the effect was partially a mirage in that de Gaulle's international monetary position was articulated at a time when the international monetary system was undergoing crisis (see Chapter 5).

Rapid domestic economic growth, one of the prime indices of modernization, has a profound effect on both the relative priority of domestic and foreign goals, and the substance of each. Once economic growth sets in as a continuous dynamic process, the value of accretions of territory and population dwindles and the "domestic savings and investment and the advancement of education, science and technology are [seen

[36] See Jacob Viner, "Power versus Plenty as Objectives of Foreign Policy in the Seventeenth and Eighteenth Centuries," *World Politics*, I (1948): 1–29.

[37] Klaus Knorr, *On the Uses of Military Power in the Nuclear Age* (Princeton, N.J.: Princeton University Press, 1966), p. 23.

as] the most profitable means and the most secure avenues to the attainment of wealth and welfare."[38] The logic of economic growth, in short, turns men's minds away from the external goals associated with the ruling groups of early modern Europe and toward the furthering of national wealth by domestic means and under conditions of peace.[39]

Domestic economic growth offers only a partial explanation of the transformation of foreign policy goals described above. In addition, the salience of low policies and the replacement of conflictual, zero-sum behavior with cooperative strategies of foreign policies are the result of the transnational character of the international system and the interdependencies that have developed among modernized states. Low policies, in this sense, derive from the interactions of citizens in various states and from the actions of governments in the interests of their citizens or their responses to private group behavior in order to assure general stability or the achievement of other goals. These other goals are themselves undermined by the scope of nongovernmental transnational and international interchanges, and may also be predominantly domestic and pertain to welfare or social services.

Another aspect of the increased prominence of low policies involves the interests of governments in building new transnational structures in order to achieve both international and domestic goals. For example, one of the motivations for creating European Economic Community (EEC, Common Market) was the expectation that it would bring increased wealth to the citizens of each member-state as a result of

[38] Ibid., p. 22.

[39] Recent economic thought on the relationship between war and economic growth falls into a great tradition of non-Marxist economic-political theory. For a history of these theories, see Edmund Silberner, *La Guerre et la paix dans l'histoire des doctrines économiques* (Paris: Sirey, 1957). Most of these theories are unsubstantiated. For another, briefer, review see George Modelski, "Agraria and Industria: Two Models of the International System," in *The International System*, ed. Klaus Knorr and Sidney Verba (Princeton, N.J.: Princeton University Press, 1961), pp. 118–19.

increased levels of trade. Thus, a principal characteristic of foreign policies under modernized conditions is that they seek cooperation rather than conflict, and conflictual or political activities take place within the context of predominantly cooperative arrangements. Plays for power or position among modernized states occur in the nonzero-sum worlds of the International Monetary Fund (IMF) and NATO rather than in predominantly conflictual arenas.

The low policies, in short, have become central to international politics among the modernized states and involve the building up of international collective goods in defense and NATO, and in international wealth-and-welfare organizations such as the General Agreement on Tariffs and Trade (GATT) and the EEC. It is within the parameters set by the need for cooperation that interplays of power and position can occur.

The collectivization of objectives in such matters as monetary and trade policies, which assume increased importance along with domestic welfare, has also set severe restrictions upon the traditional objective of independence. Since the modernized world is a highly interdependent one, both because of the existence of transnational politics and other phenomena in communications and trade, and because of policies intentionally fostered by governments that increase interdependence, the ideal view of independence has been challenged. No amount of political will can re-create a world where independence can be obtained, except at costs that no government is willing to incur. This was even more true for Gaullist France than for other modernized societies, given the primacy of national autonomy in its foreign policy objectives.

Two of the chief characteristics of foreign policies conducted under modernized conditions are their predominantly cooperative rather than conflictual nature, and the change in goals from power and position to wealth and welfare—or, at least, the addition of these new goals to the more classical ones. Both factors are accompanied by the loss of autonomy of any society in international affairs.

31

INCREASED DOMESTIC DEMANDS AND THE
ALLOCATION OF RESOURCES

It is a paradox at the heart of foreign policies in all modernized societies that increased demands on governments have resulted in a short-run problem of resource allocation, so that predominantly external goals have decreased in relative priority to predominantly internal goals. At the same time, however, increased introspection has been countered by the increased sensitivity of domestic conditions to international events as a result of international interdependence and increases in international activities taken on by the citizens of all modernized societies.

One of the distinctive features of all modernized governments, democratic and authoritarian alike, is their multifunctionality. In both ideal and actual terms, they are not merely regulative agencies in a "night-watchman" state, but are and are seen as creators and redistributors of wealth. Increasing demands on governments have helped create the modern welfare state brought about by increased politicization of citizens. A government is confronted with the "dilemma of rising demands and insufficient resources"[40] when its domestic demands are greater than the resources available to meet them, and when, at the same time, it must maintain even existing levels of commitments abroad. The demands may arise from the politicized poor who want a greater share in economic prosperity, the military who desire new weapons systems, and the government who wish to maintain public order in societies increasingly sensitive to labor and minority group disruption, etc., and are added to the "rising cost and widening scope of activities required to keep mature urban societies viable."[41] One inexorable result of these increased demands on governments is the curtailment of external commitments; another is the decreased relative priority of external goals, and both constitute an added dimension to the costs of independence.

[40] Harold and Margaret Sprout, "The Dilemma of Rising Demands and Insufficient Resources," World Politics, xx (1968): 660–93.
[41] Ibid., p. 685.

Much of the debate over the French *force de frappe* during the 1960s was specifically cast in terms of a "guns or butter" issue where there was a clear economic case to be made against the expenditure of funds on the nuclear striking force.[42] Aside from political and strategic arguments against the *force de frappe*, there were economic arguments based, on the one hand, on allocations within the armed forces, where there was fear of offsetting the balance between conventional and nuclear forces,[43] and, on the other hand, on general resource allocations, where there was a tension between resources destined for social services (social security, pensions, etc.) and those for a nuclear force.

The latter is especially the case as one looks at the leftist criticisms of the *force de frappe*. It was not just the general level of resources allocated to defense that was in question. The proportion of expenditure actually declined from 5.6 percent of the GNP and 28 percent of the budget in 1961 to 4.4 percent and 20 percent respectively in 1967. Rather, it became a question of whether a society the size of France could afford to allow 10 percent of its scientific manpower, 60 percent of its electronics industry, and 70 percent of its aerospace industry to be devoted to a nuclear striking force.[44] It is not the nuclear force that was directly called into question, but the policy of independence for which international military cooperation is based on a pre-1945 notion of defense. Modern weapons technology "requires a high level of inter-

[42] The main arguments for and against the nuclear striking force are outlined in the symposium *Pour ou contre la Force de Frappe* (Paris: Editions Didier, 1963); Alexandre Sanguinetti, *La France et l'arme atomique* (Paris: René Julliard, 1964); Club de Grenelle, *Siècle de Damoclès: La Force nucléaire stratégique* (Paris: Couderc, 1964); and Club Jean Moulin, *La Force de Frappe et le citoyen* (Paris: Editions du Seuil, 1961).

[43] In the 1968 budget nuclear armament had absolute priority over conventional forces, and this imbalance in defense was responsible for the date within the armed forces on a return to NATO.

[44] See Wolf Mendl, "Perspectives on Contemporary French Defense Policy," *World Today*, xxiv (1968): 55.

national coordination,"[45] not only for defense purposes but also for purposes of cost sharing.

It may well be that the multiplier effect of allocating resources abroad or investing them in military hardware for external purposes produces greater goods domestically than would allocations directly meeting the increased demands.[46] However, with increased politicization it is more likely that any external allocations will be highly visible, as was the case of U.S. expenditures in Vietnam, or French expenditures on a nuclear striking force, and that they will therefore be viewed as the squandering of the domestic wealth. This situation is all the more likely to arise in modern democracies where such allocations afford groups in opposition to the government the opportunity to raise questions.

In the contemporary world with instantaneous communications across boundaries, demands for increased services in one society also stem from their existence elsewhere. There are several ways that the dilemma can be met, and each of these has external effects, whether they are indirect or direct, intended or unintended. The Sprouts have summarized a number of the indirect effects as follows:

First, efforts may be made to *expand the economy*. . . .

Second, the rulers may prudentially *revise their order of priorities*. . . .

Third, the rulers may . . . *divert public attention* to other values. . . .

Fourth, the men in power may try to *change the opinions of dissenters*. . . .

[45] Ibid., p. 56. See also Alastair Buchan, *The Implications of a European System of Defense Technology: Defense, Technology and the Western Alliances* (London: Institute for Strategic Studies, 1967), pp. 9–10.

[46] Charles P. Kindleberger, for example, has argued that "vertical integration" of companies in a specific field transnationally from the procurement through the sales stages may "involve a loss for the world, though perhaps a gain for a country" (*American Business Abroad* [New Haven: Yale University Press, 1969], p. 19). Similar arguments have been made for investments in aircraft and other industries associated with predominantly military objectives.

Fifth, . . . the rulers may try to *silence dissent and opposition* . . . by threat or exercise of coercion or even
of death.[47]

In addition, these resources can be secured by various kinds
of external activities involving cooperation and compatible
efforts with other governments. One of the goals of the EEC,
for example, is a rational division of labor making available
a greater pool of resources to each of the member governments in return for giving up some domestic and external
autonomy. This pooling of resources serves to create international collective goods and also serves to increase interdependence among societies, further limiting the freedom of any
modern state to pursue a traditional policy of independence.

CHANGES IN THE PROCESSES OF
FOREIGN POLICY-MAKING

Like other processes of policy-making, those associated with
foreign policy change under modernization. Cabinet-style
decision-making gives way to administrative politics as the
information that must be gathered for policy-making increases, as the number of states and functional areas which
must be dealt with rise, and as personnel standards become
professionalized. Despite the predictions made at the turn of
the century by the ideologues of democracy, policy-making
has not been democratized as much as it has been bureaucra-
tized. At the same time great losses of control at the top
have occurred and have been well documented.[48]

[47] Harold and Margaret Sprout, "Dilemma of Rising Demands,"
pp. 690–91. Emphasis theirs.

[48] See Herbert A. Simon, *Administrative Behavior*, 2d ed. (Glencoe,
Ill.: The Free Press, 1957), pp. 172–97; Charles E. Lindblom, "The
Science of Muddling Through," *Public Administration Review*, xix
(1959): 79–88; and Anthony Downs, *Inside Bureaucracy* (Boston:
Little, Brown, 1967), pp. 49–166.

The foreign policy process in the Fifth French Republic is examined in Jean Baillou and Pierre Pelletier, *Les Affaires étrangères*
(Paris: Presses Universitaires de France, 1962), pp. 42–137.

The major transformation brought about by changes in the policy-making process has been the decreased relevance of macro-level rational actor models for understanding policy and the increased importance of both group and bureaucratic politics models.[49] Policy-making in modern bureaucracies undermines the ability of a political leader to pursue effectively any definite external goals. Rather, interest-group politics assumes greater importance and foreign policy becomes more and more a reflection of what occurs in the bureaucracies upon which leadership depends for information and position papers.

Policy-making in modern bureaucracies involves both lateral bargaining among the members of various administrative branches dealing with foreign affairs and vertical or hierarchical bargaining among members of various strata in a single organization.[50] The single spokesman in foreign affairs long prescribed as a necessity for security is made impossible by the characteristics of modern bureaucracies. Plurality in the number of foreign-policy voices is accompanied by the increased significance of routine, daily decision-making in low-policy areas that contrasts with the more unified and consistent nature of decision-making in crises and in high politics. With such increases in routine, control at the top becomes more difficult. The aspects of control of routine can be summarized under two headings, organization and size.

Organization

Modern governments are organized predominantly along functional domestic lines into such departments as agriculture, labor, and education. The domestic foreign distinction that seemed to fit the nineteenth-century model of govern-

[49] An important explication of these models is found in Graham T. Allison, "Conceptual Models and the Cuban Missile Crisis," *American Political Science Review*, LXIII (1969): 689–718.

[50] Paul Y. Hammond, "Foreign Policy-Making and Administrative Politics," *World Politics*, XVII (1965): 656–71; see also idem, "The Political Order and the Burden of External Relations," *World Politics*, XIX (1967): 443–64.

mental organization dramatically conflicts with the needs of even the predominantly domestic organizational structures of modernized governments. Here, the distinctive feature is that each of these domestic functional areas has external dimensions: most of the departments and ministries of modern governments associated with predominantly domestic areas have some kind of international bureau. The proliferation of these international bureaus severely undercuts the ability of one foreign ministry or department to control the external policies of its government, thus severely restricting the coordination of foreign policies. The problem is all the more serious insofar as one accepts the thesis that the distinction between high policies and low policies in foreign affairs has become increasingly blurred.

One way this problem is dealt with is by the formation of committees that crosscut several cabinet organizations, serving to coordinate both information and decision-making at several levels. Thus, in France, coordination of information takes place by personnel from the Quai d'Orsay assuming positions on the staffs of the Ministry of Defense, the Ministry of Finance, and the Ministry of Scientific Research. As in most Western countries, the Minister of Foreign Affairs nominally exercises control over the staffs of all departments that participate in foreign conferences and negotiations.[51]

Size

In addition to decreased control as a result of domestic orientation in modern governments, there is the added effect of coordinating a large bureaucracy dealing predominantly with foreign affairs. At the turn of the last century, one of the problems of control stemmed from the lack of coordination between the Foreign Ministry and Ministries of the Armed Forces. Thus, for example, the French armed forces often freely occupied underdeveloped areas in Africa and Southeast Asia without the knowledge of the foreign minister. Today the problem of size presents no less formidable an informa-

[51] See Baillou and Pelletier, *Les Affaires étrangères*, pp. 30–37.

tion gap at the top of large bureaucracies. With more available information than ever—with an information explosion—its channeling to the right person has become an organizational problem no Foreign Ministry has mastered.

There has been no study of changes in foreign-policy decision-making under the Fifth Republic that is in any way comparable to Grosser's study of the Fourth Republic.[52] What we do know, however, is that there was a tremendous amount of bargaining between the government and agricultural and commercial interest groups over the implementation of the Rome Treaty. De Gaulle generally sacrificed particularistic interests for a general national interest so as to preserve his freedom of action in foreign affairs. One result of this sacrifice was the disaffection of these groups, including those representing Jewish, agricultural, commercial, and military interests, which contributed to de Gaulle's defeat in the regional reform referendum of April 1969 and, consequently, to his resignation.

Modern Foreign Policies and Problems of Control

Modernization of political structures has fostered increased control over events in a society as well as in the environment in which men live, has served to create certain disabilities that impede rational and efficient foreign policies, and has exacerbated the problem of control that has always been central to international politics. This problem originates in the political organization of international society where nominally sovereign political units coexist in the absence of any hierarchical structure of political authority. The problem of coordinating and controlling these units is especially difficult under modernized conditions, for the development of interdependence among societies has eroded their autonomy to act both externally and internally, while their juridical status as sovereign states has not been significantly altered.

[52] Grosser, *La Quatrième République et sa politique extérieure.*

The problem of international stability is compounded by international interdependence (see Chapter 2). Controlling weapons and destructive power has always been the focal point of plans for peace by universal government. With the development of high levels of interdependence, all kinds of catastrophes—from nuclear holocaust to inflation or depression—tend to become worldwide phenomena, once a chain of events is begun. Thus, modernization, while it tends to bring increases in levels of coordination, also generates a series of control problems.

One reason why modern governments have lost control over their external relations is that there has been an increasing number of transnational interactions, especially among the populations of pluralistic societies in nongovernmental contexts.[53] The growth in nongovernmental external relations was one of the first changes brought about by modernization of the foreign policies and first became noticeable at the turn of the last century with the rise of the "new imperialism" characterized by the rapidly increased mobility of peoples, of money, and of military equipment. These nongovernmental external relations are associated today with the multinational corporation and other new units of international activity, which have degrees of autonomous action abroad independent of the governments to which they owe allegiance. Their external operations frequently work at cross-purposes with foreign policy goals. They also contribute a large portion of any state's balance of payments and therefore affect the monetary stability not only of a single state but also of the system of modernized states in general.

Through the structures of transnational society, a great number of dilemmas of French independence were created in the late 1960s. In trying to combat the growing control of the French economy by American corporations, for example,

[53] For an introductory discussion of the effects of transnational activities on international politics, see Robert O. Keohane and Joseph S. Nye, Jr., *Transnational Relations and World Politics* (Cambridge, Mass.: Harvard University Press, 1972).

de Gaulle demonstrated his regard for international technology as a threat to the nation-state. Although he invoked a good many bogus arguments against such investment from abroad,[54] his real argument was that to achieve first-rank France would need broad technological prowess. The problem was that in terms of general capacity to achieve this technological wherewithal, as well as in terms of the loss of economies gained by international standardization (via American companies), de Gaulle's stance appeared more that of Sisyphus or Pyrrhus than that of Perseus. With the growth of interdependence within the Common Market, American capital, if it is denied direct entry into France, can always slip through the back door from investments in Belgium or Italy. Similarly, some control over France supplying Israel with spare parts for French-made equipment even with an arms boycott was severely hindered by the transnational mobility of capital and the commitment of Dassault and others to meet French commitments to the Israelis.

A second aspect of the control problem stems from the decreasing number of policy instruments relative to the number of goals associated with any government. This problem can also be understood as the domestic side of international commitments, or the effects on domestic policies that result from international interdependence.

An optimum policy situation is one where the number of instruments available for use exceeds the number of goals desired. Under such conditions, in principle, an infinite number of policy mixes exists, in that one instrument can substitute for another, and "it will always be possible to find one among the infinity of solutions . . . for which welfare, however defined, is a maximum."[55] This is not only the most efficient sit-

---

[54] Kindleberger has shown that the argument based on the inability of the French Commisariat au Plan to control foreign corporations is contradicted by actual practice. See Kindleberger, *American Business Abroad*, pp. 81–83.

[55] Jan Tinbergen, *On the Theory of Economic Policy*, 2d ed., Contributions to Economic Analysis, 1 (Amsterdam: North-Holland Publishing Company, 1963), pp. 37–38.

uation but also the fairest, for it allows any pressure to be "distributed more evenly over the various social groups."[56] When, however, the number of instruments is less than the number of desired goals, there is no clear solution on grounds of efficiency or fairness.

It is precisely this situation that occurs with the breakdown of the domestic-foreign distinction and with increases in international interdependence. As long as the two spheres remained more or less distinct, policies in either area could be implemented with different sets of instrumentalities. As soon as the distinction is eroded, the spillover of effects from one sphere to another results in the reduction in the number of usable instrumentalities because of the following two reasons.

First, since policy instruments have recognizable effects both internally and externally, it is more and more frequently the case that any one instrument can be used for either domestic or external purposes. The effects in the other field, however, also must be taken into account. Thus, wage increases domestically can be used for the purpose of securing for a population higher general levels of living. At the same time, however, it is well known that there is a propensity to consume imported goods that increases directly with income. This has the effect of decreasing any balance-of-payments surplus in goods and services. The situation is worsened by the effect of wage increases on increasing prices and the subsequent negative effect on exports.

Second, there is a problem of consistency. What is optimally desired is that objectives are consistent. "If they are not consistent, no number of policy instruments will suffice to reach the objectives."[57] As long as domestic and foreign affairs were distinct, consistency was a problem only within each sphere. With interdependence, consistency must be faced not only in each but also in the effects that each has on

[56] Ibid., p. 41.
[57] Richard N. Cooper, *The Economics of Interdependence* (New York: McGraw Hill, 1968), p. 155.

the other. Here, the impact is both on the domestic system and on international society as a whole. Not only must domestic and foreign goals be compatible with one another, but so must the goals of a set of societies, if welfare effects are to be spread among them. However, consistency has become less and less feasible, given the economic nature of the objectives and the number and diversity of states in the system. Monetary, tax, and employment policies are affected, and so is the overall planning of the economy. French planning is a particularly interesting illustration of this point. The elaborate set of economic instruments, including industrial controls and inducements, set up during the first four French postwar plans became less and less applicable by the time the Fifth Plan was in its formulative phases. The inability of the government to control trade and monetary policies as a result of the implementation of the Rome Treaty, and the regional disequilibria created by international integration reduced the potential of domestic monetary and fiscal instruments. At first, Premier Michel Debré tried to counteract the lack of national control by projecting planning to a European level (see Chapter 7).[58] When this did not work, the elaborate planning machinery had to be transformed from an overall control of national economic development to a decentralized control of regional activities.

Together with increased international transactions associated with growing interdependence, there have also developed rising levels of transactions internal to modernized states and higher levels of national integration. It is often concluded that the increases in national cohesiveness that accompany modernization serve to counteract international interdependence. This would be true in an *in vacuo* situation. Actually, the reverse is true, and this constitutes a third area in which control has been lessened.

[58] Kindleberger has compared this projection with Jouhaux's remark in the 1930s: "If the 40-hour law is not internationalized, it will be difficult to maintain it in France," quoted in "A Matter of Ends and Means," *Interplay*, 11:4 (1968): 63.

There is a fairly simple relationship between rising levels of transactions internal to one state and increased interdependence among states. As the level of interdependencies within a state rises, as governments become more centralized, even if international transactions remain constant (and they do not), it is hypothesized that international interdependence must also increase. This hypothesis is likely to be true because sensitivity to transnational activities multiplies the domestic implications of international transactions. For example, as the levels of interdependence within a state rise, the effects of the same order of trade enlarge the implications for domestic employment as well as for fiscal, monetary, and welfare policies.

The threefold increase in the number of sovereign, if not autonomous, political entities since World War II disproportionately augments the problem of coordination and mutual adjustment, and causes the growth in the size of a bureaucracy necessary to gather information and to regulate action. A kind of change that is inevitably destabilizing for an international system compounds the problems accompanying the development of transnational society by increasing the number of interactions among governments and between governments and transnational nongovernmental organizations.

The present diversity in states is unparalleled in history. Such variety can be viewed in five different dimensions, each dimension adding to the complexity of coordination because each represents a set of conditions that must be dealt with individually. Moreover, the greater the diversity of approaches that are incorporated into executing each set of objectives, the greater is the problem of consistency in foreign-policy objectives and instrumentalities.

First, there is tremendous "unevenness of development among national societies in response to the revolution of modernization,"[59] which has been increasing recently rather

[59] Manfred Halpern, "The Revolution of Modernization in National and International Society," in Carl J. Friedrich, ed., *Revolution* (New York: Atherton Press, 1966), p. 195.

than narrowing. Second, there is great disparity in the power of states. Third, there is increased heterogeneity in the alignment of states. In fact, the development of nonalignment as an ideology of interaction rather than of neutrality or isolation is a change that accompanied the increase in the number of states. Fourth, states are differentiated according to whether they are interactionist or isolationist. Finally, governments differ along dimensions characterizing their internal organization, ranging from the democratic to the authoritarian. Accordingly, diplomatic initiatives and responses to such governments must take into account the particular context of governmental structures in other societies, and this also hinders overall foreign-policy consistency.

In addition to the great diversity that characterizes the state units in international society, there have arisen new kinds of nonstate units with impressive economic potential with which governments must interact, at least indirectly, and often directly and actively. The existence of these units has challenged the state-centered theory of international politics and has formed transnational links among societies, the importance of which varies with the state and unit in question and depends upon a variety of factors that have not yet been spelled out by theories of international relations.

These additional units can be listed under four headings. First, there are international organizations of states. Second, there are international organizations of interest groups, including political parties, unions, and business organizations. Third, there are the transnational or multinational corporations, some of which rival states in their economic power, if their net sales are viewed as equivalent to the GNP of national economies.[60] Fourth, there are other transnational groupings, such as the Vatican and the United Jewish Appeal, that deal in large transfers of capital across state lines and often to governments.

[60] General Motors, for example, with global net sales of $20.2 billion, would rank as the eighteenth most important state in such a ranking. See *War/Peace Reports*, October 1968, p. 10.

These new organizations serve both as evidence of interdependence and as important factors advancing it; they have either grown up as reflections of interdependence, or they have been specifically established for the purpose of controlling it. Since both kinds of organized entities are of wide-ranging diversity, and since they differ from the formal sovereign character of states, they have remained anomalous for international politics theory. Like all organizations, they have political aspects in all senses of the term, but they are not predominantly political organizations. Moreover, they are of such complexity and variety that the coordination and control of their activities by formal sovereign political entities has become difficult.

Conclusions

The transformations in all three aspects of foreign policies—in their contents, the processes associated with policy formation, and the control of policy effects—offer the citizens of any modernized pluralistic society opportunities of increased wealth and welfare that were unthinkable in any system with much lower levels of interdependence. They also increase the chances of instability for international society as a whole; for interdependence has increased far in advance of either the instruments capable of controlling it, or of available knowledge of its effects. There are, however, two aspects of modernization and foreign policy that ought to be further highlighted.

First, the various changes discussed above apparently pertain to all modernized societies and are affected very little by ideology or by particular sets of political institutions. To be sure, it may make some difference whether institutions are democratic or nondemocratic in particular instances. In the long run, however, the general constellation of factors that have transformed foreign policies is ubiquitous.

Second, these changes are likely to be dispersed throughout the international system far ahead of the other requisites of modernity, and are likely to characterize the foreign policies of the less modern societies either before or even in the absence of their modernization. The speed with which modernity spreads will, therefore, only increase the problems of control described above and will make more urgent the need for establishing new mechanisms of international order.

The confrontation of the ideal structures of French foreign policy with the realities of modernization was only briefly alluded to in this chapter. Illustrations of the theory will follow in the four case studies that appear in Part II. Before looking in detail at these case studies, however, the international implications of the processes of modernization need to be explained. In particular, various structures of interdependence that have resulted from these processes and that have severely restricted autonomy in foreign policy will be examined in Chapter 2.

TWO

INTERDEPENDENCIES
AMONG THE
INDUSTRIALIZED WESTERN STATES

IF tensions and problems of control in French foreign policy during the 1960s resulted in large measure from the level of interdependence between France and other societies, it is essential that the nature of these interdependencies be defined and examined in some detail. This is especially true of those interdependencies that seem to have been the greatest, namely, those between France and the other highly industrialized states in the non-Communist world. Relationships among these states were ambiguous and in flux throughout the 1960s. Changes in the political, social, and economic aspects of the relations of the societies composing the system of industrialized states stemmed, in part, from changes in the global nuclear confrontation between the United States and the Soviet Union. They can also be traced to transformations in domestic society and to an unprecedented growth among them in the mobility of capital, ideas, technology, and goods. It is the central hypothesis of this chapter that these changes were prominent characteristics of the high levels of modernization of these societies and of the persistent transformations that characterize them.

One of the paradoxes of the relationships characterizing highly industrialized societies seems to be that changes have been generally in the direction of greater interdependence. At the same time, they have been interpreted by de Gaulle and others as increasing the independence and autonomy of individual states in several fields. This paradox can be partially explained by the nature of these changes. They represented both breakdowns in the structures of international

47

politics characteristic of the 1950s and the realization that governments have greater freedom of action than had hitherto been thought.

It was only in the early 1960s that statesmen in some of these states took initiatives toward independence. This was especially the case with French diplomacy in the 1960s, where the possibilities of new diplomatic initiative latent in the new structure of international relationships among the modernized societies were first realized. Gaullist initiatives in this period were founded partially, then, on insight into the nature of contemporary international society and partially on the illusion that greater independence had become possible. French diplomatic efforts, therefore, represented the limits of independence in a highly interdependent system of international society.

The structures of interdependence characterizing the system of highly industrialized states and limiting French autonomy are the subject of this chapter. The development of interdependence between France and the other industrialized states along several axes of abstraction is examined; the reasons for which the overlapping sets of interdependencies have given the appearance of rendering independence more feasible are suggested; and certain trends that developed in international relations during the last decade and are likely to be even more significant in the future are extrapolated.

French relations with the other Western industrialized states displayed several new characteristics during the 1960s. Some aspects of these relations can be traced to national and international objectives that were peculiar to France. Others were more widespread and found their source in the more general transformation of international relations among the Western states. Both types of changes appeared to increase the potential autonomy of France in the international milieu, especially with respect to NATO, the EEC, and the international monetary system. Actually, far greater changes occurred in the direction of interdependence and curtailment of autonomy.

De Gaulle's vision of a *Europe des patries* functioning along the lines of the Franco-German Treaty of 1963, the series of French plans for reforming the international monetary system formulated between 1962 and 1968, and the French withdrawal in 1966 from the NATO command structure were all specific initiatives not only based on de Gaulle's interpretations of changes in the structure of international society and, especially, in the relative power of the major states in the world, but also on an older interpretation of modernization, which de Gaulle shared with a number of economists who wrote during the 1950s and which contrasts sharply with the central hypothesis of this chapter. In this interpretation, it is argued that modernization and its concomitant aspect of industrialization have resulted in the disintegration of even the primitive structures of world community that predated World War I. The dramatic increase in the number of nation-states, the development of nuclear weapons, the institutionalization of national planning mechanisms, and the integration of societies along national lines, according to this thesis, substantially reduced the chances for creating a worldwide community.[1]

At the same time, either by design or as an unintended consequence of national actions, new structures of international society developed that were unanticipated and, paradoxically, were highly compatible with a large number of the French diplomatic efforts during the 1960s. In this sense, they seemed to portend a new style of international collaboration that may become more significant in the future and that may be especially suited for tempering the destabilizing effects of international interdependence.

In the pages that follow, the system of states where interdependence has become greatest, the three different levels of interdependence, and their relation to French external objec-

---

[1] For a presentation by an adherent of the "disintegrationist" perspective on modernization, see Gunnar Myrdal, *An International Economy: Problems and Prospects* (New York: Harper and Row, 1969).

tives will be defined. These are strategic interdependence, systemic interdependence, and collective goods provided at the international level.

FRANCE AND THE WESTERN INDUSTRIALIZED STATES

The states with which France has been most closely interdependent can be understood as comprising a set of subsystems of international society[2] and as sharing not only similar structural characteristics in terms of their internal economic and political organization, the culture of their population, the historical context from which they developed, the mobility, educational levels, and predispositions of their members, but also several sets of relationships that are peculiar to the system which they constitute.

The high level of interdependence between France and the other industrialized Western states is a relatively recent phenomenon, which emerged over the course of the past century and which became relatively important politically after World War II,[3] and is, as will be argued below, apparently a func-

[2] Subsystems can be understood in either analytic or concrete terms. It is the latter reference that is used in this context. Analytically, a subsystem is understood as one of the infinite number of aspects of a concrete system. Thus, the global international system has political, economic, social, etc., aspects that characterize the system as a whole. Concretely, a subsystem is understood as a social system that is part of a larger system. Here the definition of a system suggested by Oran R. Young is followed. Thus, "a system will be defined as a group of actors [i.e., units] standing in characteristic relationship to each other (structure), interacting on the basis of recognizable patterns (processes), and subject to various contextual limitations" (*A Systemic Approach to International Politics*, Research Monograph No. 33 [Princeton, N.J.: Center of International Studies, 1968], p. 6).

[3] The recency of the development of high levels of interdependence has been debated along with the question of whether interdependence has increased or decreased in the twentieth century. For a review of this debate and evidence for my generalization, see Oran R. Young, "Interdependencies in World Politics," *International Journal*,

tion of the level of modernity of the societies comprising this system, for, as these societies have become more modern, the transnational aspects of modernization have served to bring them closer together. High levels of interdependence characterized certain of the relations of the Western states (e.g., defense and trade relations) in different ways and at different times. Moreover, some of the states in question are far more interdependent with one another with respect to certain activities, such as trade or monetary affairs, than they are with respect to other activities such as national security affairs. The overlapping of different forms of interdependence has made it difficult to discern the structural characteristics of international political activities among these states, a difficulty compounded by the normative implications with which the term is associated and by the bias of analysts of the Western states to focus almost exclusively on levels of strategic interactions. It is, therefore, useful to distinguish interdependence as used here from these other connotations.

The term interdependence usually has not been rigorously defined and has been associated with proponents of world federalism or various regionalisms. Thus, the growth of interdependence was frequently seen as a requisite of the abolition of interstate conflict during the early twentieth century.[4] More recently, the functionalist theory of integration saw in the creation of a common economic market the seeds of spillover for European political union. One of the fallacies in the argument of proponents of this theory is the equation of growing interdependence with the development of some form of supranational government. Such optimistic conclusions extracted from the diagnosis or prognosis of interdependence have never been warranted. High levels of interdependence among

xiv (1969): 726–50 and Edward L. Morse, "Transnational Economic Processes," in *Transnational Relations and World Politics*, ed. Robert O. Keohane and Joseph S. Nye, Jr. (Cambridge, Mass.: Harvard University Press, 1971), pp. 23–47.

[4] See Ramsay Muir, *The Interdependent World and Its Problems* (London: Constable, 1932).

states do not imply that supranational governance is either imminent or necessary. One of the great gaps of international-relations theory lies precisely in this realm. It is simply not known what forms of political or economic organization are compatible with the levels of interdependence currently characterizing international society.[5] What is known is that several forms of interdependence are highly destabilizing and that they may lead to breakdowns in domestic as well as external controls without fostering new structures of political order.

In none of the uses of interdependence outlined is there any implied normative bias. Rather, the definitions and concepts offered to describe France's relations with the other Western industrialized states are seen as analytic tools, which are helpful in understanding the most important areas toward which France's foreign policy has been directed.

The first question that is posed by the concept of interdependence can be formulated as follows: What area of the world, what collection of states or political units constitutes the contextual basis for this analysis of French foreign policies in the 1960s? In short, where have interdependencies risen internationally? After this question has been answered, the different kinds of interdependence among these states must be differentiated, and, in turn, the linkages between the different structures of interdependence must be described.

For these purposes, the universe of states interacting with France is defined as the collection of states that are characterized as highly modernized, pluralistic, or democratic, and that hold membership in various organizations purporting to represent modernized developed states (Organization for Economic Cooperation and Development [OECD]), Western states (NATO), or pluralistic states (Western European Union [WEU], Council of Europe). Most of them also appear in what Russett has identified as the "Western Community Region" of the more modernized states, based on cer-

[5] On this point, see John Pinder, "Positive Integration and Negative Integration," *The World Today*, xxiv (1968): 88–110.

tain sociocultural indices.[6] Thus, their identification in terms of certain key international organizations can be double-checked on Russett's list. Of the twenty-six countries that Russett identified as homogeneous within the Western Community, twenty appear among the twenty-three identified by comembership with France in significant and exclusivist international organizations during the period under study (1962–1969).[7] The other three—Spain, Portugal, and Turkey—are associated with France in the organizations identified as important ones. In addition, twelve of these are listed elsewhere by Russett as high mass consumption societies.[8]

These organizations formally denote the states with which France is highly interdependent along certain specified lines. What the organizational identification does is to make this list more than a mere collection of entities by indicating specified kinds of relationships. In fact, some of these international organizations—the EEC and Group of Ten, for example—were specifically created in order to encourage certain types of interdependence. In both cases French foreign policy has had to take into account the structure of the international organization in addition to the organization's member states, for these organizations have joined the member states in becoming important participants in these interaction patterns.

The overlapping memberships in the principal international organizations within which these societies interact illustrates one essential characteristic of the international system of highly industrialized Western states: namely, that these states are interdependent in different ways with regard to dif-

[6] Bruce Russett, *International Regions and the International System: A Study in Political Ecology* (Chicago: Rand McNally, 1967), pp. 14–35.

[7] The six that do not appear are Finland, New Zealand, Australia, Argentina, Israel, and Trinidad.

[8] Bruce Russett et al., *World Handbook of Political and Social Indicators*, p. 298.

ferent policy areas. At the same time, activities that occur in any one sphere, such as NATO, are bound to affect activities in other spheres, because so many of the states involved are the same, because they pursue similar, if often conflicting, objectives in the whole group of organizations, and because any changes in their objectives or in their social structures derived from activities in one sphere are bound to affect their activi-

TABLE 1

Membership in Various International Organizations
1962–1969

State	EEC	WEU	Council of Europe	NATO	OECD	Group of Ten
France	X	X	X	X	X	X
Austria			X		X	
Belgium	X	X	X	X	X	X
Canada				X	X	X
Cyprus			X			
Denmark			X	X	X	
Germany	X	X	X	X	X	X
Greece			X	X	X	
Iceland			X	X	X	
Ireland			X		X	
Italy	X	X	X	X	X	X
Japan					X	X
Luxemburg	X	X	X	X	X	
Malta			X			
Netherlands	X	X	X	X	X	X
Norway			X	X	X	
Portugal				X	X	
Spain					X	
Sweden			X		X	X
Switzerland			X		X	X
Turkey			X	X	X	
United Kingdom	X		X	X	X	X
United States				X	X	X

54

ties elsewhere. Since there is no single set of institutions by which all these activities can be ordered, it was inevitable that the "Atlantic Community" became what Hoffmann has called a "mass of ambiguities in motion, and not some kind of perfect union suddenly threatened by a willful destroyer."[9]

Analyses of the relations among the states composing an international system have usually been structured along the lines of diplomatic-strategic behavior. As a result, there is usually an emphasis placed upon conflictual aspects of the relations among the component units, or state actors, while other types of interdependence associated with those relationships are generally ignored. Hoffmann, for example, analyzes the relationship of the states in the North Atlantic area in terms of the "maze of 'diplomatic-strategic activities' "[10] that they involve, and he usually equates the relations among these states with the politics of alliance in NATO; although he seemingly intends to include the whole OECD group in his subsystem or partial-system analysis, he most frequently sees the structural characteristics of this system in terms of the fifteen states of the alliance. This predilection toward the uncoordinated aspects of statecraft is misleading. When he discusses the behavior of any state toward NATO or the OECD, Hoffmann omits constraints that result from organizational ties and focuses, instead, on the divergent policies of these states in extrasystemic matters including the United Nations, the less developed societies, or ties to the East. Hoffmann sees four layers or structural characteristics of this system, each of which stems from his bias toward a conflictual norm of interstate interaction.

1. "The layer of separateness" of fifteen more or less autonomous states in the "mere discussion forums" of the international agencies to which they belong.[11]

2. "The stratum of American hegemony."[12]

[9] Stanley Hoffmann, *Gulliver's Troubles, or the Setting of American Foreign Policy* (New York: McGraw-Hill, 1968), p. 388.
[10] Ibid.   [11] Ibid., p. 389.
[12] Ibid.

3. "The subsystem of the so-called Six of Western Europe."[13]

4. "An emergent or potential stratum . . . a possible political community of Western Europe."[14]

None of these strata outlined by Hoffmann is likely to highlight interaction patterns, which tend to be misleading and direct Hoffmann to skip a step in his argument. Hoffmann concludes, as few would deny, that without real integration in any of these strata any state can opt out of a system. France can choose to leave the EEC or NATO and partially destroy the preexisting system of interactions. To say that, however, does not mean that those interactions do not exist. Nor does it imply that they cannot be highly different from other sorts of relations. In addition, Hoffmann merely labels nonconflictual relations as such and does not elaborate, characterize, or interpret them analytically.

Thus, by omitting any analysis of the various highlighted overlapping structures among the societies of the Western industrialized system that either foster or hinder the control of transnational activities, he directs the observer's attention away from them and obfuscates the underlying cooperative nature of the relations and ties among these nations.

The relationships among the states characterizing the Western international system can be examined under several basic categories labeled structures of interdependence. Each structure of interdependence interacts with the others in nonobvious ways, can be isolated for analysis, and, though not a function of modernization, is affected by it in some way.

Interdependent behavior can be defined as the *outcome of specified actions of two or more parties (individuals, governments, corporations, etc.), when such actions are mutually contingent.* These parties, then, are interdependent with respect to specific issues rather than all activities. None of the actions involved among the parties are necessarily static, or fixed. Nor need they be consciously perceived as mutually contingent or dependent, although such perception would be

[13] Ibid., p. 390.   [14] Ibid.

necessary if interdependence is to be manipulated by one or more of the parties involved. The types of interdependence discussed below are subcategories of this general definition.

Strategic Interaction

One type of interdependence in the international system has been called strategic interaction, and is the most traditional sort found in international affairs. Strategic interaction exists *when parties that are interdependent with one another recognize the mutual contingency of their actions and consciously attempt to achieve political goals through the manipulation of that contingency.* Strategic interaction is one of the traditional motivations for the creation of an alliance. In such a case, an interdependence may be created in order to ensure a government the support of another state in case of war with a third party and/or in order to maintain some controls over the actions of the other state so as to prevent it from engaging in some activity that might lead to war. In a more general sense, strategic interaction lies at the heart of the traditional concept of international politics. Rational strategic behavior in this case is assumed to be imposed on a state's decision-makers because of the presumed fundamental anarchic structure of international society that results in a foreign-policy dilemma.

If strategic interdependence has been at the heart of international politics, its content in the Western European context changed radically in the post-World War II years. It can be illuminated by an examination of the three traditional assumptions underlying strategic interaction.

First, national borders have been impermeable to external activities. Interdependence arising from strategic interactions, therefore, did not encompass the interpenetration of societies. A corollary of this assumption has been that domestic and foreign policy spheres are largely autonomous of one another and that any state leader is free to behave strategically in international affairs and is not restrained by domestic interests.

Second, the legitimacy of the external use of force by governments existed even against an ally whose loyalty was always problematic.

Third, and perhaps most important, the rationality of governmental leadership is said to be imposed upon a political collectivity (or its leadership) in order to maximize the probability of future survival. Rational behavior, as it has become accepted in theoretical terms, is assumed to conform to the following criteria: (1) the choice of one alternative out of several; (2) an ordered and transitive rank of preferences; and (3) consistency of choice given a similar set of preferences.[15]

Such orthodox assumptions of strategic interaction have been severely undermined by the relations among the Western industrialized states. Borders have become more permeable; foreign and domestic affairs have become intricately intertwined; the rise of interest group politics domestically has restricted the rationality assumptions; and the use of force as an instrument of diplomacy has been eliminated. As Hoffmann has said, "in contrast to other subsystems, they [the Western countries] form a zone of peace. Tensions and crises among them have not led to the use of force since the end of World War II."[16]

Conventional types of strategic interaction together with the remaining factors that make such conditions invalid, if they have largely disappeared in Western states and are not likely to reappear in the foreseeable future, have a strong set of structures characterizing relations with the other highly industrialized states. For example, after 1949–1950, from the French viewpoint, the key to an ideal European order was Franco-German relations of which there were two conflicting theories known as Monnet's Europe and de Gaulle's Eu-

[15] These rationality assumptions are discussed in Kenneth J. Arrow, *Social Choice and Individual Values*, 2d ed. (New York: John Wiley and Sons, 1963), pp. 1–8.

[16] Stanley Hoffmann, "Discord in Community: The North Atlantic Area as a Partial International System," in *The Atlantic Community*, ed. Francis O. Wilcox and H. Field Haviland, Jr. (New York: Frederick A. Praeger, 1963), p. 6.

rope.[17] The former accepted a modified form of traditional strategic interaction based on both the renunciation of force and the interpenetration of societies, while the latter was based on the latent threat of force by a nuclear France against a nonnuclear Germany and cooperation without interpenetration.

De Gaulle's concept of strategic interaction in Europe was implemented in the Franco-German Treaty of Cooperation of 1963. The Treaty had its origins in a vision of a confederal Europe behind which lay at least twenty years of Gaullist political thought, but its immediate cause was the failure of the Europeans to accept the Gaullist proposals embodied in the Fouchet Plan for a confederal political union of the Six.[18] Rebuffed by the Dutch and Belgians, de Gaulle set out in the Franco-German Treaty to establish a major axis of cooperation, which would be a model for a larger European order whenever other states decided to join. The Treaty, like the Fouchet Plan, was a proposal for cooperation based on the permanent reality of the nation-state and the belief that the only legitimate forms of international interactions were those founded on the association of statesmen who harmonized the international activities of the states they represented in order to present a unified voice in foreign affairs. It was designed,

[17] On these two concepts of European order, see Jean-Baptiste Duroselle, "De Gaulle's Design for Europe and the West," in *Changing East-West Relations and the Unity of the West*, ed. Arnold Wolfers (Baltimore: The Johns Hopkins Press, 1964), pp. 171ff.; idem, "General de Gaulle's Europe and Jean Monnet's Europe," *World Today*, XXII (1966): 1–12; John Pinder, *Europe Against de Gaulle* (New York: Frederick A. Praeger, 1963), pp. 1–45; and David Calleo, *Europe's Future: The Grand Alternatives* (New York: Horizon Press, 1965), pp. 45–136.

[18] See F. Roy Willis, *France, Germany and the New Europe, 1945–1967* (Stanford, Calif.: Stanford University Press, 1968), pp. 292–311. Willis traces the Franco-German treaty to Gaullist initiatives made as early as January, 1959. See also Alessandro Silj, *Europe's Political Puzzle: A Study of the Fouchet Negotiations and the 1963 Veto*, Occasional Papers in International Affairs, No. 17 (Cambridge, Mass.: Harvard University Center for International Affairs, 1967).

in short, to form the voluntary confederation, but one full of contradictions.

The key provision in the Treaty, like that of the Fouchet Plan, was a regular consultation of heads of state and, principally, foreign and defense ministers. Gaullist objectives, in this case, were highly contradictory. For their primary motivation was a nationalist one. Like traditional alliances, the Franco-German Treaty was designed to increase the French international voice. France was envisaged as the international spokesman of Europe, while Germany was to be the industrial center. A difficulty existed in the conflict between the international ambitions of de Gaulle and the maintenance of a national framework for decision-making. Success depended on German acceptance of this Gaullist vision.

The nationalist basis of the confederal approach has been exceedingly difficult to implement, because there has been no basic consensus between French and German objectives in Europe. German foreign policy in postwar years was based until 1969 upon a set of propositions that would have been contradicted by French leadership in foreign affairs. In practice, French and German policies in the two areas most vital to Germany—the East and NATO—did not coincide. On the one hand, in Germany, the East-West split was seen as a much deeper and more fundamental one than it was in France. On the other hand, German security was wedded to the United States for the very reasons that it could never be tied to France. France could never have provided as credible a security guarantee as could the United States.[19]

Another motivation of the confederal construct was contradictory in terms of ends and means. Like traditional alliances, the Franco-German Treaty was based on a desire on

[19] See Alfred Grosser, *French Foreign Policy under De Gaulle*, trans, Lois Ames Pattison (Boston: Little, Brown, 1965), pp. 64–80, for a general analysis of these divergencies of interest. The detailed history of these differences can be found in Willis, *France, Germany*, pp. 312–65. The bases of German foreign policy are summarized in Karl Kaiser, *German Foreign Policy in Transition* (New York: Oxford University Press, 1968).

the part of de Gaulle to constrain Germany. Germany would have had to subordinate its foreign policy to France in return for a French nuclear guarantee that was aimed as much against a potential German threat as it was at the Soviet Union. For the commitment to defend Germany was based on an understanding that the communist threat had become muted, if it had not disappeared, as a result of bipolar deterrence and a satisfied Soviet Union. Such a guarantee implied a renunciation of German nuclear pretensions, which would have meant a continuous arms superiority of France in relation to Germany.[20]

Overt strategic interaction in the Europe of the 1960s was muted for several other reasons. On the level of high policies, strategic interaction was designed to re-create the conditions of French hegemony on the Continent—conditions that had become largely impossible to implement because the requisite scale of great power status had changed from the 1920s, and because of the development of a different level of interdependence discussed below. Strategic interactions within Western Europe, then, although present, never surfaced.

Thus, Monnet's Europe, as it was implemented, if not as it was intended to be established, conformed much more to the requisites of interdependence in the contemporary international system than did de Gaulle's whose vision of Europe included the realization that the requisites of strategic interaction could not be fully realized in postwar Western Europe, where national jurisdictional borders had been weakened by aspects of transnational society and the use of force had been renounced. Monnet's vision of Franco-German relations encompassed both of these new factors of politics in Western Europe, and seeing a functionalist Europe, it explicitly took into account the growth of transnational activities characteristic of the relations among highly modernized states. Monnet

[20] French foreign policy toward Germany and the limitations imposed upon France by Germany are discussed in Simon Serfaty, *France, de Gaulle and Europe* (Baltimore: The Johns Hopkins Press, 1968), pp. 139–60.

saw that the objective of conventional strategic interaction could be implemented by means other than those of strategic behavior. By creating international systemic interdependencies in a zone of peace, the old nationalisms that had been blamed for two world wars could be tempered, and the German and French economies could be linked together in order both to avoid the dangers of conflictual strategic interaction and to create a market that could simultaneously help produce greater wealth for all.[21]

Indeed, not only the growth but also the fostering of transnational society by the establishment of international institutions reduced traditional strategic interdependence in Europe just as the shifting of strategic interaction from the European to the worldwide scale by the emergence of global bipolarity, reinforced by the nuclear preponderance of the United States and the Soviet Union, had several side effects in both Western Europe and in world politics. In Western Europe, both the pattern of division left by the Russian and American armies and the development of two blocs centered on the nuclear might of a superpower established a collective good, in terms of security, or a kind of interdependence that could not exist in an atomistic world where all foreign-policy actions involve strategic behavior.

Strategic interactions, if they traditionally involved both the legitimacy of the use of force and the impermeability of the nation-state, are paradoxically hardened and eroded by nuclear weapons. As a result, Hoffmann calls the basic structure of international society muted bipolarity. With deterrence not only security becomes a function of activities pursued elsewhere but also survival becomes a transnational value. At the same time, borders and territoriality of a state become fixed. Deterrence, based on the legitimacy of nuclear weapons, denies the practicality of force because use would result in self-destruction.

[21] For a discussion of Monnet's motivations, see Pierre Gerbet, "La Genèse du Plan Schuman," *Revue française de science politique*, vi (1956): 8–20.

The shift in the traditional form of strategic interdependence from the former great powers of Europe to the two nuclear powers, the United States and Soviet Union, had a paradoxical effect on the diplomacy of the European states that de Gaulle was the first to seize upon. Without the requisites of strategic interaction—without impermeable boundaries or all-pervading external interest in security—France, like the other European states, was no longer free to engage in traditional power politics. The stakes of global power in the nuclear age require credible deterrence capability beyond the means of any nonsuperpower. The cost of building and maintaining delivery systems in an age of rapid transformation and, hence, of an increased rate of obsolescence of military hardware was too high for the French economy. At the same time, however, without the shackles of traditional strategic interdependence, de Gaulle's France was freed to pursue diplomatic theatrics and *grandes entreprises*.

The building of nuclear weapons and delivery systems, if not credible ones, the fostering of *rayonnement* by means of aid to former colonial areas, intimations of neutralism, and the pretense of a strategy of *tous azimuts* could be freely substituted for traditional strategic interactions without upsetting the patterns of global interaction. Engagement in theatrics could become, therefore, an end in itself, as the form of action assumed for de Gaulle more importance than its content or control. At the same time, however, without the shackles of traditional strategic interdependence to upset the patterns of global interaction, de Gaulle was freed to pursue not only *grandes entreprises*, including the building of second-rate nuclear weapons and delivery systems, aid to former colonial areas, and intimations of neutralism, but also diplomatic theatrics that assumed an end in itself rather than any importance in content or control of policies.

De Gaulle was a master at discerning changes in the structure of international relations. By acting in ways compatible with such changes, he fostered an illusion that he had freedom and could act and transform those structures. France's withdrawal from the NATO command structure, for example, was based on recognition both that NATO's usefulness was more limited than originally thought, and that as long as European defense was maintained as a spinoff of American defense, France could enjoy security from the alliance without paying the price of military subordination. Other examples of Gaullist adaptability include the reform of the international monetary system in the mid-1960s, French recognition of Communist China, and gestures of friendship to the Third World.

If the shift in strategic interaction from regional areas to the global system has eroded the usefulness of the most traditional of all forms of diplomatic behavior, what is its utility in the contemporary world? Has it disappeared? Or has it emerged in a new form? The answer seems to depend upon the context under analysis. Traditional strategic interaction, while it has been transformed in the relations of highly modernized states the interactions of which have become characterized by several layers of transnational activities, seems to have been revived on the periphery of the modern world.[22] Even among the more modernized states it has not wholly disappeared, and, in fact, may prove to be successful in handling certain problems of instability that arise from other forms of interdependence. A reintroduction of strategic behavior in the European context may well be evident in an area with which it is not generally associated, since it originally and classically characterized high policies, the policies of security and survival by means of the use of force. Bipolarity and the creation of security zones in Eastern and Western Europe as well as elsewhere in the world has shifted traditional strategic interaction from the security area of high politics to the welfare

[22] John Herz has seen this paradoxical effect of the reinforcement of strategic interactions at the periphery of the global nuclear confrontation—especially in the Middle East and in Vietnam—in a revision of his original thesis concerning the demise of the territorial basis of the state. See John H. Herz, "The Territorial State Revisited," *Polity*, 1 (1968): 12–34.

area of low politics. Such a shift is paralleled by an emphasis of external objectives from high- to low-policy areas, which were traced in Chapter 1.

As yet, the levels of systemic interdependence among the modernized societies have increased at rates far in advance of the available instrumentalities that may be invoked to contain them. Within Europe and among the most important monetary reserve countries, centralized decision-making in the form of transnational bureaucracies has remained extremely weak, given the problems that arise and must be resolved. In both areas, by necessity rather than by design, and especially under condition of crisis, cooperation and consultation along the lines envisaged in the Fouchet Plan have become institutionalized, especially in the late 1960s. Thus, coordination of national policies through national representatives has, in fact, become more commonplace than supranational integration.

While such forms of cooperation may be types of strategic interaction, they are also quite different from the classical case, particularly since cooperation is not based upon the decisions of heads of states as much as upon those of cabinet ministers (especially finance and agricultural ministers in the European communities) or among nonministerial officials (especially central bankers in the Group of Ten). In addition, unlike classical strategic interaction, interests are less divergent and incompatible than they are convergent and similar. For example, the interests of all states in a stable international monetary system seem to override particular national viewpoints.

Systemic Interdependence

A second way of viewing interdependence may be called systemic interdependence. Unlike strategic interaction, systemic interdependence has been less a tactic of international behavior than a description of a state of affairs. Systemic interdependence can be defined along a continuum, measured by *"the extent to which events occurring in any given part or within any given component unit of a world system affect (either physically or perceptually) events taking place in each of the other parts or component units of the system.*"[23]

In a formal sense, strategic interaction is only a subset of systemic interdependence, as both concepts are understood here. In the former and latter situations, the activities carried out by individuals representing a nation-state are contingent upon those of some other individual(s) in other states. However, that contingency need not be perceived or manipulated. The concrete situation in international politics corresponding to this type of interdependence may be understood as follows: (1) with systemic interdependence, it is assumed that borders are highly permeable with reference to certain sets of activities of both governmental and nongovernmental groups; (2) the utility of force in the relations of states enjoying some degree of systemic interdependence has become marginal by reason of treaty, or by tradition and habit; and (3) rational calculus, which was the efficiency notion built into strategic interaction, has been severely weakened by the breakdown in the distinction between foreign and domestic affairs and by the consequent permeation of national affairs by pressure group politics.

Systemic interdependencies characterize relations among those states where there exist high levels of activities of a non-security nature. Since these activities have assumed a major importance, as argued in Chapter 1, it was inevitable that they would eventually be seen in a political light by national decision-makers.

The international economic system has thus become the arena in which France interacted most intensively with the other Western states, because the traditional security focus on foreign policy seems to have lost its predominant significance for all but the superpowers. Among the other Western states, only Germany has been confronted with the security dilemmas that traditional defense policies were supposed to

[23] Young, "Interdependences in World Politics," p. 726; emphasis added.

handle. The international stalemate created by the more or less stable balance of terror and by a general security system in the North Atlantic region provided for security in Europe.[24] In spite of impressions that might be gained from such theatrics as those involved in the French proposals for reforming NATO and of the French withdrawal from the NATO command structure, security became a less important concern for French foreign policy, especially in the last two years of de Gaulle's Presidency.

In addition, international economic policy increases in significance as the industrialized states become more interdependent. Except for the superpowers, plays for power and position now have a more natural outlet in the international monetary and commercial systems than they have in the traditional areas where power politics are predominant, especially among the Western European states whose economic strength grew rapidly in the 1950s and 1960s, but whose power positions, measured in terms of the weapons at their disposal, remained marginal.

French statecraft during the 1960s in areas of systemic interdependence operated much as it did in areas of strategic interdependence. That is, de Gaulle seized upon new opportunities that he thought might enhance French independence. Like those areas associated with changes in strategic interdependence, the alleged and asserted goals of French diplomacy were highly divergent from actual practice in the areas of systemic interdependence. At the same time, however, French negotiation served to bolster the French position in that in the most systemically interdependent area—that of the European communities—France maintained a dominant position. In addition, French statecraft was most prudent in those areas where systemic interdependence rose most rapidly during the 1960s.

[24] For an enlightened discussion of the history and transformation of the system providing for security in Western Europe, see Pierre Hassner, *Change and Security in Europe, Part I: The Background,* Adelphi Papers No. 45 (London: Institute for Strategic Studies, 1968).

As systemic interdependence increases, the state's control of activities both within and outside its territory decreases. That interdependence includes the international activities of nongovernmental organizations—businesses, social organizations, and the like—that affect government policies largely in unrecognized ways. They also include a decreased number of available political instrumentalities that can be used to control domestic or external policies. Such losses of control mean that systemic interdependence must be tempered in certain political ways, either by integrating areas where it is high or by restraining its growth.

French policy in those areas where systemic interdependencies were the greatest in the 1960s—in the EEC and among the ten major monetary reserve currency countries—had a tempering or restraining effect. However, in many issue-areas, such as the international monetary system, French statecraft was overcome both by the level of systemic interdependence, which resulted in the disintegration of French monetary strength and hence the French bargaining position, and by the overwhelming preponderance of the United States in the international monetary system. In the EEC, however, almost every major policy was affected significantly by French policy, so that French statecraft was most effective in that area.

French statesmen, then, saw the political implications of international economic policies during the 1960s and used negotiations in virtually every field in which France was involved internationally to bolster the French position and to secure added benefits. The development of systemic interdependence in predominantly economic areas ranged from the EEC to the larger area of highly industrialized countries in both trade and monetary arrangements. The growth of trade among the highly industrialized states was substantial during the 1960s, and is illustrated in Figures 1 and 2 that show the rapidly increasing growth of French trade outside the franc zone and the decline in trade both relatively and absolutely within the franc zone. Reflecting a similar worldwide trend

FIGURE 1

Foreign Trade Outside the Franc Zone,
1959–1967

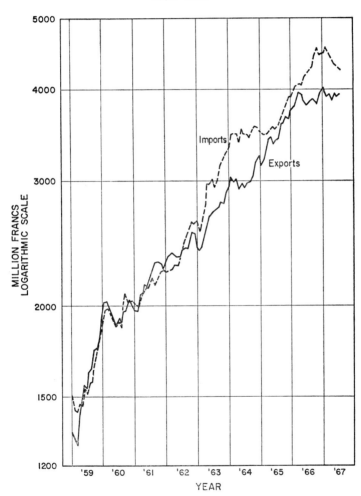

Source: Institut National de la Statistique et des Etudes Economiques,
Annuaire statistique de la France, 1967 (Paris: INSEE, 1968), p. 608a.

FIGURE 2
Foreign Trade within the Franc Zone
1959–1967

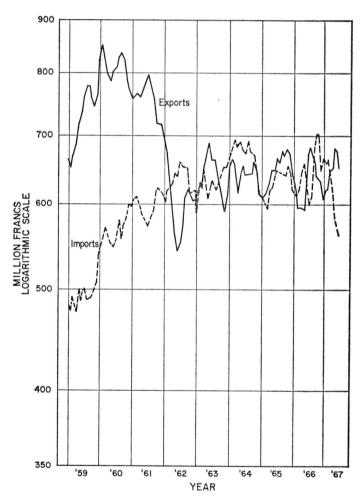

Source: Institut National de la Statistique et des Etudes Economiques, *Annuaire statistique de la France, 1967* (Paris: INSEE, 1968), p. 608d.

70

over the last fifty years, but especially over the past fifteen years, there was an increase in trade in manufactured goods with other advanced industrial countries and a relative decline in the trade of primary products with nonindustrialized countries.

Trade among industrial countries increased from 42.2 percent of global trade from 1928 to 46.5 percent in 1965—a seemingly small increase, but one that was quite marked given the intervening periods of depression and world war and the consequent retrenchment in trade.[25] French trade figures are even more impressive on this point than are the global figures because of the increased benefits of membership in the Common Market. In 1956, for example, French exports to the franc-zone countries, representing the bulk of French exports to underdeveloped or nonindustrialized areas, constituted 32 percent of all French exports, while trade within the zone represented 27.8 percent of French total trade. By 1966, that percentage dropped considerably so that only 14.0 percent of French exports went to franc-zone countries, and French trade within the franc zone fell to 13.6 percent of total French trade. Correspondingly, there was a major increase in both absolute and relative terms in French trade with the OECD and EEC countries that can be interpreted as a measure of trade with other highly industrialized countries (see Figure 1).

In those areas where systemic interdependence has grown, bilateral relationships have become more difficult to maintain. Recognition of high levels of interdependence has re-

[25] The trends in global trade are summarized in Richard N. Cooper, *Economics of Interdependence* (New York: McGraw-Hill, 1968), pp. 59–76. Cooper feels that the rapid growth of world trade from $71.4 billion in 1953 to $177.7 billion in 1966, and the concomitant relative increase in trade among industrialized countries, is due to factors that are associated with modernization, namely, "the rapid growth in the output and incomes which the industrial countries have experienced in the postwar period" as well as "changes in commercial policy, reductions in transportation costs, and broadening of business horizons" (p. 63).

sulted in the formation of multilateral organizations designed both to control any destabilizing effects of high levels of interaction and to create even higher levels of interdependence. Commercial arrangements with the other industrialized states have occurred principally in the Common Market and the GATT. By the end of the sixth round of the GATT Negotiations (Kennedy Round) in 1967 and by the time of the creation of a common market in goods and services in the EEC in 1968, the lowering of tariff barriers to trade in manufactured goods reached what many economists feel to be the lowest politically feasible level for the time being.[26]

By 1966, 60 percent of French trade was with OECD countries, and almost half of that trade was accounted for by the five other EEC countries alone. These figures reflect the predominant importance of the other advanced industrialized countries for French foreign commerce. They do not indicate their political importance, however. Commercial transactions with these other advanced states have, by necessity, been multilateral, thus imposing a positive or cooperative approach on French negotiations. However intransigent French policy within the EEC was at the time, France gained enormously from membership in it. This benefit included not only the direct boost for French agriculture[27] and general trade diversion from non-Common Market countries to Common Market countries, but also the indirect accretion of power that resulted from the common voice of the EEC countries in the Kennedy Round negotiations. Such gains in the international voice of the EEC necessitated a compromise with French in-

[26] Therefore, Common Market concerns have now shifted to non-tariff barriers to trade such as tax legislation, subsidization and transportation policies, which were not specified in the Rome Treaty. These are far more difficult to equalize than are tariff barriers. See Harry G. Johnson, "The Kennedy Round," World Today, XXIII (1967): 326–33.

[27] It has been estimated that French agricultural production rose by an additional 2.8 percent from 1963 to 1964 as a result of the Common Agricultural Policy (CAP). See Lawrence B. Krause, European Economic Integration and the United States (Washington, D.C.: The Brookings Institution, 1968), p. 94.

dependence that in this case was projected onto the European plane.

The general prosperity of the European states, then, served political ends, as was clearly illustrated by the GATT negotiations, in which Krause noted the following changes in relative European and American power:

> The dominant position of the United States in GATT evaporated with the implementation of the Rome Treaty. The United States once could have forced its trading partners to accept a compensating U.S. tariff reduction in return for the U.S. withdrawal of a previously negotiated concession. However, when the United States withdrew its concession on carpets and glass in 1962, the Common Market refused compensation and, instead, retaliated against American goods. . . . The U.S. Congress can no longer legislate a round of tariff reductions for all GATT members as it had done for most of the postwar period. . . . The Common Market is now the most important member of GATT, and can determine in large measure the success or failure of any attempts to liberalize trade.[28]

Systemic interdependence is easily confused with political integration, even though the concepts ought to be distinguished.[29] Systemic interdependence represents a state of

[28] Ibid., pp. 224–25.

[29] Interdependence is usually not distinguished from integration. This is especially true when integration is defined as a state of affairs. The economist Bela Balassa, for example, in a seminal theory of integration, defined economic integration both as a process and as a state of affairs. "Regarded as a process, it encompasses measures designed to abolish discrimination between economic units belonging to different national states; viewed as a state of affairs, it can be represented by the absence of various forms of discrimination between national economies" (*The Theory of Economic Integration* [Homewood, Ill.: Richard D. Irwin, 1961], p. 1).

Balassa's definition falls into the category which Jan Tinbergen calls negative integration. Negative integration consists of the removal of discriminations designed to maximize welfare in an area, by creating a zone of free competition. Positive integration goes beyond the re-

affairs that has resulted, in part, from the conscious removal of barriers to intercourse of all kinds, or of discriminations. It is a situation represented in ideal terms by the initial stages of the formation of the nation-state and is also characterized by the *laissez-faire* economy of the "night-watchman" state. In such a state, internal barriers to trade and other forms of intercourse are removed and the noninterventionist state allows welfare to be maximized by means of the silent hand of the market.

Integration, on the other hand, implies uniform policies in a given area and is therefore an eminently political term. Whether a description of a state or a group of states, integration implies the emergence of centralized political authority. Another sign of integration, in behavioral terms, is the existence of "political pressure groups [that] follow predominantly functional rather than regional lines."[30] As centralized authority becomes more significant and as political and economic institutions are subsequently differentiated along spe-

---

moval of discrimination. "Postive integration, or the creation both of new institutions with their instruments and the modification of existing instruments applies, in principle, to the institutions and instruments requiring centralized handling. As a minimum, this refers to measures needed to *avoid a distortion* of the process of free competition" (*International Economic Integration*, 2d ed. [Amsterdam: Elsevier Publishing Co., 1964], p. 78; emphasis his). Such measures include methods of taxation, incomes policies, market regulation, planning, etc.

If interdependence is understood as a state of affairs characterizing an area where discriminations are removed, and integration as the development of political institutions designed to control interdependence, then interdependence would be a necessary but insufficient condition for integration. Political institutions can, logically, be created in an area of low systemic interdependence, as it often is within nonmodernized states. Such a situation is not integrated and approaches what is called in French *législation dans le vide*.

[30] Cooper, *Economics of Interdependence*, p. 8. For an overview of various behavioral indices of integration, see Joseph S. Nye, Jr., *Peace in Parts; Integration and Conflict in Regional Organization* (Boston: Little, Brown, 1971), pp. 21–54.

cialized lines, regional parochialism loses its rationale. A third sign of integration is neither behavioral nor static, as are the first two, but is psychological and reflects a "sense of community"[31] that parallels the political culture of a state.

Interdependence is a concept that connotes both *laissez-faire* economics and political liberalism, and is based on both equilibrium theory and the political theory of a natural harmony of interests. Integration, to the contrary, is based on a directed economy and more conservative political thought. This political thought is more pessimistic with regard to the nature of man than is liberalism. Therefore, integration is associated with the rejection of natural harmony theory.

One of the major problems of the literature on international integration stems from overemphasis of certain specific tests or signs of political community. Whether such signs are psychological or behavioral, they tend to obscure what occurs at the level of interdependence. "To focus exclusively on tests of integration," as Cooper has shown, "would miss the importance of a process which is taking place and, which, if it is not to be reversed, will compel a higher degree of economic cooperation."[32] Such processes have characterized both the gen-

[31] Emphasis on the psychological dimension of integration can direct an observer's attention away from significant behavioral aspects of interdependence and integration. Overemphasis on psychological tests of integration is, in my view, one of the principal weaknesses of the work on integration developed over the past decade by Karl Deutsch. See Karl W. Deutsch et al., *Political Community and the North Atlantic Area* (Princeton, N.J.: Princeton University Press, 1957); and Karl W. Deutsch et al., *France, Germany and the Western Alliance: A Study of Elite Attitudes on European Integration and World Politics* (New York: Charles Scribner's Sons, 1967). See also Edward L. Morse, "The Politics of Interdependence," *International Organization*, XXIII (1969): 311–19.

[32] Cooper, *Economics of Interdependence*, p. 10. Cooper himself glosses over the distinction that must be made between cooperation and integration. Cooperation occurs even in the absence of integration, according to the logic of strategic interaction. There are also important economic differences between the two outlined in Balassa, *Theory of Economic Integration*, pp. 6–7.

eral relations of the highly industrialized states as well as the relationships among the EEC countries.

The increased levels of interdependence among the highly industrialized states came about by the conscious lowering of tariff barriers to trade after World War II. This breakdown in discrimination contrasted sharply with the high tariff and autarchy policies of these countries in the 1930s. In addition, the destruction of production capacities in Western European countries in the war years further depressed trade. Trade liberalization among these countries began with the Marshall Plan and the formation of the Organization for European Economic Cooperation (OEEC), which was instrumental in lowering trade barriers in Western Europe, and was further extended by the six rounds of tariff sessions in the GATT between 1947 and 1967. The growth in interdependence was also characterized by the institutionalization of a new international monetary system based on the IMF and ancillary agreements built around it. Monetary interdependence was an additional factor that provided a more or less stable basis for the growth in trade.

Increased levels in trade as a reflection of growing interdependence among the industrialized countries has been relatively free of any form of positive integration, except in *ad hoc* arrangements where special circumstances existed. Positive integration has been most significant in that area where both systemic interdependence and the will-to-unite were the highest, namely, in the EEC, which, like most of the other international organizations built or aborted in postwar Europe, was basically a French institution in both conception and execution. Divergent conceptions of European order were largely reflections of different strands of French thought on foreign policy. This was especially the case with respect to the technocratic, efficiency notion of Europe as opposed to the more consciously political Gaullist conception.

In addition to the rational strategic motivations that lay behind the Gaullist conception of Europe, there were motivations of a sort that parallel the conditions of systemic interdependence, that is, the welfare aspects of an enlarged market. De Gaulle clearly did not approve of the Treaty of Rome, and often said that had he been President of the Republic at the time the Treaty was negotiated, it would have been a very different document.[33] But he accepted it as it was for a variety of reasons, the most significant of which was the preoccupation with the Algerian War from 1958 to 1962. After that, he tried to extract two principal gains for France from membership in the EEC.

First was the issue of agriculture. De Gaulle saw as one of the major weaknesses in the Rome Treaty, the specific and detailed timetable established for the formation of a common market in industrial products with only a vague reference to an agricultural policy.[34] Agriculture was, however, the one area in which France could be expected to secure major advantages, and the major emphasis of French diplomacy with regard to the positive aspects of common policy formation in the 1960s was therefore in this area.

The second major benefit that de Gaulle sought to extract for France from the Common Market was related to those changes that systemic interdependence brought to strategic interactions. De Gaulle sought the traditional aim of power accretion by fostering a form of systemic interdependence. France could gain an increased voice in international politics if the power base on which France operated was enlarged. It was for this reason that there was a tremendous French concern with a common policy for the EEC countries in the GATT and IMF negotiations. This principal French concern involved the political manipulation of welfare economic

[33] See the televised interview he granted on December 14, 1965, reprinted in André Passeron, De Gaulle Parle, 1962–1966 (Paris: Fayard, 1966), p. 315.

[34] Yet during the 1957 negotiations for the Rome Treaty, French negotiators made it clear that France would consider a common market only if agriculture would constitute an important part.

77

policies and the contradictions resulting from the consequences of implementing both economic policies on such a foundation and French goals in terms of common policies that de Gaulle was unwilling to accept.

Interdependence among the EEC countries was marked by the four major political achievements of the Six in the mid-1960s,[35] each of which was heavily indebted to the French position on integration and other policies, including the establishment of a customs union, the negotiation of an agricultural policy, agreement on a united front in the sixth round of the GATT negotiations, and the establishment of a uniform value-added tax.[36] In addition, there was integration outside the governmental context among business corporations and social groups.

Each of these achievements was largely a type of negative integration, or the creation of systemic interdependence. Positive integration involving common policy formation and implementation was very low, although the long-range implications for such integration were much higher. The reasons why the creation of systemic interdependence outpaced the creation of common policies are easily summarized.

First, the Rome Treaty was far more specific on the conditions for dismantling barriers to interchange than it was on the creation of common policies.[37] The need for such common policies was elucidated, but no clear schedule was set forth for their implementation. Thus, the achievement of a customs union in the EEC on July 1, 1968, a year and a half ahead of schedule, was largely the result of the removal of barriers to internal factor movements.[38] Those aspects of pos-

[35] The first decade of operation of the Common Market is reviewed in A. E. Walsh and John Paxton, *The Structure and Development of the Common Market* (London: Hutchinson, 1968).

[36] These achievements are elaborated in Pinder, "Positive Integration and Negative Integration," pp. 100–05, to whom I am indebted for this argument.

[37] See Treaty Establishing the European Economic Community, Article 14.

[38] The specific conditions under which the implementation of the

78

itive integration involved in the customs union, particularly in the formation of common external tariffs, resulted from compromises between the former high tariff countries, France and Italy, and the low tariff countries, Germany and the Netherlands.[39] Or they were effected by mutual concessions chiefly between France and Germany on the implementation of a common agricultural policy. In general, however, the successful removal of barriers to factor movements within Europe was due to a treaty that could "more easily make effective the 'Thou shalt not' commandments than the 'Thou shalt' ones."[40]

Second, it was difficult to create common policies because of the infrastructure of the institutions of the EEC and neo-liberal economic beliefs. As indicated above, the development of systemic interdependence without the institutionalization of common policies results in a situation that is analogous to the classical *laissez-faire* economy. Factor movements are freed and are left to adjust themselves according to market mechanisms. Like the "night-watchman" state, Europe in the 1960s had no centralized bureaucracies that could implement common policies if they had been created. Rather, common policies were to be implemented by the coordination of national policies, and even this was made difficult, however, because of neoliberal economic ideas found especially in the West German government. In fact, the functionaries of

---

Treaty's timetable was advanced are reviewed in EEC Commission, *Deuxième Rapport géneral sur l'activité des communautés, 1968*, pp. 21ff.

[39] The benefits achieved by the establishment of a common market for manufactures are attributed not only to lower tariffs, but also to increases in income. See Krause, *European Economic Integration*, pp. 34–37.

[40] Pinder, "Positive Integration and Negative Integration," p. 98. Pinder adds another reason for the ease with which interdependence was increased in Europe without the parallel development of common policies, that is, the psychological factor relating to common postwar goals among the European governments to create a "new deal for Europe."

France, involved with domestic economic planning in the early 1960s, wished to institutionalize planning on a European level, but were blocked principally by the Erhard government.

Finally, common policies became more difficult to form because of the Gaullist position on supranational decision-making of any sort. De Gaulle, who viewed the nation-state not only as the highest political good but also, in political terms, as the only political authority that could receive popular legitimacy, was unwilling to surrender any decision-making power to a centralized European institution. As Pinder has pointed out, the Gaullist position was mirrored in the national bureaucracies of other states, where functionaries tended "to resist any loss of their power of unilateral decision and action which is inevitably implied in an effective procedure for taking decisions in common."[41]

Where common policies were developed during the 1960s, they resulted either from liberal motivations or from political bargains. The agreement on a common value-added tax in April 1967, for example, which had been discussed since the inception of the EEC, was designed to remove distortion in trade that accompanied divergent taxing systems.[42] Here, as in the other important achievements of the Common Market, the French view prevailed. France alone had a general value-added tax at the beginning of the treaty's implementation. The five other countries had either a cascade system, which served as an incentive to vertical concentration and was also less efficient than the value-added tax, or a mixed system.[43]

[41] Ibid., p. 99.

[42] A clue to the neoliberal implications of policies such as the TVA, or value-added tax, monopolies policies, etc., can be inferred from any of the annual reports of the Commission that are broken into sections dealing with various aspects of the community. Taxation and monopolies policies are discussed in the section entitled "Establishment and Functioning of the Common Market," which is separated from those dealing with common policies, or economic union, and common external policies.

[43] In a cascade tax system, a tax liability accrues whenever

With no common tax system, imported commodities were taxed according to the cascade system of the importing countries, and domestic or home taxes were rebated on exports. The system worked to protect local producers and was disadvantageous to the French. With common tax policies, indirect taxes on imported goods were made the same as those on comparable domestic products.

The Common Agricultural Policy (CAP), on the other hand, was less a matter of the dismantling of trade barriers than a result of a complex political bargaining process throughout the 1960s. The creation of a common market for agricultural products was far more difficult than the creation of a market in manufactured goods. Unlike the manufacturing sectors, neoliberal economic policies with regard to agriculture were desired by none of the European governments. Although the Six differed widely among themselves concerning agriculture, they also shared several common views. In none of them, for example, was agriculture submitted to market mechanisms. Each state had a national agricultural policy that had been created in the interwar period to prepare for war and to counter the effects of the depression, which had forced a depletion of monetary reserves for purposes of importing foodstuffs.

Beyond this common characteristic, there were two general types of agricultural situations. The less industrialized European countries, including Italy and parts of rural France, were distinguished by the "prevalent recourse to traditional instruments: restrictions in imports, various emergency provisions, subsidies to farmers and a few survivals of corporatist or wartime regulations."[44] In these countries there was no

---

the ownership of a product is changed. In a value-added tax system distortions to trade resulting from cascade systems are avoided by eliminating the advantages in such systems to vertically integrated companies where turnover (and hence taxing) is minimized.

[44] Manlio Rossi-Doria, "Agriculture and Europe," *Daedalus*, xciii, (1964): 345. These problems are more fully developed in François Clerc, *Le Marché commun agricole* (Paris: Presses Universitaries de France, 1964).

consistent policy for agricultural modernization. In other countries, especially Germany and the Netherlands, systems of price stabilization, policies of modernization, and income equalization between farmers and other socioeconomic groups were more highly developed. Not only, then, did well-entrenched national policies have to be changed but also highly divergent situations had to be reconciled.

The difficulties of forming a common policy for agriculture were, in the long run, overcome by the importance that the French government placed on it. From the beginning, the French made it clear that progress on the implementation of the Rome Treaty was contingent upon the successful formulation of an agricultural policy. France, with 47 percent of the community's farmland, was thought to be the principal potential beneficiary of a common agricultural policy. The French felt that if Germany and Holland would gain most from a common market in manufactured goods, they would gain most from an expanded agricultural market, especially if such a market had a price policy that would benefit French farmers. Germany, which was earmarked to pay disproportionately for this policy, was therefore interested in postponing the implementation of a common market in agriculture until after the completion of the common market in other products.

The French tactic in securing the agricultural policy was one of manipulated crisis. The French threatened to prevent the implementation of the Rome Treaty and, indeed, to withdraw from the EEC at several critical junctures throughout the 1960s. This was especially the case in July 1963, December 1964, July 1965, and May 1966. On the first two occasions, de Gaulle threatened to boycott the EEC if Germany and the other states did not agree on farm organization, timetables, an agricultural fund, and common grain prices. The French had a natural alliance in the formation of the agricultural policy with the EEC Commission. The Commission, of course, took every opportunity to strengthen EEC institutions. In the third crisis—from July 1965 to January 1966—the Commission bet on the French accepting a far-ranging centralization of EEC institutions and growth in EEC power as the price of their acceptance of French views on agriculture.[45] This price de Gaulle did not accept. In the end, the incorporation of a common agricultural policy into the fully completed customs union on July 1, 1968 was largely a product of French diplomacy and particularly of the manipulation of crises that served both to control the level of systemic interdependence and to give this control political overtones.[46]

The degree to which French policy successfully produced and manipulated crises with regard to the EEC agricultural policy illustates one of the novelties of diplomacy in an era of high levels of systemic interdependence, originally created in the EEC for certain welfare benefits that no state could receive in isolation. Since French membership was necessary for economic and political reasons for the success of the EEC, the French bargaining ploy could be successful (provided, of course, that no other state practiced crisis manipulation at the same time). But the use by the French of this tactic produced a contradictory situation for French foreign policy. For, while seeking common policies to establish a customs union, Gaullist diplomacy was unwilling to accept its logical conclusion that challenged the policy of independence.

The Gaullist policy of independence had its negative corollary in antiintegrationist measures at the supranational level, whether in defense and NATO or in economic affairs and the EEC. This antiintegrationist stance was at its peak in the

[45] The details of this, the major crisis in the EEC in the 1960s, are outlined in Miriam Camps, *European Unification in the Sixties: From the Veto to the Crisis* (New York: McGraw-Hill, 1966); and in John Newhouse, *Collision in Brussels: The Common Market Crisis of 30 June 1965* (New York: W. W. Norton, 1967).

[46] The common policy consists, most generally, of a procedure for marketing agricultural goods, a common external tariff on agricultural products, and a financing procedure partially designed to raise farming efficiency. Pricing, which was the most contentious agricultural issue, is still subject to periodic review. The policy, together with the history of crises involved in its formulation, are outlined in Walsh and Paxton, *Structure and Development of the Common Market*, pp. 56–82.

1965–1966 attack on NATO and the EEC, and was clearly outlined in de Gaulle's twelfth press conference (September 9, 1965).[47] International integration was rejected by Gaullist diplomacy because it required a dismantling of the sovereign jurisdiction of the nation-state.[48] And it was rejected for a form of cooperation that de Gaulle felt could lead to some form of confederation. In the end, this meant the acceptance of higher forms of systemic interdependence without the institutionalization of centralized transnational government. The illusion and contradiction of this position was not that interdependence implied by necessity higher levels of integration. Rather, it was with interdependence, not with integration, that national autonomy could be preserved.[49]

A fundamental aspect of systemic interdependence is the loss of autonomy in both domestic and international affairs, partly as a result of the accompanying transnational politics,

[47] See, especially, *Major Addresses, Statements and Press Conferences of General Charles de Gaulle, March 17, 1964–May 16, 1967* (New York: Ambassade de France, Service de Presse et d'Information, 1968), pp. 94–100.

[48] This does not imply that the other member governments of the EEC were any more willing than the French to accept supranational integration. But France could, in effect, be the spokesman for the German and Italian governments in this matter without the latter appearing to be the undoers of what was seen to be a desirable institution. In any case, only de Gaulle among modern statesmen had the will or capacity to articulate the nationalist position.

[49] This illusion also appears in a number of works on integration defined as community building. It may well be, as Deutsch has tried to demonstrate, that integration in Europe in the early 1960s was at a lower level than in the pre-1914 world, when measured against certain specific dimensions (Deutsch, *France, Germany and the Western Alliance*, pp. 218–39). This is especially the case with regard to psychological dimensions of statecraft. In the pre-1914 European world of closed-door diplomacy, there were some statesmen who spoke the same diplomatic language and responded to general signals of diplomatic maneuvering. Once the mobilization of mass society was introduced, and once ideologies and nationalisms developed, these aspects of community disappeared. But communal integration and systemic interdependence are quite different things.

one of the characteristics of modernization. Modernization has also been characterized by technological developments that have brought societies much closer together—developments in weaponry, in communications, in transportation, and in physical, if not social, mobility. Transnational politics, as characteristic of systemic interdependence, then arises from an increasing number of international interactions, especially among the populations of pluralistic societies, that take place largely in nongovernmental contexts.

The differences between interactions of transnational and intergovernmental systems are summarized in Kaiser's ideal-typical models that pertain particularly to the transactions within the EEC area. A "transnational society subsystem" is one where "relations between national systems are handled and decided upon by nongovernmental elites and pursued directly between social, economic, and political forces in the participating societies."[50] Intergovernmental transactions are those where "relations between national systems are handled and decided upon by elites located in governmental institutions."[51] Examples of the former are exchanges of material, capital, population, and ideas among societies, independent of governmental actions. It is precisely this type of exchange that resulted from the establishment of a customs union within the EEC. Examples of the latter are traditional alliances and new regional or global organizational activities where strategic interactions occur.

Short of any situation resembling integrated supranational government, these transnational interactions serve as breakdowns in control over the foreign activities of citizens by governments. The interactions of citizens across international boundaries may bring about situations in which governments are forced to take action, often with their freedom of choice of action restricted. This is especially the case in matters af-

[50] Karl Kaiser, "The Interaction of Regional Subsystems: Some Preliminary Notes on Recurrent Patterns and the Role of Superpowers," *World Politics*, XXI (1968): 91.

[51] Ibid., p. 92.

fecting the stability of currencies. As transnational interactions increase, the possibilities of affecting decision-making in a purely national setting, of isolation or national encapsulation, become less likely. Therefore, they make control a more difficult problem, especially because knowledge of the effects of interdependence is still limited. Kaiser concludes:

> The several crises of 1968 have shown the great potential of transnational forces as a disturbing element in the Western state system. Though in the past the notion of a general interdependence in both success and failure, notably among the noncommunist and industrialized nations, has been one of the most frequently used formulas of political rhetoric, we neither know much about the nature of the processes involved, nor have the governments been willing nor able to draw practical conclusions. Instead, the answers are sought in the old categories of the nation-state, which may well be a blueprint for another failure.[52]

Loss of control accompanying transnational politics, then, tends to result in crises of various sorts. As activities grow beyond the direct and constant observation of governments and as situations arise that threaten the status quo, governments are forced to intervene. Moreover, such situations become more common as the system becomes more interdependent. The calculated use of manipulated crisis is thus not the only diplomatic novelty of systemic interdependence. Another is the sudden occurrence of unexpected crises that force governments to collaborate in crisis management.

Fear of such crises was partly built into the Rome Treaty, and is illustrated by the logic of the economic argument laying behind it. Just as the "night-watchman" state was forced to intervene more and more in the Western economies as they developed, so it was thought the creation of a customs union would develop certain spillovers into the political sector of the European Communities. Thus, the creation of a customs union necessitated the elimination of more hidden trade dis-

[52] Karl Kaiser, "Western Europe between Inter-State Relations and Transnational Politics," mimeographed (Boston, 1969), p. 13.

tortions that could be advantageous to one or more countries, including legal obstacles, which were partially overcome with the turnover tax, various national policies on fair trade, etc., and also implied future steps toward economic union, involving the creation of common policies in transportation, global economic forecasting, monetary policies, cyclical policies, etc.

The *soi-disant* stalemate in the progress of the implementation of the more vaguely stated goals of the Rome Treaty in the late 1960s greatly obfuscated changes in policy-making and general interdependencies that had come about from the management of unanticipated crises. This is especially the case with regard to monetary policies, where the fixed exchange rates needed for a customs union delayed until 1969 the more traditional use of variable exchange rates for adjustment purposes, but where real monetary union was discounted as a possibility for political reasons. In effect, crises of the sort that have occurred in the monetary field can be expected to appear in other areas in the 1970s, and it can be expected that mixed solutions—some leading toward positive integration and others toward retrenchment—will be in order. Cooper has summarized these political solutions for the economic problems of the highly interdependent states in the Atlantic region. His suggestions are equally applicable to the more interdependent European countries. He sees three general alternatives to meet the political requisites of systemic interdependence:

(a) to accept the integration and the consequential loss of national freedom, and to engage in the *joint* determination of economic objectives and policies;

(b) to accept the integration but attempt to preserve as much national autonomy as possible by providing . . . accommodation(s). . . .

(c) to reject the integration by deliberate imposition of barriers to the integrating forces, freedom of foreign trade and international capital movements.[53]

[53] Cooper, *Economics of Interdependence*, p. 262.

Broadly speaking, then, systemic interdependence has created transnational structures that have diminished governments' control over both domestic and international affairs, and has induced governments to pursue cooperative relations with other states. As highly modern societies have become more interdependent, they also have become more susceptible to events beyond the control of their governments. The need for greater control, which exhibits itself through unexpected crises, can result in the making of new commitments and the establishment of new organizations that serve as instrumentalities for achieving these goals. Paradoxically, because of these commitments on the national level, certain kinds of control become less possible than ever. The crisis of control on the international level is thus internalized on the national level at a time when increased demands for welfare, education, and social services within each state are greater than ever, and the loss of international control is further exacerbated by the loss of domestic control.

The upshot of these tendencies toward systemic interdependence is a crisis in sovereignty that is likely to worsen appreciably in the coming decades. The crisis of sovereignty is attested to in the French case by the great concern with sovereignty in both domestic and international affairs in the 1960s.

Interdependence and Collective International Goods

A third form of interdependence that describes the relationships among the highly industrialized Western states may be characterized as public, or collective goods. Collective goods involve in formal terms both strategic interactions and systemic interdependence, as well as an additional factor that was first investigated by welfare economists. Pigou, one of the founders of welfare economics, has described this type of interdependence in the following terms:

Here, the essence of the matter is that one person A, in the course of rendering some service, for which payment is made, to a second person B, incidentally also renders services or disservices to other persons (not producers of like services), of such a sort *that payments cannot be extracted from the benefitted parties or compensation enforced on behalf of the injured parties.*[54]

The nonexclusive aspects of activities revolving about social groups and characterizing group behavior also define the relations of groups of states or interstate organizations. It should not have been surprising, therefore, that the general features of behavior involved in the supply and allocation of collective goods should also be found in international organizations and alliances.[55]

In addition to strategic interdependence, systemic interdependence, and nonexclusivity, collective goods are characterized by the principle that *once such a good is supplied by or for any one unit of a group (be it a person or a collectivity), it can also be provided to other units at either no or very little cost. Since exclusion is difficult, if not impossible, "it is of the essence of an organization that it provides an inseparable, generalized benefit."*[56] As Olson has shown, given the two principles just outlined, rational action on the part of any unit in the group would lead that unit, in the absence of co-

[54] From A. C. Pigou, *The Economics of Welfare*, 4th ed. (London: Macmillan, 1932), p. 183, quoted in William J. Baumol, *Welfare Economics and the Theory of the State*, p. 25 (emphasis his).

[55] Mancur Olson, who first applied this commonplace of welfare economics at the more general level of intergroup behavior, was also the first (with Richard Zeckhauser) to apply it to international organizations. See Mancur Olson, Jr., *The Logic of Collective Action: Public Goods and the Theory of Groups* (Cambridge, Mass.: Harvard University Press, 1965); Mancur Olson, Jr., and Richard Zeckhauser, "An Economic Theory of Alliances," *Review of Economics and Statistics*, XLVII (1966): 266–79; idem, *An Economic Theory of Alliances* (Santa Monica, Calif.: Rand Corporation, 1966); idem, "Collective Goods, Comparative Advantage and Alliance Efficiency," in *Issues in Defense Economics*, ed. Roland N. McKean (New York: Columbia University Press, 1967), pp. 25–48. The last paper combines the theory of collective goods with the theory of comparative advantage.

[56] Olson, *Logic of Collective Action*, p. 15.

ercion, to provide suboptimal contributions for the supply of a good. In addition, there is "a tendency for the 'larger' members—those that place a higher absolute value on the public good—to bear a disproportionate share of the burden."[57] In other words, by assuming rational behavior on the part of the individual members of a group, the individual's and the group's interests will differ, and individuals

> will *not* act to advance their common or group objective unless there is coercion to force them to do so, or unless some separate incentive, distinct from the achievement of the common or group interest, is offered to the members of the group individually on the condition that they help bear the costs or burdens involved in the achievement of the group objectives.[58]

With the introduction of rational calculus into the theory of collective action, its applicability to international relations becomes obvious. Interest maximization has always been a central concept of politics. With the kinds of interdependence involved in the supplying of collective goods, it would be surprising if some small state did not try to maximize its freedom of action by suboptimally paying for the cost of some collective mechanism; that is, in terms of international relations, it is likely in a situation where collective goods exist that smaller nations will attempt to receive the collective benefit and pay less than their share or nothing while also satisfying some additional goal or set of goals. In this sense, the anti-integrationist attitude of France in NATO or the

---

[57] Olson and Zeckhauser, *Economic Theory of Alliances*, p. 4. As Olson and Zeckhauser also show, there is a differing incentive for any individual to pay without coercion in large membership groups and in low membership groups. In the latter, there is greater incentive to share cost burdens. For a more general thesis concerning the provision of collective goods that is also critical of Olson, see Norman Frohlich, Joseph A. Oppenheimer, and Oran R. Young, *Political Leadership and Collective Goods* (Princeton, N.J.: Princeton University Press, 1971).

[58] Olson, *Logic of Collective Action*, p. 2.

Group of Ten can be partially explained by the theory of collective action.

Although Olson and Zeckhauser have indicated the potential use of welfare economic theory, it is not yet well enough developed to do more than prefigure a fully tested hypothesis. Generally much evidence for the applicability of the theory of collective action to international organizations, including alliances, has been adduced. However, almost no work has been done to predict the behavior of individual units at the micro-level, so that the usefulness of the theory is still limited, even though it serves to introduce the opportunities available for smaller states with respect to alliances.

French policy toward NATO during the 1960s thus cannot be understood without taking into account the kinds of interdependence that characterized that alliance. The alliance was a voluntary organization with very low levels of centralization and integration. Therefore, no coercive mechanism could assure that contributions to collective defense would reach an optimal level as defined collectively. Nor was there any incentive for individual states to contribute to the collective defense effort above a minimum. Indeed, an incentive motivated by insecurity actually diminished throughout the 1960s as nuclear deterrence and changes in American security policy from massive retaliation to flexible response were introduced. In addition, given the global change in strategic interactions discussed at the beginning of this chapter, European defense generally was perceived more and more as an automatic spin-off of American national defense policies, and was largely provided for by the fact that the United States had a credible deterrent.[59]

The theory of collective action can not only indicate the opportunity costs of actions independent or autonomous of the alliance but also can pinpoint the expected actions of

[59] See especially Frederick L. Pryor, *Public Expenditures in Communist and Capitalist Nations* (Homewood, Ill.: Richard D. Irwin, 1968), pp. 84–127.

state leadership, given the assumptions about interest maximization and specified goals. In particular, however, the specific goals of the leadership in question and the implemented strategy must be observed. In elaborating French military strategy throughout the 1960s, de Gaulle's tactics followed the general course of the unfolding of the *telos* of the Fifth Republic, as he defined it, and began with changes in the international setting of the alliance, specifically with the reassertion of European strength in the 1960s, with the perceived lowering of the Soviet threat, and with shifts in alliance structure brought about by nuclear weapons. These changes only served to reinforce differences in historical perspectives, especially between the leadership of France and of the United States.[60] Given a distinct historical perspective, with different long-range as well as immediate goals, de Gaulle was the first statesman to take advantage of the transformed security setting and to implement what was perceived to be an increase in French freedom to manuever.

The exposition of the French defense strategy in the 1960s parallels the development of the articulated rationale of the French foreign policy of independence that can be divided into three phases corresponding to important international and domestic changes.[61]

In the first phase from 1958 to 1962, de Gaulle tried to reverse what he considered to be the general trend of French

[60] These changes are described in Henry A. Kissinger, *The Troubled Partnership: A Reappraisal of the Atlantic Alliance* (New York: Mc-Graw-Hill, 1965), pp. 3–28. Kissinger's essay on structural changes within the alliance is brought up to date in Pierre Hassner, "The Changing Context of European Security." Hassner's article, written before the Soviet invasion of Czechoslovakia in August 1968, sees 1962 as a watershed in alliance relations, marking the end of the postwar global political situation and the beginning of something new.

[61] For a discussion of French military strategy within the context of French diplomacy in the 1960s, see Wilfrid L. Kohl, *The French Nuclear Force and Atlantic Diplomacy* (Princeton, N.J.: Princeton University Press, 1971). The argument is summarized in idem, "The French Nuclear Deterrent," *Proceedings of the Academy of Political Science*, XXIX (1968): 8–94. See also Chapter 4 below.

foreign policy under the Fourth Republic by reasserting French presence. Hampered by the Algerian War and the lack of what he thought were the most modern weapons,[62] de Gaulle sought to gain for France some measure of control over the direction of the Atlantic alliance. Desiring to prevent another sellout along the lines of Suez, and annoyed at the unwillingness of the United States to see the Algerian War as part of a defense effort involving NATO participation, de Gaulle felt that French global interests could be pursued only by securing a French voice in a NATO directorate. De Gaulle's motivation was clearly spelled out in his letter to President Eisenhower of September 24, 1958 (proposing a tripartite NATO directorate consisting of France, Britain, and the United States) and in his address at the Centre des Hautes Etudes Militaires of November 3, 1959 (outlining the policy of developing an independent nuclear striking force that would give France leverage over the other NATO allies).[63]

The second phase of de Gaulle's policy opened with the end of the Algerian War, with changes in the French domestic political system, and with changes at the international level from 1962 to 1963. The opening of the Sino-Soviet split, the success of deterrence in reducing the Soviet threat to West-

[62] The best discussion of the development of nuclear technology in France is in Lawrence Scheinman, *Atomic Energy Policy in France under the Fourth Republic* (Princeton, N.J.: Princeton University Press, 1965).

[63] This is a disagreement with those who see the second phase of French foreign policy, including French NATO policy, as marking an acknowledgment by de Gaulle of the failure of diplomatic initiatives from 1958 to 1959 to gain control of NATO policy and to enlarge NATO's interests to a global sphere. This argument is developed in William G. Andrews, "De Gaulle and NATO," in *Modern European Governments: Cases in Comparative Policy Making*, ed. Roy C. Macridis (Englewood Cliffs, N.J.: Prentice-Hall, 1968), pp. 92–115. The general problems for both NATO and France stemming from this second phase of Gaullist foreign policy are discussed in Carl H. Amme, Jr., *NATO Without France* (Stanford, Calif.: Hoover Institution on War, Revolution, and Peace, 1967).

ern Europe, the elaboration of the McNamara strategy of flexible response, and the development of a French nuclear striking force all served to free French foreign-policy options.[64] The changes at the international level were reinforced by those within France, where de Gaulle secured greater independence in foreign policy, allowing him to adopt new tactics to gain greater French presence by means of independence rather than by means of control over NATO strategy. The integrationist logic of the Multilateral Force (MLF) through 1963, fluctuations in the international monetary situation, and changes in Europe all pointed toward the potential of this strategy of independence. At the same time, the development of the nuclear striking force and strengthening of the franc meant for de Gaulle that France could now negotiate from a position of greater strength than had been possible before 1962.

The second phase of Gaullist foreign policy included the two vetoes of British entrance into the Common Market, the elections of 1967, and de Gaulle's assumption of extraordinary controls over the domestic economy so that he could implement a policy of economic modernization to buttress his foreign policy. The phase also involved the EEC crises of 1965, 1966, and 1967 over agriculture and the structure of Europe, the withdrawal from NATO, and the frontal attack on the dollar. The general movement of French foreign policy during this phase was one of implementing autonomy by means of the articulation of a policy of neutralism. The strategic rationale of French policy sought in ideological terms to create a third force, or a third way, unlike either American capitalism or Soviet socialism. This force was expressed in terms of a Franco-European humanitarian path of modernity and its strategic rationale was enunciated most clearly by Charles Ailleret who repeated the general outlines of French strategy as foreseen in de Gaulle's addresses at the Centre des Hautes Etudes Militaires, in 1959 and January 1968. The

[64] Charles Ailleret "Défense 'dirigée' ou défense 'tous azimuts,'" *Revue de défense nationale*, XXIII (1967): 1923–32.

self-conscious projection of the eighteenth-century Vauban fortifications to the level of France by means of nuclear weapons marked the logical conclusion as well as the termination of the second phase of Gaullist foreign policy that involved the kind of independence made impossible by both the levels of interdependence in all three senses of the term as described above, and by the underlying material base upon which it was founded.[65]

The limits of French independence are seen in the third phase of Gaullist foreign policy, which began in early 1968 and continued through de Gaulle's resignation in April 1969. During this period, the international and domestic conditions that had made plausible the policy of independence changed. Thus, the third phase is one of retrenchment and contradiction. At the international level, the invasion of Czechoslovakia in August 1968 meant that the Gaullist view on basic changes within the blocs had missed the mark: the Soviet threat appeared to be undiminished. On the domestic level, the increasing costs of the striking force led critics both within and outside the armed forces to call it into question.[66] Persistent balance-of-payments deficits had gradually weakened the franc, undercutting French international monetary policy. The events of May 1968 and the need for collaboration with the United States and Britain against Germany on monetary concerns, coupled with persistent and increasingly frequent monetary crises, all pointed to the conclusion that at the international level the limits on French independence imposed by interdependence had been reached.

While it is difficult to point out the exact effects of the existence of collective goods on the international level on

[65] For a discussion and criticism of this position, see Wolf Mendl, "Perspectives of Contemporary French Defense Policy," World Today, xxiv (1968): 50–58 and Alastair Buchan, "Battening Down Vauban's Hatches," Interplay, ii:10 (1968): 4–7.

[66] See the critical review of Ailleret's "tous azimuts" strategy in M. Fourquet, "Emploi des différents systèmes de forces dans le cadre de la stratégie de dissuasion," Revue de défense nationale, xxv (1969): 757–68.

French foreign policy, it is far easier to show that such goods do have effects both on enhancing and limiting degrees of freedom. The imprecision with which these effects can be described is a function both of the limited level of theory about them at the present time and of the interaction of domestic and foreign affairs. But a more detailed examination of the French defense policy (Chapter 4) and international monetary policies (Chapter 5) should, in the absence of deductive theory, point out further the limits on independence that result from this type of interdependence.

Modernization and the Transformation of the International System

The trends in international relationships, described above, have been the focus of much debate and controversy among scholars in recent years. The controversy not only focuses upon the question of whether, in fact, there has been an increase in the scope and level of interdependence in international society, and, if there has been such an increase, whether it has substantially altered the environment in which foreign policies are formulated and implemented, but also pertains to the following questions: Is there, in international politics, a relatively permanent focus upon the nation-state, which derives from the fragmentation of the state system into relatively autonomous political units? Or, has the emergence of new forms of interdependence established novel and unprecedented patterns of interstate interactions? Are high levels of international interdependence typical only of the present era? Or, were they even more marked in other epochs, such as the fifteenth and sixteenth centuries when the emergent state system coexisted with transnational remnants of medieval Christendom? Has the system of states been disintegrating from its more homogeneous status one century ago? Or has the web of interdependence grown tighter?

In this chapter, direct and indirect evidence has been adduced for the hypothesis that the levels and types of interdependence characteristic of the relationships among the advanced industrialized states have increased markedly. However, there is an obligation to note that this hypothesis is controversial and that the debates arising from different frameworks designed to analyze contemporary international politics are not likely to abate so long as no theoretical breakthroughs develop that can settle the matter by explaining the interrelationships among trends such as those discussed above. It is argued somewhat biasedly that changes in international relations over the past century have been dramatic and transformational, and the growth of international interdependence is a direct offshoot of the process of modernization, especially if modernization is defined in terms of the phenomenal growth in knowledge that accompanied the scientific revolution. Knowledge itself cannot be monopolized by the members of any one society and is inherently transnational. Indeed, the foundation of contemporary international society can be viewed as a direct effect of the continuously increasing "transnational stock of knowledge," to borrow Kuznets's phrase. He has argued that the basis of modern economic growth central to trends in international interdependence is "the increase in the stock of useful knowledge and the extension of its application," and has asserted that

> no matter where these technological innovations emerge the economic growth of any given nation depends upon their adoption. In that sense, whatever the national affiliation of resources used, any single nation's economic growth has its base somewhere outside its boundaries—with the single exception of the pioneering nation, and no nation remains the pioneer for long.[67]

Evidence for the linkage between modernization and the growth of international interdependence is still indirect but depends upon such phenomena as the increased incidence of monetary crises, perceived technology gaps and the political

[67] Simon Kuznets, *Modern Economic Growth; Rate, Structure and Spread* (New Haven: Yale University Press, 1966), pp. 286–87.

responses to them in Europe and elsewhere, efforts to coordinate national policies at the international level so that interdependencies can be brought under political control, and, above all, the politicization of economically derived values, a concomitant of which is the increased sensitivity of national economic policies to external activities. Each of these effects can be derived logically from the assumptions concerning modernization and interdependence argued in detail in this chapter.

The major structural features of interdependence as they are derived from the processes of modernization can be described under a set of headings that should be a useful vehicle for summarizing the argument of this chapter.

First, the development of a global international system occurred for the first time in history. This development began, of course, in fifteenth- and sixteenth-century Europe as an aspect of the age of exploration. The industrial revolution, changes in transportation technology facilitating European colonization, the development of parochialism, and the consolidation of organizations of political control in the form of nation-states all contributed to this historical process. It was not until the late nineteenth century that, with the last wave of European imperialism, the changes accompanying modernization were "extended to all other societies and resulted in a worldwide transformation affecting all human relationships."[68] This great transformation was by no means a nonviolent process. Repression on the domestic level was mirrored by international wars that resulted in the projection of strategic interaction from a European to a bipolar and global scale.

The great transformation has become so pervasive in global politics that both the instabilities that have accompanied it as well as its recency and novelty have been lost. Its instability, as well as a large measure of its stability, derives, in part, from its level of interdependence. The states of the world

[68] Cyril E. Black, *Dynamics of Modernization: A Study in Comparative History* (New York: Harper and Row, 1967), p. 7.

have historically been loosely interdependent. "Safety-valve" areas on the periphery of regions of intensive conflict have, in the past, served to release the pressures on violent international confrontation. The global city, however, has no periphery and is linked together not only by a communications network, which has made the transmittal of information potentially instantaneous, but also by a set of strategic interaction patterns. These patterns of interaction have become global by virtue of the development of nuclear weapons and ballistic missiles, which have made global security indivisible, at least as far as nuclear war is concerned.

Second, modernization has brought about the essentially transitional nature of the contemporary international system. This is the case whether one defines transition as persistent change (a fundamental feature of modern life) or whether one defines it as a transitory phase between two eras. This latter meaning has become widely held and is perhaps most generally associated with Barraclough's thesis.[69] According to him, the years between 1890 and 1960 delimit more or less the temporal span of "the great divide between two ages in the history of mankind," namely, the ages of modern and contemporary history. The conjuncture of the societies of the world into one social system derives, then, from the processes of modernization and the corresponding scientific, technological, and industrial changes that have "acted both as a solvent of the old order and as a catalyst of the new. They created urban and industrial society as we know it today; they were also the instruments by which industrial society subsequently expanded into the industrially undeveloped parts of the world."[70]

Third, the revolution of modernization on international society involves the paradox of change, not only continual innovation of the sort described in exponential growth curves but also continual destruction of outmoded institutions. Some

[69] Geoffrey Barraclough, *An Introduction to Contemporary History* (New York: Basic Books, 1964), p. 2.
[70] Ibid., p. 43.

of these institutions represent universal values that have been replaced by other institutions characterized by particularism or vice versa. The other two logical combinations between particularism and individualism also abound. Thus, international society over the past seventy to one hundred years has been characterized not only by both fragmentation and integration, by the collapse of the universal norms of European diplomacy and their replacement by the fragmented norms of modern nationalism, by the breakup of empires and the proliferation of nation-states, by the collapse of a universal economic standard of value (gold) and its replacement by a mixture of various and differing standards, *but also* by the growth of various kinds of transnational activities, especially among the set of highly industrialized countries, including the increased mobility of capital, of labor, of technology, and of goods and services. Such fragmentation and integration are of the essence of the revolution of modernization in contemporary international society.

Fourth, in the twentieth century there exists a lag between perceptions and reality. In a world undergoing continuous change, no individual decision-maker is able to formulate policies or make decisions toward a stable environment. Perceptions and decisions inevitably are based on experience gained in the past and therefore in a world rather different from the present or future. This lag between perceptions of the world and actual conditions may result in the formulation of policy or the making of decisions that are not only counterproductive but also potentially capable of resulting in violence.

Fifth, transnational activities have grown to a scale greater than ever before in history, especially with regard to the fundamental basis of the kind of society that the processes of modernization has apparently produced, a society based on a phenomenal growth in knowledge, which, as argued above, is inherently transnational. Since the growth of transnational activities has occurred predominantly in those areas of the world that are most modernized (the highly industrialized societies of the West), they are not coextensive with the limits of global society. Rather, the consequent gap between the highly developed and less developed sectors of the international system has exacerbated the dilemmas inherent in other aspects of international society today.

Sixth, there has been a revolution in the geographic conceptualization of international politics. If there is something that marks international politics from other forms of politics or social affairs, it is that it is inherently a geographically based discipline. Statecraft has, therefore, traditionally been structured by calculations of distance, but the revolution in communications and transformations that accompanied industrial growth served to revolutionize the concept of distance and to transform it into one based on dynamic processes, especially those pertaining either to time or to costs. The increased abstraction of international affairs inevitably reverts to basic geopolitical concepts of distance—measured, however, in terms of time (as in the delivery of nuclear warheads between the Soviet Union and the United States) or of costs. Thus, wherever modern communication and transportation linkages exist, they have tended to counteract the political limits of the states and have made cities, such as London, New York, and Paris, much closer to one another for certain functional purposes than they are to adjacent areas. Similarly, the psychological distances between disparate cultures have been reduced, and simultaneously, the probability of conflict among isolable areas has increased. Bottlenecks of transportation that exist wherever such modern linkages terminate also call for new instruments of control to alleviate anxieties produced in the nonmodernized world when that world is confronted by phenomena completely alien to it.[71]

Finally, there has been the apparent merging of political and economic phenomena in the mid-twentieth century. Many of the dilemmas outlined in these two theoretical chapters result from our predisposition to think separately in terms

[71] See Albert Wohlstetter, "Strength, Interest and New Technologies," in *The Implications of Military Technology in the 1970s*, Adelphi Papers No. 46 (London: Institute for Strategic Studies, 1968).

of political and economic activities. In an age when both domestic and international politics take place primarily in terms of the allocation of economic resources, only holistic accounts will suffice for adequate explanation. The politicization of economic affairs and the creation of economic value for political goods is what the contemporary transnational age is about. Politics and economics can no longer be conceptualized as independent of the other.

Each of these structural characteristics of international interdependence served to limit French independence during the 1960s in ways to be detailed in the remaining chapters. However, the case study in itself does not prove these generalizations concerning transformations in the norms and processes of international affairs, but at best only adduces indirect evidence for them. On the one hand, the theoretical statement embodied in these two first chapters has been concerned with an interpretation of international affairs that is incomplete. The hypothesized trends in relations among advanced industrialized societies omit a great deal of the substance of contemporary international affairs, including asymmetries in military potential and economic development that may alter significantly the selected conditions. Moreover, the linkage adduced between modernization and increased interdependence must be tentative since no direct ties were specified. On the other hand, empirical evidence for the hypotheses must come from a wider context if they are to be confirmed with greater confidence. Not only the foreign policies of other highly modernized societies but also those of a number of less modernized historical and contemporary societies must be examined.

II

FRANCE AND THE PROBLEM
OF INDEPENDENCE
IN AN INTERDEPENDENT WORLD

INTRODUCTION

THE theoretical analysis in Part I pointed up a set of problems that ought to be prominent in the foreign policy of any
highly modernized society. The politics of resource allocation
to define and support foreign and domestic goals, the salience
of foreign economic policy, the exigencies of crisis diplomacy,
and the impingement of international interdependence on
domestic economic policy necessarily figure significantly in
public debates in all such societies if the general argument is
valid. At the same time, the manner in which a political leadership handles these problems depends inevitably on the requisites of its own peculiar circumstances, including its political traditions and the immediate social issues that confront
it. The interplay between the general problems of foreign policy that face France and the other highly modernized societies
and the way in which one society addressed them is the subject of the remaining chapters.

The choice of the general subject of French foreign policy,
of the individual problems selected for analysis, and of the
period that delimits this study were made in the hopes that
the selection would provide a severe test for the theoretical
framework. France in the 1960s was quickly transforming
and modernizing, and did not seem to be the sort of society
for which traditional diplomatic style could be effective, at
least in the long run. Yet, the existence of that style seemed
to illuminate clearly the theoretical foreign policy problems
discussed in Part I.

Modernized societies are extremely complex. For them, as
has been seen, the distinctions between high defense policies
and low economic policies that de Gaulle tried to maintain
no longer exist. Nor does the traditional sharp distinction between foreign and domestic affairs exist. Rather, this kind of
society is highly interdependent with other such societies, and
inevitably, tensions that are volatile and difficult to reduce or
to control permeate them. Spectacular initiatives seem only to

exacerbate the frictions and dilemmas inherent in the foreign policies of modern societies.

The case study is limited to the period from 1962 to 1969, although the examination of aspects of earlier foreign poli cies is made when warranted. The terminal point is far more obvious than is the initial point. The departure of de Gaulle from the Presidency in 1969 on a nominal issue of domestic governmental reform represents a tacit admission of his failure in delineating a foreign policy and conveniently serves as a final point in this examination because he maintained a consistency in foreign policy objectives that is difficult to find in other modernized states.

The starting point of 1962 is particularly relevant. A series of factors relating to the interactions of domestic and foreign policies, on the one hand, and of foreign policy and the structure of international society, on the other hand, served to foster the illusion after 1962 of increased French autonomy. The illusion resulted from situations internal and external to France that were products of the past or prospects for the future.

In 1962 the major legacies of postwar French foreign policy were liquidated, especially the Algerian War and the dismantling of the colonial empire. The end of the Algerian War had a double effect on French foreign policy. On the one hand, it put to an end one of the major problems that had led to *immobilisme* and eventually to the downfall of the Fourth Republic, and that plagued the early years of the Fifth Republic. Decolonization not only ceased to be the major external problem of France but also served to build up hopes for domestic unity; it marked the end of the colonial legacy and the possibility of reintegrating a society whose splits had been exacerbated; and it also freed resources tied down by colonial conflict, so that they could be used for other foreign and domestic ends.

In addition to marking the liquidation of the major foreign-policy issues of the postwar period, 1962 marks, in an institutional sense, the beginning of the unfolding of the *telos* of the

Fifth Republic. The Constitution of 1958 was drafted in a political context that had little to do with the realities of the social and political situation of France in 1962, and "owes its parentage [not only] to an established doctrinal tradition [and] the particular ideas and experiences of its authors," but also to "the combination of immediate political circumstances."[1] In each case, there were great changes by 1962. The doctrine upon which the principal framers of the Constitution, de Gaulle and Michel Debré, had been in accord in 1958 pertained specifically to the political context of the Fourth Republic. The Fifth Republic Constitution was designed to resolve historical problems that France in 1962 no longer faced, especially the problems of a weak political system with numerous parties and chronic instability. It was also designed to isolate the international or foreign and domestic spheres from one another, to insulate them so that they would have little mutual effect. According to the 1958 Constitution, the President, elected by a college of 81,764 electors, 76,359 of whom represented metropolitan France (and 51 percent of whom represented communes of less than 9,000 inhabitants),[2] was in charge of those functions concerned with international affairs. The Prime Minister, as head of the Cabinet, was concerned with domestic functions. By 1962, however, the situation of 1958 had changed. De Gaulle, under the pressing need to negotiate the end of the Algerian War, changed his mind on the constitutional order.[3] He still felt,

[1] A. Nicholas Wahl, "The French Constitution of 1958: The Initial Draft and its Origins," *American Political Science Review*, LIII (1959): 358.

[2] See Dorothy Pickles, *The Fifth French Republic*, 3d ed. (New York: Frederick A. Praeger, 1966), pp. 130–31.

[3] On the constitutional changes of 1962, see William G. Andrews and Stanley Hoffmann, "France: The Search for Presidentialism," in *European Politics I*, ed. William G. Andrews (Princeton, N.J.: Van Nostrand Co., 1966), pp. 77–138; Bernard E. Brown, "The Decision to Elect the President by Popular Vote," in *Cases in Comparative Politics*, ed. James B. Christoph (Boston: Little, Brown, 1965), pp. 181–203; François Goguel, "Réflexions sur le régime présidentiel,"

as in 1958, that the chief concerns of the President were to be in the realm of foreign affairs. However, he felt that he could not accomplish this by maintaining a Presidency elected by a representative college, or by separating domestic and foreign functions in governmental operations.

The 1962 constitutional revision had, therefore, two aspects. The formation of a Presidency subject to plebiscite was designed to increase the legitimacy of the chief executive by tying the office directly to popular sovereignty so that he could be the single national representative. This would have the effect not only of giving the presidential office the power and dignity needed to implement international goals but also of assuring that the presidential regime would be maintained in a post-de Gaulle Fifth Republic. The institutionalization of an executive subject to plebiscite furthermore crystallized a tradition that had been realized through periodic eruptions in French history and that had been associated with the two Napoleons and Pétain. Connected with antiparliamentarianism, the creation of such an executive was based on a notion of political legitimacy derived directly from the populace. The executive could relate directly to it without the intervention of any intermediary political bodies.[4]

Second, the change to a Presidency subject to plebiscite meant that the President would be in charge of all policies, both domestic and foreign. By 1962 de Gaulle had realized that the initial ideas, which he had shared with Debré in 1958, on reforming the Parliament had failed and that domestic policy-making had more and more come to bypass

---

Revue française de science politique, XII (1962): 289–311; Georges Laval, "Réflexions sur le régime politique en France," *Revue française de science politique*, XII (1962): 813–44; Pickles, *Fifth French Republic*, pp. 130–31.

[4] The development of policy-making as a process of direct confrontation between the executive subject to plebiscite and interest groups is traced in A. Nicholas Wahl, "The Fifth Republic: From Last Word to After-thought," in *Lawmakers in a Changing World*, ed. Elke Frank (Englewood Cliffs, N.J.: Prentice-Hall, 1966), pp. 49–64.

Parliament and to result from processes of direct confrontation between the executive and various interest groups. Such policy-making required that the executive be in charge of domestic as well as foreign affairs.[5]

In addition, de Gaulle realized by 1962 that the execution of foreign policy made it necessary not only that the powers of the President be implemented along the lines incorporated into the 1958 Constitution but also that the domestic sectors be mobilized as well. This mobilization had two aspects. One dealt with the material basis of national power, while the other pertained to the psychological and sociological bases of national unity. For de Gaulle the Presidency was to be the office from which foreign policy would be conducted. The foreign policy would be comprised of *grandes entreprises* as a means of regaining the national unity that had been absent from French society. French society had been split by the issues of communism and decolonization. Foreign-policy undertakings were one means of gaining that national unity. At the same time, it was perceived as the requisite of national action abroad. A singularly defined national interest meant that the nation had to be mobilized to fulfill it. In this respect, the President had to mobilize not only the population for *grandes entreprises* but also the material resources to sup-

[5] The performance by the executive of functions that de Gaulle and Debré had assumed would, in 1958, be in the hands of parliament and the Prime Minister was symbolized by the change of Prime Ministers in 1962, when Pompidou succeeded Debré, by the change in the rhetoric which identified the President no longer as the *arbitre* among conflicting interests, but the *guide* of the nation, and by the incorporation of the President into the Cabinet and the transformation of the Cabinet into a collective decision-making body. There is some disagreement whether Debré and de Gaulle originally shared the same views on the separation of domestic and foreign affairs and the reform of the parliament in 1958. Wahl suggests that they did share a common interpretation of the 1958 Constitution. Hoffmann feels they did not and de Gaulle could turn to the implementation of his own notions only after the end of the Algerian War. Contrast Wahl, "The French Constitution of 1958," with Andrews and Hoffmann, "France: The Search for Presidentialism."

port those undertakings. The modernization of society and the concomitant technological development of French industry to support a nuclear arsenal became the great domestic counterparts to a foreign policy of independence and *grandes entreprises*. The mobilization of domestic society, in this sense, also began in 1962, not only because the end of the Algerian War freed the resources for other tasks, but also because the general basis of the French political system as it would exist for the next five or six years was then established.

Third, in 1962 modern French society begins to emerge. By 1962 France had become a modernized society of high industrial capacity and mass consumption. Modernization in France, to be sure, had begun centuries before. On the basis of several criteria of modernity, France was the first modern European nation-state. For example, the centralization of French administrative structures and the establishment of a national bureaucracy were salient characteristics of the *ancien régime* in France. In addition, France was the first society in which mass political mobilization occurred. Both aspects of modernity occurred in France before the development of other modern social features. Industrial modernization, for example, was "abrupt instead of continuous and incremental."[6] After World War II, French industry became modernized at a relatively rapid pace. This was true in terms not only of physical well-being but also of psychological orientations. For example, in 1958 only 20 percent of French households had refrigerators, while in 1962, 40 percent had them. Ten percent in 1958 had television receivers, while in 1962 the number had doubled to 20 percent. Similar sudden increases in possession of consumer goods characteristic of modern societies could be found in automobiles, washing machines, and phonographs.[7]

[6] Henry Ehrmann, *Politics in France*, 2d ed. (Boston: Little, Brown, 1971), 304–19. See also Bernard E. Brown, "The French Experience of Modernization," *World Politics*, xxi (1969): 366–91.

[7] Institut National de la Statistique et des Etudes Economiques, *Annuaire statistique de la France*, 1967 (Paris: 1968), p. 704. It should

With regard to psychological outlooks, the most noticeable change was the widespread orientation to the future rather than to the present or to the past, which occurred immediately after World War II. For example, French industries were rebuilt in the aftermath of World War I with the same equipment, even the same bricks, as the war-ruined factories that were being replaced. After World War II, industries were usually modernized with the latest equipment, machines, and building structures.[8] Planning for economic growth rather than maintenance of economic stalemate became the salient feature of the national economy. In virtually every major sector of the French economy and political system, orientations toward the status quo were replaced by those toward the future. The number of societies and organizations involved in planning for the future or looking to the future also proliferated.

The change in orientation toward the domestic aspects of society was also, although more slowly, confronted in foreign affairs. As Hoffmann and others have indicated, the corollary of the stalemate and status quo society in terms of foreign affairs was the maintenance of a status quo international system in which French equality and stature could be sustained, albeit artificially. While this foreign-policy tradition lingered long after the development of modernization in domestic society, it also passed. By 1962 one of the important changes in French foreign policy was its orientation to the future and to change in international society rather than maintenance of the preexisting order.[9] French society, in

be noted that by 1967, 67 percent of French households had refrigerators, 53 percent television, and 55 percent automobiles.

[8] See the discussion on this in Charles P. Kindleberger, *Economic Growth in France and Britain, 1851–1950* (Cambridge, Mass.: Harvard University Press, 1964), pp. 88–134. Evidence of awareness of this change was incorporated into the title of the Plan, which was for reconstruction *and* modernization.

[9] The change in orientation from past or status quo to future orientations is the theme which unites an extraordinary number of books

short, reached the age of high mass consumption at the same time that the colonial legacy was eliminated and that a political foundation of the Fifth Republic was laid.

Fourth, the ideals and norms of French foreign policy articulated by de Gaulle gave it a new direction which provided the philosophy behind the Fifth Republic as reconstituted in 1962 and which was the major theme of French foreign policy in the 1960s. All of the other three factors gave the appearance of supporting a policy of independence and autonomy in foreign affairs. The liquidation of the past resulted in a sharp reduction of French commitments abroad, the breadth of which, in part, forced France to tie its security to that of the Western alliance. The reconstitution of the political regime of the Fifth Republic under the unifying command of the *guide*, de Gaulle, gave the appearance that domestic society as a whole could be mobilized to serve the national interest as defined by the President; and the modernization of French domestic society fostered the appearance that independence was possible in international activities, an illusion sustained by changes in the international system, particularly the nuclear stalemate between the Soviet Union and the United States. This meant not only that French defense was provided by the United States as a function of American security without France having to contribute to an alliance structure but also that great degrees of freedom of action were

---

on France written in recent years. Laurence Wylie has discussed this change in terms of village life in *Village in the Vaucluse*, 2d ed. (Cambridge, Mass.: Harvard University Press, 1964). It is the general theme of Stanley Hoffmann et al., *In Search of France* (Cambridge, Mass.: Harvard University Press, 1963); of R. L. Wagner et al., *La France d'aujourd'hui* (London: George G. Harrap, 1964); and of John Ardagh, *The New French Revolution* (New York: Harper and Row, 1968). The same general changes are summarized in Robert Gilpin, *France in the Age of the Scientific State* (Princeton, N.J.: Princeton University Press, 1968); and in Harvey Waterman, *Political Change in Contemporary France; The Politics of an Industrial Democracy* (Columbus, Ohio: Charles E. Merrill, 1969).

available without fear of endangering French security. Another illusion was that the high-policy security area constituted all of international events, while still another was that in matters of high-policy French actions could significantly affect the structure of the international system. The latter view ignored the growing interdependence between France and the other North Atlantic states along dimensions constituting other areas of foreign policy.

The progressive dispelling of this compounded illusion meant that de Gaulle's main heritage is not likely to be found in foreign policy. Rather, the legacy of political and social institutions, which de Gaulle constructed in moments of domestic and international crisis, are likely to have their most lasting effects on domestic rather than on international politics.

It is not difficult to understand the reasons for this. First, the fundamental trends of Gaullist foreign policy were not idiosyncratic, but were initiated under the Fourth Republic. These included the dismantling of empire, the fostering of linkages with Germany, the maintenance of strong ties with former colonies, the *force de frappe*, anti-Americanism, *détente* with Russia and the Eastern bloc countries, and the general vision of *rayonnement*. Traditions, such as those de Gaulle followed, are not readily changed in the conduct of foreign affairs.

Second, where de Gaulle's style was most startling and spectacular, it *was* highly idiosyncratic and also unpopular. It was self-defeating and led to the failure of the most noteworthy Gaullist efforts. Tactics which smacked of *renversement des alliances,* diplomatic tergiversations, the "empty chair" and "tactical no" used in relations with those states where cooperation was fundamental to success all proved to be unpopular both at home and abroad after their initial hypnotic effects were dissipated. De Gaulle's arrogance in ignoring major foreign concerns of domestic interest groups built up hostility to his foreign policies with increasing momentum. Of all the major domestic groups, only the Communists were content with Gaullist foreign policy. Even among them, satisfaction was neither constant nor all-pervasive. Farmers and businessmen were dissatisfied by policies toward the EEC, while workers were increasingly dissatisfied with limitations on wage increases that were established for reasons of foreign commercial and monetary policy. The important and politically active Jewish community was alienated by the General's Middle Eastern policy after the Six Day War, while, for some military interests, that policy only added to the frustrations engendered by what was considered to be an impractical and unrealistic defense policy. Finally, the mood of a population interested in economic well-being was depressed by highly visible projects of huge cost—the *force de frappe*, Concorde, foreign aid, nuclear submarines, missiles, and the like. These projects seemed to enhance the General's international stature, but deprived the population of the fruits of modernization and economic growth.

These tensions in French foreign policy in a set of specific issue-areas will be examined in four case studies. Before that, the role of the pursuit of autonomy and the general limitations on its attainment in the French context will be anlayzed in Chapter 3.

In Chapter 4 the politics of national priorities in Gaullist France are discussed in detail in order to elucidate the origins of the "dilemma of insufficient resources" in the 1960s as well as the various political tactics used by the government to maintain its ideal of defense autonomy. The shifting of foreign-policy goals from areas of high policy to those of low policy are further examined in Chapter 5, which has as its specific focus France's international monetary policy. The limits upon an independent French foreign policy derived from international interdependence and from France's internal weaknesses are discussed in both chapters.

The attempt by de Gaulle to manipulate politics in the European Communities through a policy of crisis management is contrasted with the occurrence of unanticipated international crises in Chapter 6. Both sorts of crises are discussed in a special theoretical section, which spells out some of the implications for crisis diplomacy that were outlined in the discussion of international interdependence in Chapter 2.

Finally, in Chapter 7, the external constraints on domestic policy are illustrated within the context of changes in French economic planning procedures during the 1960s. Reasons for the failure of the attempt to project planning to the European level are elucidated, as are changes in French domestic decision-making.

THREE

LIMITATIONS ON GAULLIST
FOREIGN POLICY

DE GAULLE's foreign policies have a coherence belied by two
sets of fundamental contradictions. First, they pertain to the
antithesis between the general objective of political and
economic independence or autonomy in international affairs
and the need for relinquishing independence, if not sovereignty, in order to attain other domestic and external objectives of equal priority. Second, they derive from the unintended consequences of the pursuit of autonomy. Both the
tensions deriving from the conflict between policies of
independence and the reality of interdependence, and from
the unintended consequences of French policies are specifically modern phenomena. In a period when interdependence
was at appreciably lower levels, tensions arising from either
set of factors would have been minimal. Interdependence
would not have eroded either domestic or external policies,
and the unintended consequences of foreign policy activities
would not have reverberated throughout the international
system or pervaded domestic politics. These tensions reflect
the strong conflict between norms of foreign and domestic
policies, developed during the centuries-long period of the
formation of the modern state and the actual forms of
behavior that derive from the increased salience of transnational processes among the highly modernized states.

The first set of contradictions is illustrated within every
sphere of foreign policy associated with de Gaulle's France,
from functional areas such as defense, agricultural, and monetary affairs to geographic areas such as policies toward the
EEC countries, Britain, the United States, and the Soviet
Union. They are striking because of the central role of the

pursuit of autonomy in Gaullist foreign policy. It was, in de Gaulle's view, the great enterprise of the nation.

In order to be prosperous, to be masters of ourselves, and to be powerful, we French have done a great deal. Much remains for us to do. For progress demands effort. Independence is not free. Security is costly. That is of course why the state, whose role and *raison d'être* is to serve the general interest, has no right to let things go. . . .

This policy is not an easy one. The world abounds with sirens that sing to us the sweetness of renunciation, unless, annoyed at seeing us indifferent to their seduction, they raise toward us a noisy chorus of invectives. But without our being cocksure, in the interest of everyone as much as in our own, our ship is pursuing its course. There is absolutely no chance that, choosing the easy way, we would allow France to be pushed into the background.[1]

Independence as a policy for France had implications for both international society and for the domestic organization of the French state.[2] Internationally, the maximization of

---

[1] *Major Addresses, Statements, and Press Conferences of Charles de Gaulle, May 19, 1958–January 31, 1964* (New York: Ambassade de France, Service de presse et d'information, 1964), pp. 223–25. The selection is from a speech delivered in Paris April 19, 1963.

[2] The general objective of independence and changing tactics used in its pursuit were de Gaulle's lifelong vocations characteristic of a certain far more widespread intellectual tendency. The similarities between de Gaulle's views on independence and foreign policy as expressed in his memoirs and those of Charles Maurras, *Kiel et Tanger* (Paris: Bibliothèque des oeuvres politiques, 1910) are traced in Pierre Hassner, "Une France aux 'mains libres,' " *Preuves*, No. 204 (February, 1968), pp. 48–57. De Gaulle's views on independence derive from his *idée de la France*. This notion of France was one shared with the nationalist tradition of both Renan and Bainville. The various strands of this tradition are outlined in Raoul Girardet, ed., *Le Nationalisme française, 1871–1914* (Paris: A. Colin, 1966); and in Pierre Vergnaud, *L'Idée de la nationalité et de la libre disposition des peuples dans ses rapports avec l'idée de l'état* (*Etudes des doctrines politiques contemporaines*) *1870–1950* (Genève: Librairie E. Droz, 1955).

French independence was seen to depend not only upon the establishment of a balance of power between the superpowers but also on the prevention of cooperation between them that would lead them to impose their wills on other states. Domestically, independence was seen to depend on the modernization of the French state including the establishment of a modernized economy with large corporations, the development of nuclear capability and the institutionalization of scientific research and development.[3] The manipulated external and internal environments were thus viewed as instrumentalities designed to strengthen independence. The goal of independence had, for de Gaulle, a theoretical foundation in the permanent reality of the state as the fundamental organization of political life. The state, for de Gaulle, was "an instrument of decision, action and ambition, expressing and serving the national interest alone."[4] In de Gaulle's

[3] For a statement of the French view on the relationship between modernization and independence, see Robert Gilpin, "Scientific Research and National Independence: The French View," in *France in the Age of the Scientific State* (Princeton, N.J.: Princeton University Press, 1968), pp. 3–16. De Gaulle's televised speech of April 27, 1965 is a paean to independence. It covers all of the various domestic and foreign themes that he has associated with the concept. See *L'Année politique, 1965* (Paris: Presses Universitaires de France, 1966), pp. 431–32.

[4] *The Complete War Memoirs of Charles de Gaulle*, trans. Jonathan Griffin and Richard Howard (New York: Simon and Schuster, 1964), p. 780. De Gaulle also clarified the link between his concept of domestic capacity and foreign independence as two aspects of a single situation: "For today, as ever, it was incumbent upon the state to create the national power, which henceforth would depend on the economy. The latter must therefore be directed, particularly since it was deficient, since it must be renovated, and since it would not be renovated unless the state determined to do so. This was, in my eyes, the chief motive of the nationalization, control and modernization measures adopted by my government. But this conception of a government armed to act powerfully in the economic domain was directly linked to my conception of the state itself. I regarded the state not as it was yesterday and as the parties wished it to become once more, a juxtaposition of

118

view, this action function of a state required a complete separation of foreign and domestic affairs. An independent policy formulated in terms of the action function is one that is imposed neither by outside forces, as NATO decisions were imposed by the United States, nor by internal weakness, as a result of surrendering policy to particular interest groups.

If complete autonomy was the basic goal of Gaullist foreign policy, interdependence severely curtailed it. This limitation on independence established the fundamental tension of recent French foreign policy that is best exemplified in those areas of statecraft that have become the weathervanes of modernity, namely, areas of foreign economic policy toward other industrialized states. It is in such areas that limits imposed by interdependence on both domestic and foreign affairs are most vivid, especially insofar as security concerns have become less important for France, given the requisites of great power status in the nuclear age and the general stalemate in the political utility of military force resulting from deterrence.

For example, in international monetary policy, de Gaulle consistently followed a policy, after 1961, of limiting France's dependence on the United States in particular and on the institutions associated with the international monetary system in general. He did this in three ways. First, he tried vigorously to maintain the franc as a strong currency. Second, he converted dollar reserves into gold, "whose nature does not change, which can be transformed indifferently into bars, into ingots, or into coin, which has no nationality, and which is held eternally and universally as the inalterable fiduciary

---

private interests which could never produce anything but weak compromise, but instead an institution of decision, action and ambition, expressing and serving the national interest alone. In order to make decisions and determine measures, it must have a qualified arbitrator at its head. In order to execute them, it must have servants recruited and trained so as to constitute a valid and homogeneous corps in all public functions" (ibid., pp. 779–80).

value, *par excellence.*[5] Third, he used changing tactics in international monetary negotiations to restructure the international monetary system in such a way as to increase French influence.

French international monetary policy had other implications that also had importance in other industrialized states. The maintenance of a strong currency necessitated monetary stability at home, thus limiting not only inflation but also domestic growth. The conversion of dollars into gold served to diminish international liquidity, thus limiting the available investment capital from abroad. Such capital was, in fact, needed to strengthen French industry.[6] But, in terms of limitations derived from interdependence, de Gaulle was not willing to alter the basic system of international monetary arrangements. Thus, if the period of monetary negotiations "has been marked by disagreements and has given way to pressures, a minimum of international solidarity has, however, been maintained."[7] In other words, there were limits on

[5] Press conference of February 4, 1965, reprinted in André Passeron, ed., *De Gaulle Parle, 1962–1966* (Paris: Fayard, 1966), p. 177.

[6] Of course, one of the aims of de Gaulle's international monetary policy was to limit American investments in France in order to free the economy from too great a dependency upon the United States. In this respect, French monetary policy was supported by a policy restricting direct American investments in France. With the increased free movement of merchandise within the Common Market, however, American investments in other EEC countries could be converted directly into material, which entered France freely without France gaining from direct investments. After realizing this, the French changed their policy toward direct American investments without altering substantially their monetary policy. For further discussion of this point, see Charles P. Kindleberger, *Europe and the Dollar* (Cambridge, Mass.: MIT Press, 1966), as well as *American Business Abroad* (New Haven: Yale University Press, 1968). See also Allan Johnstone, *United States Direct Investment in France: An Investigation of the French Charges* (Cambridge, Mass., MIT Press, 1965); and Robert Gilpin, "The Dimensions of the American Challenge," *France in the Age of the Scientific State*, pp. 39–76.

[7] "Les Etapes de la négotiation monétaire internationale (1961–1968)," *Problèmes économiques*, No. 1901 (November 28, 1968), p. 10.

autonomous action that derived not simply from the commitment to participate in and to maintain a viable structure of international monetary relationships, but from a high level of interdependence between France and other states participating in these monetary arrangements. The monetary crisis of November 1968 and France's drawing upon the monetary resources of the other industrialized states of the West demonstrated strikingly the limits on autonomous international monetary policy derived from interdependence. It was a sign of failure of seven years of foreign policy in this area.

These limitations were impediments to the attainment of domestic as well as external objectives. It has been already suggested that one requisite of pursuing a forceful monetary policy was the maintenance of a strong currency that necessitated monetary stability and antiinflationary policies that served to bolster the balance of payments. But maintenance of economic stability was not consistent with the fostering of economic growth. The implementation of an *ad hoc plan de stabilisation* in 1963 meant that the economic and social goals of French indicative planning during the period of the Fourth and Fifth Plans had to be relinquished.

There is a further, secondary effect on external objectives, which stems from the internal effects of monetary policy. This effect involves the incompatibility of economic growth and economic stability, and the need for economic growth to fulfill external objectives. The attainment of objectives by means of external monetary policy imposed a policy of economic stability on the domestic economy. Economic growth, however, has been a requisite of modernization and technological advance for the fulfillment of domestic needs in terms not only of the increased general welfare of the population but also of the development of technological capacity that was perceived to be translatable into national power. In this sense, French planning, which could not be fulfilled by the imposition of a *plan de stabilisation,* was a prime instrument of external independence. The more stability substituted for growth, the less feasible did the transformation of the economic system become and the less possible the pursuit of the kinds of independent activities for which de Gaulle felt economic growth was a requisite.

The same interplay and tensions between autonomy and dependence, on the one hand, and between external and domestic policies, on the other hand, found in French monetary policies, also characterized policy in other areas, such as defense, NATO, agriculture, and the Common Market. They were all particular manifestations of the general contradiction between the independent pursuit of foreign policy objectives and the constraints derived from interdependence.

A second set of contradictions in recent French foreign policy derived from the unintended consequences of the pursuit of autonomy. De Gaulle's style of statecraft produced antagonism elsewhere that made the implementation of French objectives more difficult. These unintended consequences plagued Gaullist policies from the beginning of the Fifth Republic. Undermining the general objective of French policies in the most important areas in which they were pursued, they characterized especially French relations with Germany, the United States, and Britain. For example, intransigence in the EEC or the policy of the "empty chair" in 1965 served less to influence others to come to terms with the French position than it reduced French influence in general. This was true not only of the antagonism that de Gaulle's style produced but also of the mimicking of the style by others who made cooperation more difficult. His intransigence fostered obstinacy in others, reducing in the long run not only French influence over other states but also the degree of independence that the French could pursue in implementing any particular policy.

The unintended consequences of the policy of independence resulted in failures in French policy rather than in the successful pursuit of French autonomy. To some degree the use of negative tactics was imposed upon de Gaulle by French weakness and by the policies of the United States and Germany. Even so, autonomy and independence in the contemporary world were generally illusory, the principal aspect of which pertained to the attainment of goals by collaborative actions or by activities that occurred regardless of the policies pursued by any single government. In order to obtain the fruits of interdependence, which often gave the illusion of independence, collaboration with other governments was required. De Gaulle irritated the governments of all the states with which such cooperation would have been possible.

The unintended consequences of French foreign policy may have been greatest with respect to Germany. Grosser, for example, found with respect to the consequences of French policies toward Germany "the likelihood that the worldwide scope of General de Gaulle's policy will, in the end, lead to the predominance of Germany in Europe,"[8] in economic as well as defense affairs. He isolated France from Germany by his policy of cooperation with Russia, by his nuclear policy, and by his unwillingness to cooperate in matters of economic integration and defense. He consistently acted against the spirit of the Franco-German Treaty of 1963; he did not consult with Germany on either the French withdrawal from NATO in 1966 or on the talks with Britain in February 1969 concerning the substitution of a larger European free trade area to replace NATO as the treaty specified. Consequences of this behavior included the strengthening of German-American and German-British ties and the greater autonomy of German foreign policy.

Foreign policies are, of course, always in danger of being undermined by their unintended effects. Modernization of domestic society and growing interdependence with other societies, however, increase this danger disproportionately. On the one hand, with respect to policy formulation, the modernization of a society is accompanied by an increased role for interest-group politics. As interest groups must be satisfied more and more in the policy-making process, rational planning in foreign policy becomes more difficult to maintain, and

[8] Alfred Grosser, *French Foreign Policy Under de Gaulle*, trans. Lois Ames Pattison (Boston: Little, Brown, 1967), p. 133.

particular interests are sacrified to a more general concept of national interest (with the subsequent loss of some of the leadership's domestic support). On the other hand, with respect to interdependence, rational planning becomes even more essential. Interdependence depends upon strategic interactions for its implementation. The goals associated with any state in its foreign relations thus become dependent upon the actions of decision-makers in other states. And, it may be hypothesized, as the system of interactions becomes more interdependent, unintended effects assume a more important role in the successful pursuit of any set of objectives.

Actual behavior, in short, has served to undermine the norms associated with the conduct of foreign policy in the modern world, especially in international economic relations, where interdependence is greatest. In effect, the economic aspects of statecraft have become the most significant areas of political relations among industrialized societies. In spite of appearances to the contrary, these relations are primarily cooperative rather than conflictual. In all of the basic economic areas of policy-making, including politics in the EEC since 1966 and in international monetary arrangements since 1962, French foreign policy never challenged the basis of cooperation. Much more than a bare minimum of cooperation has been maintained, because in an interdependent system no society can afford to do without reciprocal arrangements. The lack of opposition to cooperation is true both of domestic and external goals. For example, the structure of France's domestic monetary system and the ability to trade externally are dependent upon the existence of structures of an international monetary system.

The tensions created between the priority of independence and the need for cooperative and collaborative relationships, and stemming from growing interdependence reflect the need to control the effects of interdependence as well as the inadequacy of the national framework for controlling these effects completely. In short, the levels of interdependence among highly industrialized societies have increased much more rapidly than the levels of control at a time when interdependence has greater and greater impact in limiting the implementation of both domestic and foreign policies.

General Limitations on French Autonomy

The tensions stemming from the priority that had been placed on independence and the undercutting effects of interdependence are not, of course, the only ones that characterized recent French foreign policies. Other tensions associated with the quest for French independence were more traditional ones, while still others reflected recent French history.

Traditional limitations on the implementation of foreign policy objectives are those material or psychological factors that impede the attainment of specified goals. The recognition of these limitations can lead to the curtailment of commitments in order to balance ends and means; or, they can lead to the making of new types of commitments that are specifically designed to increase the material base of a nation by the creation of certain kinds of interdependencies. Other limitations may not be recognized at all and may lead to foreign policy failures.[9]

The traditional limitations stemming from technological weakness or from lack of resources can lead to the sharing of resources with other societies and consequently to higher

---

[9] Traditional limitations on statecraft have been summarized by Harold and Margaret Sprout as follows:

"1. Limitations that derive from the level of technology (tools and skills) available.

"2. Limitations that derive from perceptual and/or apperceptual behavior:
   a. Lack of opportunity to perceive limiting factors.
   b. Failure to perceive perceivable limiting factors.
   c. Defective recognition or assessment of limiting factors perceived.

"3. Limitations that derive from insufficiency of resources to cover all technically feasible commitments and desires" (*An Ecological Paradigm for the Study of International Politics*, Research Monograph No. 30 [Princeton: Center of International Studies, 1968], pp. 35–36).

levels of interdependence. For example, the relatively modest
level of French nuclear armament and delivery capacities
has made the goal of independence in defense particularly
difficult to maintain. By the end of 1968, such limitations led
to pressures within the armed forces for greater cooperation
with France's NATO allies.[10] They were also one reason for
de Gaulle's agreement to collaborate with the British on the
creation of a supersonic transport. International cooperation
of this sort, designed to overcome absolute physical limitations or those stemming from the inability to pursue a wide
spectrum of objectives at one time, has a long history in international politics. It is, for example, the traditional impetus
for nations to form alliances and coalitions.

Alliances and "alignments are always instrumental in struc-
turing the state system, sometimes in transforming it"[11] because they increase the power available to any state. The
Franco-Russian rapprochement beginning in 1890 and leading eventually to alliance served, from the French point of
view, to increase the power of France against Germany. Alliances, however, also increase interdependence, and are often
designed to do so. This is the restraining function of alliances
best exemplified by the alliance system designed by Bismarck
not only to isolate France from the other continental powers
but also to restrain both Austria and Russia in the Balkans.
French investments in Russia prior to World War I, which
"made up a quarter of all French ownership abroad,"[12] were
encouraged in order to tie the ally to France for strategic rea-

[10] Georges Suffert has written that "the great dream of a French
nuclear and modern army is worn down month by month on the solid
rocks of reality. Military staffs have learned that the gap in the preparation of nuclear matters has grown. Some of them whisper that this
gap cannot be overcome. However, the nation must be defended. Faces,
once again, are turning enviously toward America" (*L'Express*, January 20–26, 1969, p. 3).

[11] George Liska, *Nations in Alliance; the Limits of Interdependence*
(Baltimore: The Johns Hopkins Press, 1962), p. 12.

[12] Herbert Feis, *Europe, The World's Banker, 1870–1914* (New
Haven: Yale University Press, 1930), p. 52.

sons and to prevent Russia from withdrawing from the alliance.

The levels of interdependence that arose from alliances prior to World War II were apparently much lower than those of the postwar period when interpenetration of political and economic life became possible on a large scale for the first time. The manipulation of interdependence can still have the same political overtones, however. The functionalist approach to European integration was specifically and consciously designed to create high levels of interdependence in a way that was qualitatively different from the restraining function of alliances, although the traditional motives for alliance were present. For example, like traditional alliance policy, the Schuman plan was for France a *renversement des alliances* from London and Moscow to Bonn. It was also designed to increase French power. "For the initiators of the Schuman plan, indirectly approved by the Social-Democratic opposition in Germany, European integration had to permit France a much larger political role because she would use the economic potential of Germany, thus depriving Germany of the political weight that she would find necessary to face a sovereign France."[13] But the unique feature was the tying together of key sectors of the French and German economies as a means not only of restraining the recently created government in Bonn but also of increasing the general welfare of Western Europeans. Schuman indicated in his press conference of May 9, 1950 that

> the mission imparted to the Common High Authority [of the Coal and Steel Community] will be to insure in as rapid a time as possible: the modernization of production and the improvement of its quality; the supplying under identical conditions of coal and steel on the French and German markets as well as on the markets of other member countries; the development of common exports toward third

[13] Alfred Grosser, *La Quatrième République et sa politique extérieure* (Paris: A. Colin 1961), p. 237.

countries; the equalization of progress in the living conditions of workers in these industries, etc.[14]

If limitations on the attainment of external goals traditionally have been derived from the levels of available technology and resources to cover a wide spectrum of commitments, they have also been derived from cognitive failures. Like the other two types of limitations, cognitive limitations continued to play an important part in Gaullist foreign policy, already discussed in terms of the unintended consequences of Gaullist foreign and domestic policies that designed to increase independence. They have another dimension as well, more accurately defined by "defective recognition or assessment of limiting factors perceived."[15]

The cognitive failure characteristic of Gaullist foreign policy pertained, in particular, to French policy toward Germany. De Gaulle's "grand design" for Europe was abstractly based on the Fouchet Plan and concretely on the Franco-German Treaty of Cooperation of 1963. The Gaullist bet in this sense was placed upon cooperation with Germany that would result in an independent but geographically limited Europe with a strong economic base, where German political ambitions would be linked to French global pretensions. If Germany was to be the industrial base of independent Europe, France was to be both its breadbox and its spokesman. The bet proved increasingly to be a bad one. This occurred not only because German security was wedded to the United States rather than to France but also because after 1965 German economic growth significantly outstripped that of France to such a degree that Germany became, in effect, the more significant spokesman. French interests in independence throughout the 1960s coincided with those of Britain far more than with those of Germany. De Gaulle's recognition

---

[14] Robert Schuman, press conference of May 9, 1950, quoted in Grosser, *La Quatrième République et sa politique extérieure*, p. 234.
[15] Sprout and Sprout, *Ecological Paradigm*, p. 36.

of this coincidence of French and British interests developed very slowly and did not become evident until February, 1969, with the proposal to Ambassador Soames of a free trade area under the four-power direction of France, Britain, Germany, and Italy. The overtures to Britain in early 1969 were not merely another example of the policy of *renversement des alliances*, but were a significant avowal of the failure of six years of policy toward Germany.[16]

There was, in summary, a mixture of contradictions in French foreign policy during the 1960s. The most significant ones stemmed from the interplay of independence and interdependence, on the one hand, and from the unintended consequences of certain policies, on the other hand. Both of these contradictions are predominantly modern and reflect decreasing levels of control over the effects of foreign and domestic policies that, to be sure, have been developing for over a century, but that have assumed significant divergence only in the 1960s. In neither case is there any reason to assume that tensions would have been significantly reduced if de Gaulle had not been President of France. Perhaps they would not have been so clearly crystallized, but they do not stem only from the designs of a single individual. Rather, they typify the foreign policies of any highly modern state in its relations with other modern states in contemporary international politics. Other limitations, as discussed above, were more traditional ones that affect any state. Since the analysis of the foreign policy of a state is a mixture of both generalized and unique factors, it is worthwhile to examine those tensions in recent French foreign policy that relate to France's particular

16 De Gaulle actually realized the potential of alignment with Britain rather than Germany. But either state serving as a partner in a European directorate posed a dilemma for him. German material strength was matched by British economic power, with the exception that Britain was hampered by a weak reserve currency. Britain, however, posed a threat with its imperial avocation, which was much like that of Gaullist France, and by the belief on the part of de Gaulle that Britain, like France, was an original nation-state.

historical experience, especially since they exacerbated those already discussed as they reinforced the quest for autonomy in foreign affairs.

TENSIONS IN FRENCH FOREIGN POLICY DERIVED FROM FRENCH HISTORY

An additional set of tensions in French foreign policy stems less from modernized rather than from particular French conditions that are based on social conflict and historical traditions. These tensions played a role not only in Gaullist foreign policy but also predated de Gaulle's coming to power. Since they overlap with tensions derived from specifically modern phenomena and since they are analytically separable from these other tensions, it is useful to examine them as well.

This set of contradictions accompanied secular changes in the international position of France that stemmed from general changes in the structure of the international system during the last century. As a result of these changes, there arose a sharp dialogue in French foreign-policy traditions, both of which predated French decline. The nationalist tradition, although it included several strands of political thought and ideology ranging from monarchism to republicanism, has stressed independence, *grandeur*, status, and *grandes entreprises* in foreign policy. The balance-of-power tradition was upheld by its proponents as realism and was denounced by its critics as defeatism, especially after 1871. It too presents confusions, because it also appeared in various schools of political thought. Moreover, both foreign-policy traditions were imposed upon various cleavages in French society that had more to do with domestic than with foreign affairs. These cleavages include those between the friends and enemies of the Revolution of 1789, and clericalism and anticlericalism.[17]

[17] These various cleavages as they had persisted into the Fourth Republic are outlined in Philip Williams, *Politics in Postwar France* (London: Longmans, Green, 1954), pp. 1–62.

The nationalist tradition is the more relevant, for it is the one in which de Gaulle belongs. This tradition predated the Franco-Prussian War by more than two centuries, but did not become part of a dialectic in French politics with the realist school of thought until after that watershed. It was then that realization of change in France's security position on the European continent presented a cultural crisis of identity that challenged the myths of French nationalism. The challenge was worked out, in part, in the dialectics of ideal views on foreign policy. The transformation in the perceived and actual position of France in international affairs resulted at that time in a sharp contrast between two ideal versions of that position. This contrast reflected the tensions between the myths of nationalism that had developed in terms of relations between France and other states, and the actual position of France in the international system. The contrast between ideals and reality was the basic contradiction of French foreign policy from the Franco-Prussian War until the early 1960s, when the loss of Indochina, the Suez expedition, and the independence of Algeria and the sub-Saharan colonies ended any pretensions to French global power. Afterward, only certain aspects of the nationalist school lingered on in Gaullist foreign policy.

The nationalist tradition of French foreign policy stems from the central focus in French policy on international position. It is the heritage of Louis XIV and the policy of *grandeur* that had been central to a specific interpretation of the ideal structures of French foreign policy for four hundred years. This link to the *ancien régime* is threefold. First, it pertains to the apotheosis of the French nation, defined in terms of the relations between the French monarchs and other monarchs as well as with other civilizations. Second, it has to do with the pursuit of *grandeur* as a transcendental goal of French policy. Third, it is the link between the French international mission and French geography. Each of these elements had been challenged before the end of the nineteenth

century. The general transformation of the structure of international society between the mid-nineteenth century and
1960 made the nationalist dream an impossible one to fulfill.

First, then, the national component of French statecraft
is unique not only because France was the earliest of the
modern nation states but also because the national myth that
surrounded the formation of the nation encompassed the
ideal of civilization, merging both particularistic factors and
universal traits. Specifically, the French monarchs, even of
the Gothic period of the twelfth century, idealized their
heritage. According to this norm, they were the heirs not only
of the Gauls, but of ancient civilization, including its pagan
and Christian elements. This heritage gave the French special
privileges as the defenders of civilization. The merging of the
monarchy, church, ancient tradition, and the nation reached
its apogee under Louis XIV,[18] and continued not only
in French literature but also in certain myths of French foreign policy throughout the nineteenth century into the twentieth. According to the national myth, French culture was
identified with that of Western civilization. In the words of
a German admirer of that myth, "France carried forward the
ancient idea of civilization into the modern world, not, however, because she has deliberately accepted it, but because it
is inherent in her. It is a primary formal category of the
French nature."[19] The argument is traced in foreign-policy
terms as follows: If France is the representative of Western
civilization, then France must be a great power. To be a great
power, France must maintain an independent role in the

---

[18] The argument is based on one summarized in Ernst R. Curtius,
The Civilization of France: An Introduction, trans. Oliver Wyon (New
York: Vintage Books, 1962), pp. 1–35. Curtius traces the merging
of the Gallican and Roman traditions via the French monarchy. Even
in republican periods, he argues, three basic ideas stemming from the
monarchical development are translated into republican terms: (1)
world history as the history of civilization; (2) the concern of civilization with the development of freedom; and (3) France, the leader of
civilization in the "march of freedom" and, therefore, of states.

[19] Ibid., p. 9.

world. If the population, territory, and resources of the nation limit the degree to which France can play this role, then policy must find some artificial, synthetic, and rational substitute for natural greatness.

It is at this point in the national argument that presuppositions of the rational tradition in France must be introduced. The rational tradition in France stems not only from the Enlightment heritage but also from the baroque intellectual tradition of the Age of Absolutism. According to this tradition, man can order the world to conform to his image of it; that is, history begins with the word rather than the deed. If the statesman, as the embodiment of the nation, can manipulate concrete reality, then effective policy is not only a possibility but also an obligation to the French as representatives of Western civilization. Such a policy can assure the development of the world system along lines compatible with France's national goals, provided that France has the superior tools to implement them. The international system is then no longer characterized by haphazard anarchy, but becomes a work of art created by the French mind, similar to the order that is characteristic of French gardens.[20]

The second element, the policy of *grandeur*, is also a heritage of the *ancien régime*, and especially of the foreign policy of Louis XIV.[21] Under the *ancien régime*, *grandeur* was characteristic of the monarch rather than of the nation as a whole. Louis XIV, for example, always distinguished between the body politic and the prince who directed it.[22] Glory for Louis,

[20] The form of baroque positivism that has characterized French politics under the name of Cartesianism is fully argued in Carl J. Friedrich, *The Age of the Baroque, 1610–1660* (New York: Harper and Brothers, 1952).

[21] *Grandeur*, like the other elements of the nationalist tradition, did not apply to the regimes of all the monarchs, nor even to all those of the *ancien régime*. Rather, it is one of the elements of a tradition by which Louis XIV, Napoleon I, and Napoleon III, Chateaubriand, Clemenceau, and de Gaulle are joined.

[22] While many aspects of his rule changed during his reign of fifty-four years, his doctrine of royal sovereignty remained virtually constant.

as for the other monarchs of the *ancien régime*, was a complicated congeries of elements. Whatever its particular form, it
was always translated into empirical terms by means of
grandes entreprises. Glory was transformed after the fall of
the monarchy to reflect upon the nation as a whole rather
than on the king. For Louis, "the concomitant of glory is high
reputation—a fragile thing—which the prince must constantly seek and to which they [the subjects] must subject themselves . . . ."[23] If glory reflected in modern times upon the nation rather than upon the person of the monarch, it was no
less a goal of French foreign policy. Nor did its varied nature
change, except that it was no longer measured in terms of military pursuit. Glory under the Third, Fourth, and Fifth Republics, however, was still understood as derived from

> great enterprises foreign and domestic: in putting a French
> prince on the Polish throne, and in building the Languedoc
> Canal. There is glory in overcoming difficulties that cannot
> be avoided, but not in creating such difficulties, nor in rash
> action. There is glory in work toward the improvement of
> society and in spending money for public needs. There is
> glory in keeping one's word at the expense of one's im-
> mediate interest. And there is glory in moderation, in
> maintaining one's dignity, in curbing one's pride, in over-
> coming one's resentment, and in that mastery of oneself
> that ensures the conquest of one's natural inclinations by
> reason. Indeed, it is reason that guides us on the path of
> true glory.[24]

See Andrew Lossky, "The Nature of Political Power According to
Louis XIV," in *The Responsibility of Power: Historical Essays in
Honor of Hajo Holborn*, ed. Leonard Krieger and Fritz Stern (Garden
City, N.Y.: Doubleday, 1967), pp. 107–22.

[23] Ibid., p. 114.

[24] Ibid. This element of French diplomatic style is central to the
understanding of French foreign policy, but has been largely ignored.
Lossky's argument is derived from other studies on glory in French
statecraft, including Gaston Zeller, "Politique extérieure et diplomatie
sous Louis XIV," *Revue d'histoire moderne*, VI (1931): 124–43.

The pursuit of *grandes entreprises* in foreign and domestic affairs is always the clue to this nationalist tradition in France. It was the element that distinguished Louis XIV from his successors, Chateaubriand from Villèle,[25] Clemenceau from Caillaux and de Gaulle from his predecessors in the Fourth Republic. *Grandes entreprises* reflect the political belief that a nation is only as great as its ideals and visions and the degree to which they are pursued.

A final element in French preeminence is the perceived geographical basis of grandeur. It is difficult to overestimate the bearing of geopolitical factors on French foreign policy because of the centuries-long identification of French political culture with the physical environment of the French state. The French have long integrated this physical setting with notions about the state in international affairs and, more importantly, with an abstract conception of the French nation.[26] From this strong identification has come a traditional fascination with geographic determinism and geomysticism. Geographical determinism has been socialized into French culture. Virtually all French geography texts begin with a mystical, idealized account of the geopolitical setting of the hexagon of France.[27] Not unnaturally, this creates a special

[25] De Gaulle was fond of Chateaubriand, whom he quoted with admiration for leading the French "by dreams" (*War Memoirs*, p. 141). Chateaubriand took the great risk of sending an interventionary force of 100,000 men to Spain in 1823, which the liberals predicted would end in disaster. Instead, it was a success, which reinforced the Bourbon monarchy and ensured the loyalty of the French army. Chateaubriand claimed this great undertaking to be the most important political event in his life. See François René Chateaubriand, *Mémoires d'outre-tombe* (Paris: Garnier, n.d.), IV, p. 285. For a general interpretation of Gaullist foreign policy along these lines, see Hassner, "Une France aux 'Mains libres.'"

[26] The relationship between geography, history, and nationalism in France is stressed in Derwent Whittlesey, *The Earth and the State: A Study of Political Geography* (New York: Henry Holt, 1939), pp. 129–65.

[27] A current geography text illustrates the degree of socialization. See André Blanc and Lucien Pernet, *Géographie; Classe de troisième*

perception of the international setting that permeates French society.

Like most myths, those of French geopolitical determinism have a strong foundation in fact. In the most general terms, France is situated approximately halfway between the North Pole and the Equator, is approximately 620 miles across, in the general shape of a hexagon, and contains a rich variety of agricultural and other economic resources. Climatic variation allows a rich spectrum of cultivation, while the centralization of economic and political forces in the Paris basin has resulted in a political and cultural dichotomy between Paris and the provinces. The borders of France are both natural and historical and include from west to north counterclockwise: the Atlantic Ocean, the Pyrenees, the Mediterranean, the Alps, the Rhine, and to the northeast, the European plain and North Sea.

These three images of France, legacies of the *ancien régime* central to the mythology, or idealized version, of the position of France in the world, were challenged by the transformation of international society that began in the nineteenth century —by the recognition of demographic decline domestically, which was taken as a sign of national decline, by the challenge of Britain throughout the century, and of Germany after 1870–1871. Paradoxically, however, it was only after the Franco-Prussian War and the rise of mass nationalism that the national myth in foreign policy reached its apogee. For it was then that the bitter dialectic took place. From 1871, the ideal image of France, which was defined in terms of recognition by others of French preeminence through reflected glory and by the central position of France in the internation-

(Paris: Librarie Hachette, 1966), p. 5. The first chapter is entitled "The Place and Role of France." It includes a map of the world on which France is placed at the center and around which is drawn a circle the radius of which includes all of the land areas of the world. The text points out that France is the microcosm of the world, located midway between the North Pole and the Equator.

al system, bore a diminishing relationship to the actual position of the French state in the international system.

Fears of decline began with the end of the Napoleonic Wars and the beginning of the Restoration. At that time both the liberals and Ultras, for different reasons, wanted the monarch to pursue an active foreign policy. The liberals stressed ideological elements. They wanted France to set an example as a republican regime. The Ultras wanted an active foreign policy to legitimize the restored monarchy. In general, a passive policy was pursued for fear that any active policy would lead to trouble with Britain or Russia. The rise of Britain as the world's leading industrial power led to fears that French relative preeminence on the continent would be lost. To this was added fear of national decay as evidenced by demographic stagnation and decline. Historical pessimism, then, first arose in the early part of the nineteenth century as a result of the awareness that other nations were growing industrially and demographically at much higher rates than was France. This was accentuated in the last half of the century by the unification of Germany and Italy that resulted in France becoming the second most populous state in Western Europe for the first time in modern history. An indication of the pervasive awareness of the demographic challenge to French security was the rise of demographic studies in France, which had already become highly developed by the end of the nineteenth century.

The relative decline in French population between 1800 and 1900 can be observed in Table 2 below. The absolute figures actually hide the relative standings of the different states. Germany and Italy were unified only later in the century, while the Austrian and Russian populations were composed of mixtures of ethnic groups that prevented the intensive mobilization of populations that was much more readily accomplished in the more highly integrated French political system. Moreover, France's population of 35.8 million in 1850 remained more or less stationary for a century while the populations of her neighboring states increased vigorously. The increase of the population by approximately 5 million inhabitants between 1850 and 1900 was almost entirely the result of the dissemination of public health measures that increased life expectancy rather than the net reproduction rate that was negative for several years. The same factors were operative in the forty-year period between 1900 and 1940, when the total French population declined for several years as a result of France's loss of 1.7 million soldiers and civilians during World War I and the subsequent loss of unborn generations.

More interesting than these figures were the policy reactions within France. The demographer Spengler has argued that

for at least three quarters of a century the Devil of Declining Growth has been present at French council tables, at policy-making conferences, and in the minds of strategically situated decision-makers. The Devil has not always been

TABLE 2

Population of Selected European States, 1800-1900

	1800		1850		1900	
States	Population in millions	Percentage of European population	Population in millions	Percentage of European population	Population in millions	Percentage of European population
France	28.2	15.0	35.8	13.6	40.7	10.0
Russia	40.0	21.0	57.0	21.8	100.0	24.0
Britain	16.0	9.0	27.5	10.5	41.5	10.6
Germany	23.0	13.0	35.1	13.0	56.4	14.0
Italy	18.0	9.2	25.0	9.2	32.5	8.4
Austria	28.0	15.0	36.0	13.7	50.0	12.0
Total	153.3	82.2	216.4	81.8	321.1	79.0

Source: M. Reinhard and A. Armengaud, *Histoire générale de la population mondiale* (Paris: Editions Montchrestien, 1961), p. 226.

present in the flesh, since that is not the way of devils. But he has always been at the shoulders of the holders of power, and they have usually taken him into account implicitly when not explicitly.[28]

But the problem was not only in the minds of policy-makers. It also was widely prevalent among the public in the nineteenth century. A best seller of 1868, Prevost-Paradol's *La France nouvelle*, exhorted the French to expand to North Africa in order to procreate rapidly, so that France could maintain her greatness in the face of the rapidly growing Anglo-Saxon powers, and thus avoid the fate of Athens and Sparta in the age of Rome. His book ends with the following hope: "May the day soon come when our fellow citizens, close pressed in our African France, will overflow into Morocco, Tunisia, and finally establish that Mediterranean empire which will not only be a satisfaction for our pride, but which will certainly, in the future state of the world, be the last resource of our greatness.[29]

Spengler found two policy responses to counter the perceived decline in French power due to population stagnation.

On the one hand, measures designed to stimulate natural increase and immigration were proposed and after a time adopted to a slight degree. On the other hand, efforts were made to enlist sources of strength that might make up in part the relative deficiency in French military manpower and economic strength. . . .

In this second category fall, besides France's search for

[28] Joseph J. Spengler, "Notes on France's Response to her Declining Rate of Demographic Growth," in *Demographic Analysis*, ed. Joseph J. Spengler and Otis T. Duncan (Glencoe, Ill.: The Free Press of Glencoe, 1956), p. 587. See also Joseph J. Spengler, *France Faces Depopulation* (Durham, N.C.: Duke University Press, 1938); and idem, *Economie et population: les doctrines françaises avant 1800, de Budé à Condorcet* (Paris: Presses Universitaires de France, 1954).

[29] Quoted in Raymond Aron, *Peace and War; A Theory of International Relations*, trans. Richard Howard and Annette Baker Fox (Garden City, N.Y.: Doubleday, 1965), p. 678.

allies, her utilization of savings for international purposes, her post-1870 colonial ventures, and some of her military manpower policies.[30]

Actually, this account oversimplifies the policy responses to demographic decline. For ever since 1871 men representing the two schools of thought outlined above have challenged each other on this as on other questions of foreign policy. On the one hand, there were such figures as Jules Ferry, architect of the imperial policy of the 1880s, and General de Gaulle, who felt throughout the 1940s and 1950s that only an imperial France of 100 million people could retain *rang* in the contemporary age of superstates.[31] On the other hand, there were the critics of the imperial expansion in the late nineteenth and early twentieth centuries, and the European integrationists of the 1950s, who felt that by looking beyond the shores of Europe, France would divide her resources and be too weak to be defended against a perpetual German menace.

The realist school, exemplified by the theory of Jules Cambon, stressed French weakness rather than French strength. This tradition stressed balance rather than *grandeur* and *grandes entreprises* as the means of strengthening France's position. It looked upon *grandeur* and balance as opposing principles of statecraft. *Grandeur*, while it could be pursued as an instrumentality of balance on the part of a weak state, or as an element of a revisionist policy, could not be pursued as an end in itself while balance was being maintained. Thus, Cambon saw balance as the main tradition of French foreign policy and *grandeur* as an aberration.[32] Like the nationalist school, the realist school also stressed geography. Cambon,

[30] Spengler, "Notes on France's Response," p. 595.

[31] Compare the ideas on population and empire of Paul Leroy-Beaulieu, an earlier popularizer of colonization, with those of Ferry and de Gaulle. See selections from Leroy-Beaulieu and Ferry in Girardet, *Le nationalisme français*, pp. 86ff., p. 106. De Gaulle's notions are outlined in Roy Macridis, ed., *De Gaulle: Implacable Ally* (New York: Harper and Row, 1966), p. 84.

[32] Jules Cambon, "France," in *The Foreign Policy of the Powers*, ed. Hamilton Fish Armstrong (New York: Harper and Row, 1935), pp. 3–24.

for example, asserted that "the geographical position of a nation, indeed, is the principal factor conditioning its foreign policy—the principal reason why it must have a foreign policy at all."[33] He did not, however, look upon the idealized account of French geography, nationalism, and *grandeur* as constituting the mainstream of French foreign-policy tradition. He looked at the balance of power as the central doctrine of French foreign policy and found Louis XIV and Napoleon out of the tradition. Rather, the realist tradition is said to be based on the prudential statecraft of Richelieu and Henry IV and the policy of security.

The dialogue between the realists and the nationalists was, in summary, a reflection of French decline. The nationalist tradition stressed French *rang* and independence. The heroes of this school of interpretation were those who put independence as a primary task of statecraft, the villains those who renounced complete autonomy.[34] The dialogue between schools stemmed from the changes in the international position of France after 1871. This change represented a momentous and stark discontinuity in international political history. It reversed the relative power of France and Germany on the western extremity of the European continent and transformed the structure of the balance of power in Europe as it had been known for two centuries. Prior to the French defeat at Sedan (1870), the balance of power on the continent in geographic terms was based on a string of powerful and more or less equal states surrounding the political vacuum of Germany, the "safety valve" that secured the independence of the peripheral states and prevented any local crisis from developing into a general conflagration. After 1871 with the establishment of the most powerful state at the center of Europe, the security of each of the states on the periphery was linked intimately to its policies.

The relationships that were changed by the creation of a

[33] Ibid., p. 3.
[34] For a summary of this dialogue in the nineteenth and early twentieth centuries, see Gordon Wright, *France in Modern Times: 1760 to the Present* (Chicago: Rand McNally, 1960), pp. 378f.

central state whose territory was contiguous with that of states on the west and east compounded other transformations brought about by technological innovations. The development of railroad networks and new forms of communication, in addition to changes in weaponry brought about by mass-produced steel, made possible levels of destruction that had been unprecedented. In addition, the mobility of armies was greatly increased, as was the ability to direct them from greater distances. Both kinds of changes served to revolutionize more traditional conceptions of both space and time so that security could be measured less in terms of physical distances and more in terms of time needed to prepare for defense against attack.[35]

Not only was the structure of the European system transformed by the unification of Germany at its geographic center but also French preeminence was permanently ended. A. J. P. Taylor noted that "it was the moment when the myth of *la grande nation*, dominating Europe, was shattered for ever."[36] On every relevant dimension, France lost her lead to Germany on the continent. French population in 1860 was 37.4 million, greater than any other power except Russia (63 million) and far greater than that of Prussia (18.5 million). After 1870 Germany's population stood at 41 million, and the French population, with the loss of Alsace-Lorraine, stood at 36 million.[37] The French expenditures on armaments were 1.6 times those of Germany, but they failed to increase at the same rate as Germany's, so that by 1914 the German expenditures were 2.3 times those of France.[38] The widening

---

[35] One of the paradoxes of this change was that although foreign policy in the European states became highly defensive, military strategy was based on the fast offensive. See essays on Moltke, Schlieffen, du Picq, and Foch in *Makers of Modern Strategy: Military Thought from Machiavelli to Hitler*, ed. Edward M. Earle (Princeton, N.J.: Princeton University Press, 1942), pp. 172–233. See also George H. Quester, *Deterrence before Hiroshima* (New York: John Wiley and Sons, 1966).

[36] A. J. P. Taylor, *The Struggle for Mastery in Europe, 1848–1918* (London: Oxford University Press, 1954), p. 210.

[37] Ibid., p. xxv.   [38] Ibid., pp. xxvii–xxix.

gap between French and German capabilities could also be measured in terms of pig iron production, steel production, and general manufacturing.

The immediate effect of German unification was to limit the main options open to French policy-makers. It immediately ruled out any policy of independence. France had to be aligned with other powers in order to maintain her basic security. Freedom of international movement was limited to three options that Liska has summarized.

> The oldest option is an offensive or defensive alliance with the strongest available Eastern European power or powers of the moment; it was to permit a vigorous policy toward the strongest or most aggressive of the Germanic powers in the middle of the continent. Another option is an alliance with the Anglo-Saxon island power or powers in the West; this connection has traditionally legitimized a weak French government and both reinforced and restrained it in foreign affairs. The third option is a stabilizing alliance of self-confident but non-expansionist French government with the conservative Germanic power in the center of Europe.[39]

Shortly after German unification, a fourth choice became available to French statesmen in the form of increasing the population and resources of France by the accretion of colonial territories and peoples. Each of these options had its spokesmen after the Franco-Prussian War and was pursued in some form by de Gaulle either between 1940 and

[39] George Liska, *Europe Ascendant: The International Politics of Unification* (Baltimore: The Johns Hopkins Press, 1964), p. 68. Liska maintains that these options were open to French foreign policy "for two and a half centuries," and that the unification of Germany "reduced French alignment alternatives on major European issues to a Western alliance with one or both of the Anglo-Saxon powers, or an Eastern-European alliance" (ibid.). His original judgment is faulty insofar as the change brought about by German unification eliminated the option of independence that had previously existed. Moreover, his omission of the option of reconciliation with Germany was a mistake, for this option was a very real one, even in the aftermath of the Franco-Prussian War.

1945 or between 1958 and 1969. Thus, German unification was a permanent challenge to French independence and created a dilemma for French foreign policy that continued to exist at least until the end of the Algerian War, by necessitating French expansion or alliance with Russia in order to enhance security. By the 1930s, the realist tradition of balance on the continent, which links Laval to his predecessor Caillaux and his successors Monnet and Pierre Mendes-France, had an almost continuous reign at the Quai d'Orsay.[40] By 1962 the illusion of the possibility of independence in terms of superpower stature was permanently terminated. Instead, independence was transformed into a concept of global neutralism based on superpower deterrence.

The transformation in the structure of the international system was limited, however, neither to Europe nor to the period from 1870 to 1871. There was a more general transformation associated with the revolution of modernization, which one scholar has called transition from modern to contemporary society.[41] This revolution occurred from 1871 to 1962 and further exacerbated the tension that existed between the goal of independence, defined in terms of great power status for France and the possibility of attaining such status. This period is characterized by the transformation of the European state system, which typified modern history from the Renaissance through the nineteenth century, into the contemporary worldwide international system. It was during this transitional era that foreign policy decisions made in the capitals of Europe grew to have less and less influence

[40] See Richard D. Challener, "The French Foreign Office: The Era of Philippe Berthelot," in The Diplomats, 1919–1938, I, ed. Gordon A. Craig and Felix Gilbert (Princeton, N.J.: Princeton University Press, 1953), pp. 49–85; and Elizabeth R. Cameron, "Alexis Saint-Léger Léger," ibid., II, pp. 378–405.

[41] See Geoffrey Barraclough, An Introduction to Contemporary History. The political history of European decline is traced in Hajo Holborn, The Political Collapse of Europe (New York: Alfred A. Knopf, 1966); John Lukacs, Decline and Rise of Europe (Garden City, N.Y.: Doubleday, 1965), and in René Albrecht-Carrié, One Europe (Garden City, N.Y.: Doubleday, 1965).

upon events beyond Europe, and even within Europe. In short, the transitional period was that time span whereby the European state system, which was once the dominant international system, became a subordinate subsystem of the international system.

The transition began with the emergence of power centers outside Europe, which eventually became the dominant political units of international society. The initial phase of the transitional epoch was first apparent in the Far East, where Russia, the United States, and Japan, became the primary political units. Within the period there existed several watersheds that can be perceived as transformational in character and that also often served to reinforce the illusion that Europe remained the center of the international system as well as dominant within it. For example, the withdrawal of the United States and Russia from European politics after World War I, the maintenance of global empires of the European states during the interwar period, and the central position of Germany in that period as a destabilizing factor in the international system all contributed to the deception that the European system was still the dominant system in international politics, and that the relations among the European states formed the central structures of global international relations. By 1945, of course, the European system had collapsed, and the Soviet-American relationship tended to structure the other major relationships within international society.

The tensions arising from the continuity of tradition in terms of French foreign-policy objectives and the transformation of the international system that made those objectives unattainable and unrealistic had passed by 1962, when the end of the Algerian War terminated any French hopes of regaining great power status.

The aspects of French statecraft central to this study are predominantly those that reflect French modernity rather than those that originate in the now outmoded goal of great power stature. This is true in terms of attempts to control policies directed at targets outside of France as well as in terms of the kinds of international relationships involving

France that have been selected for study. The relationships that will be analyzed in the following chapters are those between France and other highly modernized societies of the West for which problems of control are similar to those that France has faced in recent years. It is the particular interplay between these highly interdependent relationships and the basic national framework of political decision-making that is of interest. It represents the same kind of tension that is derived from the contradiction between interdependence and independence and that Grosser described in other terms in his study of the external policies of the Fourth Republic. He felt that

> all the questions that have been asked in postwar France regarding external policy issues can be reduced to a single question: how can equality and dependence be reconciled? Conquered Germany will not always experience occupation and chaos. How can her return to sovereignty be reconciled with effective control of her evolution? The age of colonial empires has come to an end. How can access of dependent peoples to autonomy be reconciled with their membership in a French union? France is no longer one of the great powers. How can her will to be treated as an equal be reconciled with military and economic aid from others?[42]

Grosser's analysis of the dilemma seems quite correct, if for the wrong reasons. The problem has not been one of reconciling particularistic and conflicting policy goals, but the central tension and fundamental conflicts of objectives in French foreign policy are being faced by all modernized pluralistic societies. These will become more difficult to handle in the future than in the past. It is the particular way in which the problem has been confronted by French foreign policy that makes it a particularly interesting case to study.

[42] Grosser, *La Quatrième République et sa politique extérieure*, pp. 397–98.

146

FOUR

WELFARE VERSUS WARFARE
DEFENSE AUTONOMY AND THE DILEMMA
OF INSUFFICIENT RESOURCES

DE GAULLE predicated his concept of national autonomy upon the belief that it required an independent foreign policy and that the requisite of such a policy in the international system of the 1960s was a credible nuclear defense force. He derived this belief from his notions about the nature of international politics and from his own understanding of French history.

> If you consider our history, whether in the case of the Merovingians, the Carolingians, the Capetians, the First or Second Empires, the First, Second, Third, Fourth, or Fifth Republics—you will see that considerations or necessities of defense were always at the origin of the State and of the regimes that came into being, one after another. Conversely, every invasion, every national disaster has without fail brought about the fall of whatever regime was in power. If, therefore, a government lost control of its essential responsibility, it would thereby lose its justification.[1]

One of the central tasks upon de Gaulle's assuming the Presidency of the Fifth Republic was the development of a program implementing what he felt was required for maintaining an independent defense posture and, therefore, an independent foreign policy. This program included the creation of the first five-year Program Law for military equipment that outlined investment priorities for rebuilding the French defense

[1] Speech to officers at Ecole de Guerre, Paris, November 3, 1959, quoted in Roy Macridis, ed., *De Gaulle: Implacable Ally* (New York: Harper and Row, 1966), p. 133.

establishment, for the full implementation of the atomic weapons program that had been started under the Fourth Republic, and for the reorganization of the French armed forces.

The de Gaulle program for French defense was an attempt to fulfill a highly idiosyncratic view of both French foreign policy and of the nature of international politics in the contemporary world. In trying to implement that program, however, de Gaulle was confronted by a problem of resource allocation, which is faced by the leadership of practically all other modernized societies in the world; namely, how to fulfill traditional foreign-policy goals in a period when new demands are being placed upon the government by vocal and highly politicized segments of the population for a greater share of governmental expenditure on welfare, education, and social services, and when that society has grown so highly integrated that it has become vulnerable to external and internal stress on an unprecedented scale.

The interplay between the ideal of autonomy in defense and foreign policy, and exigencies for predominantly domestic economic programs is the subject of this chapter. In it I review the dilemma of rising demands and insufficient disposable resources explored in Chapter 1, describe in some detail various means by which de Gaulle tried to isolate defense spending from other items in the French budget in order to maintain his priority on foreign policy, and trace the inexorable course played by domestic contingencies in reversing the priorities of the French government. Here, too, the subject is treated in terms of both the particular limitations on foreign-policy expenditures in France and the general limitations on such policies in all highly industrialized societies. The general case is made especially clear by the way de Gaulle emphasized the primacy of foreign policy in his governmental program. Even though, in short, a policy based on the primacy of foreign policy may have been idiosyncratic to de Gaulle, an examination of its implementation serves to highlight the

148

dilemmas confronting all modernized societies in adjusting the allocation of their economic resources to political needs.

THE IDEAL OF AUTONOMY IN FRENCH SECURITY

Of all aspects of Gaullist foreign policy, security has perhaps been the one most frequently discussed and examined in the scholarly literature on France,[2] and its predominance is easily understood. De Gaulle's emphasis on the primacy of the nation-state in international relations, his withdrawal from the military organization of NATO in 1966, the development of the French nuclear striking force, and the refusal of the Gaullist government to sign and ratify either the partial Test Ban Treaty or the Nonproliferation Treaty were, in fact, central foci of French foreign policy during the 1960s.

As is argued in Chapter 1, de Gaulle's ideal in foreign policy was an affirmation and strengthening of all aspects of the autonomy of the nation-state. Since, in de Gaulle's view, international society was an arena in which anarchy was tempered by equilibrium, it was the primary responsibility of the political leadership to provide for the external defense of the state and, therefore, to develop an independent security capacity. This was true not only for defense but also for the broad spectrum of national policy. Gilpin argued that

> to decrease its dependence upon the United States and to balance German industrial power, the French have sought to establish a French capacity in all the sciences and technologies believed to be important for military power and economic competition: atomic energy, computers, elec-

[2] See Wilfrid L. Kohl, *French Nuclear Diplomacy* (Princeton, N.J.: Princeton University Press, 1972); Edward A. Kolodziej, *Patterns of French Foreign Policy, 1958–1967* (McLean, Va.: Research Analysis Corporation, 1968); and Wolf Mendl, *Deterrence and Persuasion: French Nuclear Armament in the Context of National Policy, 1945–1969* (London: Faber and Faber, 1970).

tronics, high-performance aircraft, space technology, and so forth. . . . In short, the French sought to compete against the two superpowers across the broad front of science and advanced technology.[3]

De Gaulle recognized that such a strategy could be thought of as quixotic for a state the scale of France in the era of superstates. After all, France did not have a market the size of that of the United States or the Soviet Union, nor did France possess the manpower or technological capacity to support a large land-based military force. However, de Gaulle saw in the international politics of the post World War II period a significant transformation in the nature of military power that, in the military potential of states of such disproportionate scale, provided an equalizer found in nuclear technology and in French participation in a global system of deterrence. As de Gaulle argued in 1964,

the field of deterrence is thus henceforth open to us. For to attack France would be equivalent, for whomever it might be, to undergoing frightful destruction itself. . . . Indeed, since a man and a people can die only once, the deterrent exists provided that one has the means to wound the possible aggressor mortally, that one is very determined to do it, and that the aggressor is convinced of it.[4]

[3] Robert Gilpin, "Technological Strategies and National Purpose," *Science,* CLXIX (1970): 443. Gilpin compares the strategies of developing technology across the broad spectrum of national potential as exemplified by France, with two other such strategies: scientific and technological specialization (e.g., Sweden); and importing foreign technology (e.g., Japan).

[4] *Speeches and Press Conferences* (New York: Ambassade de France, Service de Presse et d'Information, July 23, 1964). For a general discussion of the role of deterrence in French foreign policy, see Wladyslaw W. Kulski, *De Gaulle and the World* (Syracuse, N.Y.: Syracuse University Press, 1966), pp. 93–151. Kolodziej contrasts Beaufre's strategy with that of Gallois in the context of Gaullist diplomacy in "French Strategy Emergent; General André Beaufre: A Critique," *World Politics,* XIX (1967): 417–42.

Whether such an equalizer could in fact be found through the development of a French nuclear striking force is less relevant than its credibility which de Gaulle believed was fostered by the international setting after 1962 with the stalemate between the superpowers and the economic recovery of Europe. Neither the subtleties of the French strategy of deterrence are reviewed, nor is a critique of that posture in strategic terms offered since such criticism abounds in scholarly literature about France as well as in the political writings of French journalists.[5] Rather, the general and particular limitations on French defense autonomy in the Gaullist years will be analyzed abstractly.

The general conditions that made a policy of autonomy somewhat credible, it will be recalled, stemmed from fundamental changes in the international system in the early 1960s including: (1) the stalemate in the confrontation between the United States and the Soviet Union that reinforced the autonomy of smaller states and resulted in the emergence of polycentrism and intimations of international multipolarity;[6] (2) the consequent emergence of policies of accommodation, if not détente, between the two blocs of superpowers and their

[5] See especially, Raymond Aron, *The Great Debate*, trans. by Ernst Pawel (Garden City, N.Y.: Doubleday, 1965), pp. 100–44.

[6] Stanley Hoffmann articulates these changes convincingly in *Gulliver's Troubles, Or the Setting of American Foreign Policy* (New York: McGraw-Hill, 1968): "As a result of the nuclear stalemate, he has argued, confrontations have been, when direct, nonmilitary . . . As a result, a kind of *de facto polycentrism* occupies the forefront of the stage, in which almost anyone who wants can play. Old-fashioned multipolarity resulted from the distribution of coercive power, but this polycentrism results from the devaluation of coercive power" (p. 34). With regard to the emergence of multipolarity through the proliferation of nuclear weapons, Hoffmann argues that "the spread of nuclear weapons exploits *and* reacts against the muted bipolar contest and the rise of polycentrism. As long as there is no change in the basic structures of the international milieu, the possession of the *ultima ratio*, nuclear weapons, increases a nation's power of inflicting death and makes it virtually inevitably a party to any settlement of issues in which it has a stake" (p. 44).

allies; (3) the economic recovery of the European states and the growth of the European communities, which facilitated their attacks on the de facto monetary hegemony of the United States; and (4) recognition by the partners in NATO that the United States government would automatically provide for their defense through its own deterrent system.[7]

These general conditions were coupled with the set of goals pertaining to defense autonomy that de Gaulle attempted to implement, as a result of his diplomatic-strategic rationale based upon his idiosyncratic style and his view of France's role in human history. For de Gaulle, no great nation could afford to relinquish its autonomy since it could not entrust any aspect of its destiny to outsiders whose interests were not wholly compatible with its own. Thus, France could not consign its defense to either NATO or the United States since France would no longer control its destiny. Distrust of the United States stemmed also from de Gaulle's humiliation by Roosevelt during World War II, when the latter refused to recognize de Gaulle as the representative of the French state. It was reinforced by such experiences as the Suez venture of 1956, when the Franco-British-Israeli armies invading Suez and the Sinai peninsula were forced to retreat under American pressure. Added to these experiences, the debate in the

[7] The "public good" aspect of the American deterrent has been much commented upon (see Chapter 2). Frederick L. Pryor has adduced much empirical evidence for this phenomenon in developing the following arguments: "First, the smaller nations of a defense alliance have a greater tendency to cut their relative defense expenditures after joining an alliance than larger nations. Other things being equal, among nations of a single alliance one would expect the ratio of defense expenditures to the GNP to vary directly according to the absolute value of the GNP. . . .

"Second, since it is possible to trace the reaction curve of a single nation to changes in defense expenditures by other nations in its defense alliance it is also possible to trace the reaction curves of the other nations and to determine the equilibrium amount of defense expenditures for all nations within the alliance" (*Public Expenditures in Communist and Capitalist Nations* [Homewood, Illinois: Richard D. Irwin, 1968], p. 96).

late 1950s and early 1960s over the control of the NATO deterrent led de Gaulle to foresee circumstances in which détente between the superpowers might become for the United States more important than its European link. Since de Gaulle conceived of a role for France among the front-rank nations, he felt that such a state had to have the means to influence the future of international society—the wherewithal which, given the requisites of military potential in the 1960s, inevitably meant the need to possess an independently owned and maintained nuclear striking force.

As in other strands of Gaullist diplomacy, plans in foreign affairs converged with important domestic considerations in the implementation of the French nuclear option. In particular, there was the need to reorganize the armed forces after the termination of the Algerian War in order to decrease the threat of a revolt by the armed forces against the state. The legitimacy of the government in the eyes of important sectors of the armed forces had been a critical problem in France since its defeat in June 1940 and de Gaulle's own appeal from London, which had signaled the beginning of the French resistance. It was exacerbated by the series of defeats suffered in colonial wars after World War II, including Algeria, and by the acceptance of revolutionary warfare doctrine by the army that might also be used against the French state.[8] In order to reintegrate the armed forces after the Algerian War, de Gaulle undoubtedly felt that he had to streamline it, put in its command a new leadership whose loyalty was unquestioned, and give it a new set of tasks. The creation of a strategic nuclear force at the heart of a French defense structure as well as the withdrawal from NATO served, therefore, to give the army a new mission, just as it served to fulfill de Gaulle's own foreign policy objectives.[9]

[8] These themes are analyzed thoroughly in John Steward Ambler, *Soldiers Against the States; The French Army in Politics* (Columbus, Ohio: The Ohio State University Press, 1966).

[9] This is the argument of Edgar S. Furniss, Jr., *De Gaulle and the French Army: A Crisis in Civil-Military Relations* (New York:

The key to this reorganization of the armed forces—the most important such reorganization since Napoleon's—was detailed in a new approach to defense planning begun under de Gaulle's administration. This was the creation of a five-year Program Law in which the government articulated long-term military planning in the context of total budgetary priorities. Although the decision to create a nuclear capability had been made before de Gaulle reassumed power in 1958, this Program Law represented the first overview of French defense efforts. Law 60–1305, approved by the French Parliament on December 8, 1960 defined the government's long-term plan to build three defense systems: (1) the strategic nuclear force (*La Force nucléaire stratégique*, FNS); (2) the interventionary forces (*Forces d'intervention*); and (3) the territorial defense forces (*Forces de défense opérationnelle du territoire*, DOT).

The core of the reorganization was the strategic nuclear force (FNS) and it remained so through subsequent revisions of French long-term defense options. As a British observer of the French defense establishment, Mendl, has commented, "the 'Force Nucléaire Stratégique' was the centre piece and all other aspects of national defense served to complement it."[10] Plans called for the creation of a fission bomb deliverable by aircraft by 1964. In a second stage fusion bombs were to be developed along with ballistic missile delivery systems (hardened silos as well as submarines) by 1970.

The FNS was to be supplemented by other forces capable

The Twentieth Century Fund, 1964). For a thorough study of the reforms in the trend national defense, see Bernard Chantebout, *Organisation générale de la défense nationale en France depuis la fin de la seconde guerre mondiale* (Paris: R. Pichon and R. Durand-Auzias, 1967).

[10] Mendl, *Deterrence and Persuasion*, p. 110. In his view, the first five-year program for defense was predicated on the termination of the Algerian War, which had consumed much of the resources devoted to defense and limited French freedom of action. The Program Law of 1960 was the first concrete step for Mendl in the implementation of de Gaulle's "grand design" for Europe which depended upon the existence of a French deterrent force.

of fighting either nuclear or conventional battles, and the interventionary forces were also to be available for service in the French Community on short notice. The territorial defense system was to provide security within France in case of attack from outside. The set of three systems were to have cost the government 31.160 billion francs over the five-year period ending in December 1964.[11]

Although the major objectives of the first five-year plan were met by the end of 1964,[12] the second Program Law (1965–1970) demonstrated certain long-term problems, and new hurdles had to be overcome if the deterrent force was to become fully operational. In particular, weaponry had been discovered that was technologically feasible but far surpassed the financial resources of France, thereby forcing the military planners to make fundamental choices, which first became obvious in 1963 when the goals of the defense system, formulated in 1958, were radically changed from a capacity to strike, intervene, and survive (*frapper, intervenir, survivre*) to one to deter, intervene, and defend (*dissuader, intervenir, défendre*).[13]

The unanticipated increase in the projected costs of the FNS, especially those due to needed investment and capital expenditures, were to result in plans to expend 54.898 billion francs during the 1965–1970 program.[14] Moreover, expenditures for the tactical forces and the territorial defense forces were to be curtailed while the FNS was to receive priority.

[11] For details, see *La Défense: La politique militaire et ses réalisations* (Paris: Notes et études documentaires, No. 3343, December 6, 1966). This study also examines briefly the politics of defense expenditures within the armed forces and cabinet. No general study on this important subject now exists.

[12] By 1964, France had created a plant to produce enriched uranium, had carried out a series of atomic tests, and had operationalized the defense system through the development of Mirage IV delivery craft and the purchase of C–135Fs for refueling. In addition, submarine and missile prototype development had begun.

[13] See *La Défense: La politique militaire et ses réalisations*, p. 22.

[14] The Program Law covered only part of the proposed military expenditures over this six-year period. The total was to reach 80 billion francs.

Thus, the French planned to develop, during the implementation of the second stage of its defense program, three nuclear submarines, each equipped with sixteen nuclear warhead missiles and a series of hardened silos.

The planned development of French strategic forces thus paralleled closely the development of both its own rationale and that of French foreign policy as outlined in Chapter 2. The first phase (1958–1962) consisted, it will be recalled, of reversing the general trend of French foreign policy during the Fourth Republic by reasserting French presence in the world. After the close of the Algerian War, de Gaulle began to affirm French independence by combating what he felt was the integrationist logic of NATO. By 1967 de Gaulle moved toward the culmination of his foreign-policy program by articulating a general foreign policy of neutralism and independence in international conflicts from the Soviet-American global confrontation to the Arab-Israeli conflict in the Middle East. This was reflected in defense policy in the strategy of *tous azimuts*, which represented a France fortified with its deterrent system against an attack from any place in the world.

The foundations of this policy of autonomy were extremely weak, as the events of May 1968 clearly demonstrated. Although the logic of the strategy may have been impeccable in military terms, the costs of implementing it were obviously beyond the capacity of France. The May riots against the regime thus concretely symbolized the limits of potential French defense autonomy. Demands for domestic government expenditures and for increased personal consumption became so high that governmental priorities were forced to be reversed, and those resources of French society that had been allocated for the policy of *tous azimuts* had to be reapportioned for domestic purposes.

The Increased Burden of Defense

The reversal of French defense policy reflected the French situation, and is a condition of all highly industrialized states;

the dilemma faced by the Gaullist government in trying to marshal resources to implement its defense policy is apparently only a specific instance of a more general problem. As was argued in Chapter 1, what the Sprouts have called "the dilemma of rising demands and insufficient resources" seems to be a condition in all highly industrialized societies. Specifically, it appears to be a result of the coincidence of the increased politicization of the members of such societies as well as of the more general level of responsibility, which their governments have assumed in order both to satisfy demands placed upon them by their citizens and to maintain public order.[15]

Demands placed upon governments in modern industrialized states as well as their needs for fulfilling general social goals in terms of shares of the national product include the following:[16] (1) demands for increased personal consumption in an era when people want their fair share and when their expectation of material improvement is constantly rising; (2) needs for education as educational costs increase as more people expect to achieve higher levels of education and, as the society requires a more highly educated population in order to maintain itself; (3) allocations for investment expenditures and research in order to support the goals of technologically based societies the achievement of which depends upon the maintenance of continuous technological advance; (4) the need to maintain a defense establishment in order to assure the external security of the society when the cost of new and sophisticated military hardware continuously increases; (5) allocations for nonmilitary external purposes, including foreign aid programs; (6) allocations to maintain public order within urbanized societies that have apparently

[15] The processes by which these phenomena converged in the formation of the modern industrialized state are brilliantly outlined in Edward Hallett Carr, *The New Society* (London: Macmillan, 1951).

[16] For a more thorough review of these demands, see Margaret Sprout and Harold Sprout, *Ecology and Politics in America: Some Issues and Alternatives* (New York: General Learning Press, 1971).

become more fragmented or "corporatist"; and (7) other allocations, including those for environmental purposes in order to maintain the viability of the physical habitat.

If these demands are simultaneously increasing on governments in highly industrialized societies, there must be some important choices made with regard to the allocation of public funds and the definition of governmental priorities, especially in those areas where the distribution of governmental funds is imperative and those where relative and absolute cutbacks can be made. In France the government gave priority to defense and other external expenditures. At the same time, however, the thrust of new demands placed on the government was toward increased expenditures for predominantly domestic purposes. Given the inexorable increase in the latter priorities, a clash between the two was inevitable. The Gaullist government tried through a variety of mechanisms and political tactics to limit the demands placed upon it for domestic ends and to maintain its defense program.

Allocations of governmental expenditures in various sectors in France, including those for security purposes in recent years, poses the dilemma of increasing demands and insufficient disposable resources to meet them. According to the hypothesis outlined in Chapter 1, in all highly industrialized societies, an increase in governmental expenditures for social services (education, welfare, and other predominantly domestic concerns) results in a squeeze on expenditures for security and other external purposes, including foreign aid, and reflects the salience of introspection as well as of low politics.

The squeeze on defense expenditures ought to reflect not only a short-term trend beginning after World War II but also the results of long-term processes of modernization. Governmental allocations ought also, therefore, to be examined over a longer period of time, as exemplified in the period from 1868 to 1968. The long-term data on trends in governmental expenditures ought to reflect the increasing multifunctionality of the modern welfare state and ought to demonstrate that during the nineteenth century the French government, like the governments of all relatively nonmodernized societies, allocated resources predominantly for purposes of defense and for administration. As the society became more highly industrialized and as new demands were placed on the government, the relative priority of security and administrative expenditures should be expected to fall, while other sorts of allocations should rise.

These trends are precisely those that were found through an examination of the French budget for both the short-term and long-term periods. Table 3 summarizes French defense expenditures as a percentage of the government's budget and GNP from 1960 to 1970. For the period, French expenditures for defense declined precipitously in both categories.[17]

TABLE 3

The Total French Defense Expenditure as a Percentage
of the Total Government Budget and GNP, 1960–1970

Year	Budget	GNP
1960	25.1	6.4
1961	24.8	6.2
1962	23.1	6.1
1963	22.4	5.5
1964	22.2	4.6
1965	22.5	4.3
1966	21.8	4.1
1967	20.7	4.1
1968	20.0	4.0
1969	17.8	3.6
1970	17.6	3.4

Sources: B. Tricot, "Le Budget des Armées pour 1965," *Revue de défense nationale*, xxi (1965): 1691ff.; G. Heidt, "Le Budget de la Défense Nationale pour 1970," *Revue de défense nationale*, xxvi (1970): 21.

[17] The planned share of GNP for defense by 1975, according to the Third Program Law for defense was 3.1 percent. See Roger Antiphon, "Le Budget de la Défense Nationale pour 1971," *Revue de défense nationale*, xxvii (1971): 21.

Part of this decline was due to the termination of the Algerian War. But at the same time new expenditures were made on costly equipment for the new French army. Even so, new demands were being created that cut into the budget for the nuclear striking force resulting in a large relative reduction in the percentage of the budget devoted to defense.

The larger trend is illustrated in Figure 3 that presents the percentage of the French budget appropriated for defense over the period from 1868 to 1968 (exclusive of public debt).[18] During the last third of the nineteenth century, defense expenditures increased from 35 percent of the budget in 1871 to almost 50 percent at the outbreak of World War I and, even before the arms race in the intervening years, rarely fell below 40 percent of the budget. This markedly contrasts with the period after World War II when, after a series of colonial wars, the proportion of governmental expenditures on defense fell below 20 percent. Even during the 1950s, when the French were fighting in Indochina and Algeria, defense expenditures were held below the proportion they had attained during the more than forty years of peace after 1871. Other foreign expenditures similarly declined during the 1960s, for example, the flow of aid to less developed countries.

[18] Unless the public debt is excluded from a long-term analysis such as this, the results are likely to be misleading. This is the case whether defense expenditures are examined in terms of the total government budget or as a percentage of the GNP. Before and during the nineteenth century, the public debt was almost entirely due to the cost of past wars, and it constituted a large part of governmental budgets. In France, the cost of servicing the public debt was between 30 percent and 44 percent of the budget between 1868 and 1910, when it was nearly erased by inflation. Although the public debt increased to 54 percent of the budget in the mid-1920s, it was reduced to approximately 25 percent before the outbreak of World War II. Since 1945 it has remained nearly constant at 7 percent of the budget. See Institut National de la Statistique et des Etudes Economiques, *L'Annuaire statistique de la France, Résumé rétrospectif* (Paris: 1966), pp. 490–92. For the origins of the public debt in France in the nineteenth century see Francis W. Hirst, *The Political Economy of War* (New York: E. P. Dutton, 1915), pp. 237–52.

FIGURE 3

Annual Expenditures on National Defense* as a Percentage
of the Budget, 1868–1968 (public debt excluded)

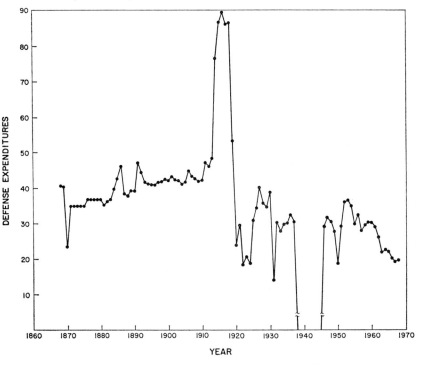

Source: Institut National de la Statistique et des Etudes Economiques,
Annuaire statistique de la France, Résumé rétrospectif (Paris: INSEE,
1966).

  * Longitudinal data for expenditures on national defense are not completely comparable because the budgetary system in France has changed
and expenditures on the nuclear striking force have been hidden in
allocations for a variety of ministries. From 1868 to 1917, data in this
figure include official expenditures for the Ministries of the Navy and
War, Armament, and Manufacture for War. From 1917 to 1937, data
come from budgetary allocations for the Ministries of War and Navy.
Data for subsequent years include total military expenditures. Ordinary
expenditures for the funding of the armed services have been separated
from capital expenditures.

French foreign policy during the Gaullist years had its negative and positive characteristics. Negatively, de Gaulle tried to enhance French autonomy and independence by denying other governments a say in some aspect of French destiny, and he used the "tactical no" in the EEC and NATO, as well as of other instrumentalities of Gaullist antiintegrationist policy. Positively, de Gaulle followed the policy of *rayonnement* of French culture. This aspect of French foreign policy consisted of fostering the use of the French language in international forums and of support for educational and cultural efforts abroad largely in former French dependencies. It also consisted of military, general budgetary, and technical assistance. The French aid program assumed, in the final analysis, a variety of positive goals, including the maintenance of a French presence abroad that might have, at some future point, allowed de Gaulle to lead a third-force movement independent of the superpowers.

Like the nuclear weapons program, the French aid program was a keystone of French foreign policy. In fact, France led all of the other developed societies in the proportion of its GNP allotted for aid, well above the 1.0 percent level prescribed by the OECD for its decade of development in the 1960s. But, in the face of rising domestic demands, both general defense expenditures and resources apportioned for aid could be cut. The dramatic decline in the French aid effort that resulted from new demands on the government is illustrated in Table 4. As can be seen, there was a marked decline in the flow of official and private resources from France to recipient countries in the less developed areas of the world during the course of the decade. The flow of official funds was exactly halved from 1.38 percent to 0.69 percent of the GNP. The flows of private capital sloped less rapidly, but still markedly, from 0.79 percent to 0.55 percent of the GNP, and do not show the same tendency to decline continuously as do official flows. Rather, they appear to respond more sensitively to domestic and foreign market pressures.

The decline in the proportion of expenditures for the major foreign-policy programs of de Gaulle was matched by dra-

matic increases in expenditures in other areas. As could be
expected from the general argument above concerning pro-
liferating new demands placed on the government under the
impetus of higher expectations for well-being, these increases
occurred in government expenditures for higher education,
for social services, and for new housing. Figure 4 shows the
increase in expenditures for public education. These expenditures first increased markedly with the reforms of Ferry and
other radicals adopted between 1879 and 1886 that were designed to expand the public school system in France in order
to legitimize the Third Republic and to counter the influence
of the Church in French society. The increase after World
War I was not as dramatic as the graph would imply, since
the down curve between 1913 and 1918 reflects the extraordinary defense expenditures during the war. From 1950 to
the mid-1960s, however, there is a steep upward trend as the
share of the budget for education increased from 6.91 percent

TABLE 4

Flows of French Resources to Less-Developed Societies
as a Percentage of GNP, 1960–1969

Year	Governmental revenues	Private resources	Total flow
1960	1.38	0.78	2.16
1961	1.41	0.69	2.10
1962	1.30	0.56	1.86
1963	1.01	0.46	1.47
1964	0.89	0.57	1.46
1965	0.75	0.55	1.30
1966	0.69	0.53	1.22
1967	0.71	0.44	1.15
1968	0.69	0.66	1.35
1969	0.69	0.55	1.24

Source: OECD, *Development Assistance: Efforts and Policies of the
Members of the Development Assistance Committee* (Paris: 1970),
pp. 180–83.

of the budget in 1950 to its peak of 18.23 percent in 1965—a share almost as high as that of the budget for defense.

The growth of the public educational system in France after World War II was extremely rapid. Although the primary and secondary school systems grew during this time, their expansion was by and large an accommodation to the increase in France's population base after the war. The

FIGURE 4

Annual Total Expenditures on Public Education
as a Percentage of Budget, 1868–1968 (public debt excluded)

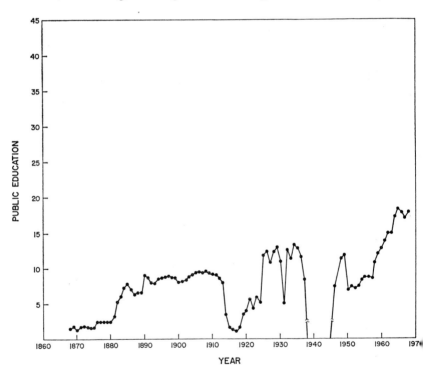

Source: Institut National de la Statistique et des Etudes Economiques, *Annuaire statistique de la France, Résumé rétrospéctif* (Paris: INSEE, 1966).

growth of higher education, however, was much more rapid. As Table 5 indicates, the number of students enrolled in French universities during the 1960s increased at an average rate of 11.3 percent per year between 1958 and 1966— an increase from 214,000 to 502,000 that reflected the growing demands upon that system by a society the economic growth of which had become based on an advanced level of technology requiring a higher and more generalized level of educational attainment.[19] Similar increases occurred in the 1960s in all of the other highly industrialized societies of the West, which indicates that the trend was generalized.[20] Even

TABLE 5

University Attendance in France, 1958–1966

Year	Number of university students in thousands	Percent of total school attendance
1958	241	2.73
1959	225	2.72
1960	249	2.94
1961	277	3.19
1962	315	3.50
1963	362	3.99
1964	406	4.37
1965	455	4.84
1966	502	5.28

Source: EEC Statistical Office, *The Common Market Ten Years On: Tables 1958–1967* (Brussels: 1968), p. 95.

[19] By 1970 this figure had reached 600,000. In a little more than a decade, the total population in schools of higher education had tripled. See Henry W. Ehrmann, *Politics in France*, 2d ed. (Boston: Little, Brown, 1971), p. 73.

[20] The similarities as well as the national differences in educational policies and problems are reviewed in several series published by the OECD. See especially the series entitled *Innovation in Higher Education*, and *Reviews of National Policies for Education*.

with the expansion of the system of higher education, public demands fell notably short of satisfaction. As the events of May 1968 demonstrate, this growth in the system of higher education accentuated the need for structural reforms in the university system in France as in other European societies. In spite of the increase in enrollments in institutions of higher learning, and in a significant measure because of it, new demands were placed on the institutions requiring even further expenditures by the central government.[21]

The same patterns exhibited in expenditures on higher education as well as the problems associated with the reform of its institutions can be found in allocations for social services, for social security, for housing, etc. In each case, expenditures, while they increased to meet growing needs, did not rise as rapidly as demands placed on the system,[22] and the French government under de Gaulle faced the same dilemma that the governments of all other modern industrialized societies have —the dilemma between rising demands for a wide variety of governmental expenditures and insufficient resources to meet those demands. The dilemma arose even though de Gaulle

[21] Ehrmann describes the problems of higher education in France succinctly: "But the troubles besetting the system were not only due to quantitative pressures. The teaching methods practiced at the lycées proved entirely inappropriate for the socialization of the lower middle classes which were winning entry into secondary education. Increased social mobility and the modernization of the country resulted in a situation in which the university and the economy have grown out of phase. Because the universities failed to respond to the demands of mass education, the students' dissatisfaction with the content and methods of their education was frequently combined with anxieties about their professional careers. For others, a minority, the haphazard efforts of the system to serve the needs of the society by providing training for skills were distasteful because, in their eyes, such a design subjected higher education to the demands of technocratic capitalism" (*Politics in France*, pp. 73–74).

[22] The growth of the social security system in France is fully described in Wallace C. Peterson, *The Welfare State in France* (Lincoln, Nebr.: University of Nebraska Press, 1960). For detailed analyses of these domestic problems, see John Ardagh, *The New French Revolution* (New York, Harper and Row, 1969), pp. 203–30, 391–433; and Ehrmann, *Politics in France*, pp. 17–39, 304–19.

was insensitive to problems of resource allocation since for him policy was a matter of will and morale. The demands for domestic expenditures increased over the century-long period beginning with the creation of the Third Republic but, as the data on expenditures indicate, accelerated after World War II as France became a highly industrialized society.

The obvious target of these demands, as was evident in May 1968, was the legitimacy of the political order that had placed its highest priority on expenditures for external purposes. After May 1968, both de Gaulle's and Pompidou's governments reordered priorities. Foreign-policy expenditures were curtailed in order to make a larger pool of resources available for domestic purposes without drastically raising taxes. In addition, both governments reversed the policy of autonomy pursued during the mid-1960s and began to collaborate with foreign governments in order to reduce the costs of their foreign policies. De Gaulle's movement away from the policy of autonomy and independence was evident in the monetary crisis of November 1968 when his government sought the cooperation of Britain and the United States against pressures from Germany. The change in France's policy toward Europe with plans for a monetary union and the admission of Britain into the EEC under Pompidou were the logical culmination of this trend. Both de Gaulle and Pompidou, moreover, reevaluated the French position with regard to Western defense, increased bilateral defense cooperation with the United States, and staunchly supported the maintenance of the level of U.S. troops deployed in Europe.

Even during de Gaulle's Presidency, issues of resource allocation were posed in political debates as an alternative between expenditures for defense and national glorification, and those for modernization of domestic social institutions. The choice was summarized clearly by Bonnefous as follows:

> She [France] will realize at her own expense that it is impossible to continue a costly military policy, an independent nuclear policy, a policy of aid to the overseas countries, and, at the same time, to develop her own national terri-

tory, to modernize her economy, to train the adequate number of her technologists and to renovate her educational system.[23]

To some extent de Gaulle had foreseen arguments and pressures against the primacy he placed on foreign-policy goals. He viewed the French people as one with the capacity both for greatness and for mediocrity,[24] their institutions as capable of both partisanship and unity, and, therefore, provided in the constitutional mechanisms of France certain political instruments that would enable him to carry on his foreign policy with unity and to counter the pressures for reversing his priorities.

The tactics of leadership of any advanced industrialized society in maintaining autonomy in the face of reduced defense expenditures can be best analyzed through de Gaulle's solution to this dilemma.

GOVERNMENTAL OPTIONS ON ALLOCATIONS FOR DEFENSE

Confronted with rising domestic demands and with a limited resource base for fulfilling the claims of his foreign policy of autonomy, de Gaulle was forced to make important choices in the allocation of French resources that carried with them long-term effects on both French society and foreign policy. Until spring 1968, he chose to isolate foreign policy from future domestic claims to ensure both its fulfillment and its continuity after he had relinquished power. The choices his gov-

[23] *Les Milliards qui s'envolent: l'aide française aux pays sous-développés.* (Paris: Fayard, 1963), p. 7, as translated in Kulski, *De Gaulle and the World,* p. 354.

[24] His characteristically ambivalent attitude to the French people is summarized in the closing paragraphs of his war memoirs: "Old France, weighed down with history, prostrated by wars and revolutions, endlessly vacillating from greatness to decline, but revived, century after century, by the genius of renewal!" (*The Complete War Memoirs of Charles de Gaulle,* trans. by Jonathan Griffin and Richard Howard [New York: Simon and Schuster, 1967], p. 998).

ernment made, however, served to politicize many groups in French society whose demands for a larger share of the national wealth had not been met. In fact, de Gaulle's foreign policy and its ostensible primacy in political affairs seemed to lead many of these groups to believe that Gaullist foreign-policy expenditures could better have been spent on programs with a more obvious domestic impact than the development of a nuclear striking force or a missile launching capability. The compounding of these demands seems in large measure to be responsbile for the speed with which the student revolts of May 1968 spread through French society to workers striking for higher salaries and greater benefits.

In retrospect, the budgetary choices of the French government from 1962 to 1968 thus appear to have enabled it to pursue its foreign policy with relative isolation from domestic demands for a short-term period. Over the long term, the general policy seems to have been less successful as a strategy for assuring foreign-policy success and continuity since the reaction to it was so widespread and deep within French society. Nonetheless, in coping with the dilemma concerning expenditures, the Gaullist government seems to have used each of the tactics available to the government of any highly industrialized society:[25] (1) efforts can be made to expand the resources available to the government by some combination of an increase in the rate of economic growth of the society and an increase in the taxing domain of the government; (2) the government may revise its priorities "either to bring the commitments and demands and the resources more nearly into balance or to relieve pressure in the domestic political boiler";[26] (3) efforts can be made of a diversionary nature to win the support of voters to the government's policies; (4) the opinions of dissenters can be manipulated in order to change them, to reduce their credibility, or to silence them; and (5)

---

[25] The description of these tactics are borrowed in modified form from Sprout and Sprout, "The Dilemma of Rising Demands and Insufficient Resources," pp. 690–93.

[26] Ibid., p. 690.

collaborative efforts with other governments can be undertaken in order to reduce the costs to the government of certain domestic expenditures, or to reduce expenditures made
in order to fulfill foreign-policy goals.

Economic Expansion

The fostering of economic growth as a means to increase the
resources available to support the French defense policy was
one of the options used by the governments of the Fifth Republic during the 1960s. This strategy was coupled with a
series of planned constraints on the expansion of private consumption, so that a greater share of the society's GNP could
be devoted to investment in defense related sectors. By this
means, public demands for increased social services, educational, and other domestic expenditures could be simultaneously satisfied with the fulfillment of the goals of the government's defense program. The planned growth of the national
product was 5.5 percent from 1960 to 1965 and 5.0 percent
from 1966 to 1970 according to the targets of the Fourth and
Fifth Economic Plans.[27] Since investments were to increase
at a substantially higher rate, private consumption was to increase at a lower rate. During the Fourth Plan, forecasts for
private consumption were at an annual growth rate of 4.0
percent, while during the Fifth Plan they were reduced to
3.5 percent.[28]

[27] See Chapter 7. Actual increases were, however, quite different:
1960, 7.04 percent; 1961, 5.08 percent; 1962, 6.68 percent; 1963, 5.74
percent; 1964, 6.58 percent; 1965, 4.65 percent; 1966, 5.51 percent;
1967, 4.74 percent; 1968, 4.24 percent (all in constant prices), OECD,
Economic Surveys, France (Paris: 1970), p. 71. Yet it is important
to emphasize the extraordinary increase in French economic growth
after World War II. In contrast to the annual growth rate of 2 percent to 2.5 percent before the war, average productivity per man-hour
has increased at a yearly average of 5.0 percent since 1949. See J.-J.
Carré, P. Dubois, and E. Malinvaud, *La croissance française: un essai
d'analyse économique causale de l'après-guerre* (Paris: 1972).

[28] "The reduction in the increase in individual living standards is
thus marked, and it is being done, without any doubt, against the gen-

The planned expansion of the economy had its desired effect on the level of public consumption. As Table 6 indicates, the public consumption's share of the GNP decreased with the transition from the Fourth to the Fifth Republic and with

TABLE 6

Consumption, Governmental Expenditure, Savings and
Investment as Percentages of the GNP in France,
1949–1968

Year	Private consumption	Government	Savings and investment
1949	64.73	14.12	21.02
1950	63.63	14.61	19.95
1951	64.55	14.79	18.60
1952	64.98	16.89	17.74
1953	66.05	16.93	16.35
1954	65.66	14.56	17.57
1955	66.25	13.36	18.25
1956	66.39	14.43	20.52
1957	66.41	14.32	20.56
1958	65.48	13.45	21.45
1959	65.03	13.95	19.68
1960	60.33	14.01	23.80
1961	60.72	13.83	23.60
1962	60.99	13.48	24.65
1963	61.79	12.97	24.74
1964	61.20	12.61	26.30
1965	61.02	12.37	25.59
1966	60.54	12.04	27.10
1967	60.57	11.90	27.26
1968	61.03	12.01	27.10

Source: Institut National de la Statistique et des Etudes Economiques, *L'Année statistique de la France, 1968* (Paris: INSEE, 1969), p. 638.

eral tendencies of French society" (Jean Boissonat, "Le Ve Plan et la crise de la planification française," *Esprit*, No. 335 [February 1965], p. 391).

the implementation of the Fourth and Fifth Economic Plans. Governmental expenditure's relative share of the GNP similarly decreased, while investment increased by more than 10 percent above its nadir during the Fourth Republic. Even though two colonial wars were fought during the Fourth Republic, private consumption was at a level significantly above that during the 1960s. Undoubtedly, this was the result of several additional factors beyond the incentives given by the government to corporations for increasing their investment. For example, implementation of the Rome Treaty probably spurred on some businesses to invest in order to increase their competitiveness in the Common Market. In any case, the effect was a decrease in relative share of private consumption that partly represented the efforts of the government to implement its foreign policy.

The steep increase in French research and development efforts and the role of the government in it are indicated in Table 7. In per capita terms, such efforts increased from 40 percent of those in the United States in 1961 to over 71 per-

TABLE 7

Comparisons of National Research and Development
Expenditures for Selected Countries, 1961 and 1967
(U.S. = 100)

Country	Government financed		Industry financed		Total		Per capita	
	1961	1967	1961	1967	1961	1967	1961	1967
United States	100	100	100	100	100	100	100	100
France	10	19	10	16	10	18	40	71
Germany	8	13	15	22	10	17	34	55
Japan	5	10	17	22	10	15	19	30
United Kingdom	19	15	25	24	21	18	74	67

Source: Keith Pavitt, "Technology in Europe's Future," *Research Policy*, 1 (1971–1972), p. 216.

cent in 1967.[29] Although total French efforts were about equal to those of other states of similar scale, the government-financed efforts were higher since they were primarily found in the high priority defense sectors. As Table 8 notes, French investment in nuclear research and development was second to that of the United States of all the states noted in the table. In per capita terms, however, it was more than twice that of the United States in 1969 after its tremendous growth during

TABLE 8

Comparisons of Governmental Expenditures on Research and Development, 1961 and 1969 (U.S. = 100)

Polity	Defense				Nuclear				Space			
	Total		Per capita		Total		Per capita		Total		Per capita	
	1961	1969	1961	1969	1961	1969	1961	1969	1961	1969	1961	1969
United States	100	100	100	100	100	100	100	100	100	100	100	100
Canada	1	1	7	8	5	7	49	64	0	0	0	2
France	6	11	23	46	35	52	139	211	0	5	1	21
Germany	2	6	7	19	14	38	44	128	0	4	0	13
Belgium	0	0	1	1	2	3	31	56	0	0	0	7
Netherlands	0	0	1	4	2	4	25	70	0	0	0	6
EEC*	8	17	12	26	52	98	77	149	0	10	0	15
United Kingdom	17	14	57	51	32	27	113	99	1	3	2	10
Sweden	1	1	30	33	6	4	135	95	0	0	0	4
Norway	0	0	2	5	1	1	32	42	0	0	0	2
EFTA†	18	15	51	46	39	32	111	95	1	3	2	9
Japan	0	0	0	1	4	11	7	22	0	0	0	0

Source: Keith Pavitt, "Technology in Europe's Future," *Research Policy*, 1 (1971–1972), pp. 216–17.

* Italy excluded.

† Austria, Switzerland, Denmark, and Portugal excluded.

[29] In 1967 the per capita research and development expenditures in France and the other countries in Table 7 peaked. By 1970 this level fell to 65 percent of the U.S. level in per capita terms.

the decade. French investment in space technology, although much lower, increased in the 1960s and was significantly higher than any of its European neighbors.

The resources required for these expanded investments by the French government in defense related production could be obtained only through a coherent economic program that would enable the French economy to possess a highly industrialized sector. De Gaulle began a program to modernize and stabilize the French economy when he first came to office in 1958. The Rueff plan for a 17.5 percent devaluation in December 1958 was designed to restore the balance-of-payments situation that had progressively deteriorated during the Fourth Republic (see Chapter 5), and was coupled with tariff reductions in the EEC and the GATT that were to encourage French industries to compete internationally.

Reality stood in the way of full achievement of the economic miracle for which de Gaulle had hoped. In 1962 de Gaulle was forced to accept an interim *plan de stabilisation* to fight the reemergence of inflation. Accordingly, credit was restricted, prices and wages were frozen selectively, and public expenditures reduced for fear that the strong franc, an instrument of Gaullist foreign economic policy, would be weakened. The cost was a doubling of unemployment and the slackening of expansion in the name of foreign-policy goals. Here were the origins of the cumulative grievances held by various groups against the government's foreign policies. Unemployment remained high for French standards through the next four to five years and the purchasing power of workers was restricted, and their grievances were compounded by complaints from the agricultural sector, especially from farmers who never achieved the promises held out to them by the CAP in the EEC.

Although the general public in France was somewhat ambivalent toward defense expenditures per se, a majority saw some link between those expenditures and their curtailed consumption. Polls of public opinion in 1963 and 1964, for example, indicated that a declining, but marked percentage felt the government did not have the means to build a nuclear striking force.[30] At the same time, over 60 percent felt that the government ought to have spent more on education (64 percent), health and social welfare (61 percent), housing (77 percent), and roads and transportation (80 percent), while a large sector of the population felt that less should be spent on military defense (40 percent) and foreign assistance (44 percent).[31]

Increasingly throughout the 1960s with the increased defense expenditures and other allocations for the *grandes entreprises* of the Gaullist government, the French public felt

[30] "In your mind, can France make the expenditures required by the nuclear striking force?"

	Yes	No	No response
April 1963	15%	52%	33%
April 1964	29	45	26

Institut Français de l'opinion publique, *Sondages, Revue Française de l'Opinion Publique,* xxvi (1964): 53. The mixed support for the nuclear striking force was reported in ibid.

"Do you believe that France ought to have its own nuclear striking force?"

	Yes	No	No response
July 1962	39%	27%	34%
January 1963	42	31	27
July 1963	37	38	25
August 1963	34	37	29
November 1963	39	37	24
April 1964	39	40	21

The same range of breakdown in opinion occurred through the poll of 1966.

[31] See Johan Galtung, "Public Opinion on the Economic Effects of Disarmament," in *Disarmament and World Economic Interdependence,* ed. Emile Benoit (New York: Columbia University Press, 1965), p. 173. French opinion on these issues correlated strongly with those of Norway in terms of rank order correlations (0.99) which led Galtung to argue that "this similarity in preference is due more to the degree of development France and Norway have in common than to their NATO membership, particularly since the items in the question mainly reflect domestic allocation policy in very general terms" (ibid., p. 174).

that it was not receiving a fair share of economic and material gains. The number of grievances seemed to increase as did the sector of the disaffected public. As Ehrmann has argued,

> the feeling of having been denied a fair share in an expanding economy, the abnormally low rate of minimum wages, the longest working hours in Europe, unpopular reforms, especially those of the social security system [which increased worker costs and decreased payments] and also a widely felt need for recognition of trade-union activities at places of work, motivated the workers' demands in private and public enterprises.[32]

In spite of salary and fringe benefit increases during the early and mid-1960s, laborers did not gain as much as administrative and white collar workers, but rather received smaller increases, and the government was more or less content to perpetuate this situation, postponing added benefits for workers under the belief that given weak union organization in France, political pressures from the unions would be minimal.

The events of May 1968 were to prove the government wrong. Spurred on by the quickness with which the government responded to student demands for reforms in the educational system, the idea of a mass general strike quickly spread among the French working classes. The Grenelle agreements and subsequent general contracts with workers that were signed after May 1968 satisfied many demands of the workers who received relative increases in their income and purchasing power. For example, the minimum average wage increased by 35 percent as a result of the Grenelle agreements. Between 1968 and 1971, the average hourly wage of workers increased by 20 percent, that of civil servants by 16 percent, while that of administrators (cadres) increased by only 12

[32] Ehrmann, *Politics in France*, p. 189. See also Stephen S. Cohen, *Modern Capitalist Planning: The French Model* (Cambridge, Mass.: Harvard University Press, 1969), pp. 238–39.

percent, whose increases before 1968 had been markedly
higher than those of other categories of workers.[33]

In summary, the joint policies of expanding the French
economy and simultaneously limiting the share in economic
growth of private consumption freed resources that the
French government could allocate for investment and for
defense. The general economic policy was a successful, but
short-term venture in implementing the policy of autonomy.
It finally resulted in increasing the demands placed upon the
government for spending in the domestic public sector that
had been curtailed for the government's defense program.
The result was the need after 1968 to fulfill unsatisfied demands for housing, for private consumption, for social services, transportation, and for other aspects of low policies, or
economic and welfare expenditures, and a reordering of the
defense program to such a degree that it meant a virtual renunciation of the policy of autonomy.

Revising Governmental Priorities

Governments may solve the dilemma posed by the allocation
of resources for external versus domestic purposes by redefin-
ing priorities, a strategy, of course, which de Gaulle's government wanted to avoid at almost any cost. To reverse priorities would have undermined the government's rationale
since the ideology of the Gaullist state was based on *une
certaine idée de la France* stemming from the international
role of France. For de Gaulle influence in the world was the
mission of the French people and was the underlying idea
behind the constitutional and other administrative reforms
of the Fifth Republic.

One of the basic bulwarks against a reversal of de Gaulle's
priorities was a reform of the budgetary process that had
characterized politics in the Third and Fourth Republics.
Philip Williams wrote as follows: "It was the great legislative
event of the parliamentary year, the chief occasion for criti-

[33] See *Le Monde*, March 30, 1971, pp. 19–20.

177

cizing governmental policy and administration, and an opportunity for aggrieved interests to press their case on a ministry which needed every vote it could get. So crucial was it to the survival of governments that it provoked half the votes of confidence in the Fourth Republic."[34] Several additional reforms were created in the Fifth Republic limiting the ability of Parliament to amend or transform government bills including budgetary bills. These reforms were buttressed by the fact that the government also possessed a majority in Parliament. Now the administration rather than the representative body was to be the key political institution responsible for initiating the budgetary process.

In the new reforms, the Finance Minister steered the passage of his bill. He first presented it to the Finance Committee of the Assembly, one of the six standing committees, and the only committee able to make amendments to the bill, since amendments not discussed in committee were to be prohibited on the floor of the Assembly. The Finance Minister could also submit the bill to a package vote, thus prohibiting votes on separate clauses or amendments and thereby limiting the influence of individual members of the Finance Committee or the Assembly. In fact, the right of individual representatives to propose new public expenditures was completely abolished. Finally, the budgetary process, which had dragged out over seemingly interminable sessions during the Fourth Republic, was to be submitted to a rather rigorous timetable. The Assembly had forty days to vote on the budget after it was first presented. If it did not vote on it, the bill would then lay before the Senate for two weeks. If after seventy days no decision was taken on the budget, the government could bring it into force by ordinance unless the Assembly explicitly rejected it.

In spite of the predominance of the government in the

[34] Philip Williams, *The French Parliament* (1958–1967), (London: George Allen and Unwin, 1968), p. 76. See also Pierre Delvoyé and Henri Lesguillons, *Le contrôle parlementaire sur la politique économique et budgétaire* (Paris: Presses Universitaires de France, 1964).

budgetary process under the Fifth Republic reforms, the budget still provided opportunity for major debates over the general priorities of the government. Moreover, it did not overcome the politics of resource allocation, but shifted to behind the scenes negotiations within the Finance Committee and within the administration itself.[35] In the end, however, the process enhanced the autonomy of the Cabinet in establishing its priorities among different and often conflicting national goals.[36]

If general budgetary expenditures had been relatively insulated from parliamentary control by these reforms, defense expenditures had been even more removed and protected as a result of another innovation in Fifth Republic resource allocation processes designed, in part, to separate the government's foreign policy from short-term political interests. This innovation led to the passage of five-year Program Laws for defense that rationalized the government's defense posture and forecast the relative allocations for the five-year period as a whole. In addition, of course, yearly budgets for defense are submitted to the parliament.[37] But the five-year Program Law provided the Minister of Defense with a significant lever

[35] This shift in the principal locus of budgetary politics from parliamentary to administrative bodies makes the politics of national priorities extremely difficult to study in the case of France. I wish that I had been able to gain some insights into this process through interviews with responsible officials, but I found those whom I interviewed to be as closed-mouthed privately as they were publicly.

[36] Williams claims that the decline of Parliament in the budgetary process has occurred in all highly industrialized states as a response to long-term changes. In France, however, this loss of parliamentary control is more pronounced because of the reforms created by the constitution writers of the Fifth Republic (*French Parliament*, p. 83).

[37] A large amount of defense expenditures, especially on the secret nuclear and space programs, are hidden in the French budget under other rubrics. I have, obviously, ignored these additional expenditures in these remarks. This technique is, of course, prevalent in all democratic countries and is another instrument available to the government to enable it to maintain its overall priorities. See also Pierre Sudreau, *L'Enchaînement* (Paris: Librairie Plon, 1967), pp. 178–83.

179

in these yearly battles for governmental resources with his counterpart in the Ministry of Finance. As Secretary-General for Administration in the Ministry of National Defense Long has argued, ". . . the existence of a plan gives at the very least a very strong basis to the ministry for claiming each year the amounts which, in absolute value and in annual increases, are needed to enable him to achieve the objectives as they were forecasted in the plan."[38]

The process of decision-making institutionalized after de Gaulle returned to power in 1958 served, then, as an assurance that the priorities established by the government could withstand some pressures of special interest groups within French society or in the parliament. Here one can find the main constraint on domestic demands that might alter or reverse the implementation of programs designed to achieve the government's goals. With five-year Program Laws for defense, capital expenditures for long-term projects such as missiles, miniaturation, aircraft, submarines, etc., had an additional assurance of continuity. For example, even before the Third Program Law (1971–1975) went into effect, two thirds of the planned investment expenditures were necessitated by plans that had been developed in the previous two programs.[39]

Even with these institutional supports, however, the defense program progressively yielded to increasingly urgent domestic demands during the course of the 1960s. The degree to which these demands progressively cut into the defense program can be seen through a juxtaposition of the goals of the first two plans with the actual planned expenditures of the third long-term military program. It will be recalled that the original five-year plan for defense called for a tripartite de-

[38] Marceau Long, "Financement de la politique militaire française," *Revue de défense nationale*, xxvi (1970): 548.

[39] For an analysis of the relative lack of degrees of freedom, or choice, in defense expenditures, see Jacques Isnard, "Le tiers des investissements militaires pour l'armement nucléaire," *Le Monde, Sélection Hebdomadaire*, August 6–12, 1970, p. 7.

fense system. The center of the system was to be the strategic nuclear force (FNS) consisting of a first stage of fifty-eight Mirage IV bombers, to be replaced by four nuclear submarines armed with sixteen nuclear warhead missiles each, and eighteen to twenty-seven hardened silos by 1975. The deterrent force was to be supplemented by the tactical forces (one army of five mechanized divisions with a tactical nuclear weapons capacity), tactical and airborne interventionary forces, the Atlantic and Mediterranean fleets, and the territorial defense force that was to be used against fifth columns and for fighting within French territory. The three forces had been outlined in 1958 in a two page *Instruction Personnelle et Secrète* (IPS) issued by de Gaulle to the Minister of the Armies. Their design took into account all the forms of warfare observed by the French over the previous twenty years: atomic, conventional, and subversive. The creation of these three forces were to enable France to pursue a defense policy of neutralism, or of *tous azimuts*, by the late 1970s.

The implementation of the French defense program never met its stated goals. Although its costliness was gradually revealed, it was the events of May 1968 which, as in the case of our analysis of the French economic base, suddenly demonstrated the inability of the French government to continue to fund it. As an observer noted in *Le Monde* in the summer of 1968,

> the army staffs scarcely speak any longer of a "force tous azimuts" which, in the minds of its supporters, was to see light by 1980. The Events of May and the prospects of a reordering by next year of military financial credits have overcome this ambitious and costly project. Now the most optimistic supporters foresee the implementation of the military program by 1990; others find it preferable, under present conditions, to cancel an operation which will be depreciated even more by the arms race.[40]

[40] Jacques Isnard, "La France disposera en 1975 d'une capacité nucléaire égale à celle d'un B-52 américain," *Le Monde*, July 11, 1968, p. 14.

The major constraint on the full implementation of the government's military program stemmed from the need to limit the overall amount of money expended on defense at a level below 5 percent of the GNP. The French program was simply too costly to be implemented within these budgetary bounds. The chief reasons for this costliness were the unanticipated costs and the relatively unknown total cost of the "second generation" of the French nuclear arsenal. But unanticipated costs turned up even under the First Program Law (1960–1965) providing for military equipment, for example, the costs of the Pierrelatte uranium separation plant, of atomic test sites, atomic stockpiles, aircraft, etc.[41] When it came to the second stage of the French program with ballistic missiles and submarines, these costs increased even more.

The general way in which the government tried to meet these unanticipated costs was by sacrificing the two ancillary forces (tactical forces and territorial defense forces) and by placing the bulk of French military expenditures on the nuclear striking force. The rationale for this was that if the deterrent was central to the French program, the major defense goals could be met by focusing upon it alone. Given the general international situation and the relatively low probability that warfare would break out in Europe, the government could then simultaneously cut costs and meet both domestic and defense needs. Mendl described the situation in 1968, both before and after the events of May as follows:

The budget for 1968 continued to mark the trend which gave absolute priority to nuclear armament and which pursued the modernization of one service at the expense of another. For the first time the navy disposed of greater credits for nuclear equipment than the air force. The army credits continued to lag far behind those of the other two services. Even credits for the development of the Pluton [tactical nuclear] missile had to be postponed. The economic crisis of

[41] See Sudreau, L'Enchaînement, pp. 181–83.

the spring and summer 1968 caused further postponements and cuts in a programme whose fulfillment receded steadily into the future.[42]

Thus, in constant francs, the FNS cost 34 billion rather than the forecasted 27.4 billion francs[43] under the Second Program Law. This cost forced the government to reduce expenditures on its other forces even at the risk of establishing a disequilibrium among the three forces. As a result of these reductions in expenditures, the production of AMX–30 tanks was delayed and a large number of projects for the land-based forces were canceled including plans to develop MIRVs and nuclear-powered hunter submarines.[44] The general consequences of these economic constraints was a postponement of plans both for creating the strategic nuclear forces and for modernizing the conventional forces. Even during the period of the Second Program Law, two rather than five French divisions were modernized and chances for the complete modernization of French forces by 1975 were dim.[45]

If the general budgetary squeeze forced a slow reevaluation of French military planning, the *coup de grâce* to those plans came with the events of May as can be seen in the subsequent increased costs of two items: (1) personnel costs stemming from the general salary increases granted governmental employees; and (2) the *gendarmérie*, or internal security forces of the army, the costs of which were itemized in the defense budget and the size of which was expanded. Between 1969 and 1971 operational costs for personnel increased by 15.4

[42] Mendl, *Deterrence and Persuasion*, pp. 113–14.

[43] *Le Monde*, November 12, 1969, p. 8.

[44] Institute for Strategic Studies (ISS), *Strategic Survey, 1970* (London: 1971), p. 23.

[45] The inability of the French economy to sustain the government's defense program was admitted by Pompidou's first defense minister, Michel Debré, who, soon after assuming office, announced plans for reforming the French armed forces, including a previously announced reduction in military service for conscripts from eighteen to twelve months.

percent,[46] even though 1.5 percent of the military and civil positions in the armed forces were eliminated. The bolstering of the *gendarmérie* was an even more obvious social burden included in the military budget. The events of May had demonstrated the need for increasing the capacity of the government to maintain social order. Not only was the *gendarmérie* to receive equipment for riot control (special training, tear gas, etc.), but also the internal security force was to be increased by 2,591 positions (an amount almost equal to the reduction in military and civilian personnel attached to the armed forces).

In short, even with a set of institutionalized processes designed to guarantee the fulfillment of the foreign-policy goals of the government, budgetary pressures forced the government to revise substantially its priorities. By the time de Gaulle resigned from the Presidency there were grave doubts that the successor government would be able to continue a program designed to provide France with a defense system autonomous of that of other states. The total French defense forces were granted an ever diminishing share of both the GNP and the budget of France, even though their budgets increased each year. Such increases, however, were more and more taken up by the rising cost of the strategic nuclear forces, which reached 35 percent of the defense budget for the period of the Third Program Law, and were also accounted for by additional costs of personnel, equipment, and the *gendarmérie*, which meant that the Gaullist military program could not be immediately realized. The question whether France could afford that military program, first raised in the early years of the Fifth Republic, was now mute. The urgent need of the government to meet rising social demands and domestic costs meant that de Gaulle's military program was no longer taken seriously at the highest cabinet level in France, even though official declarations still acknowledged the plan.

[46] This was an increase from 9.7 billion francs to 11.2 billion francs. ISS, *Strategic Survey*, 1971, p. 24.

Diversionary Politics

A third means by which a government may assure the achievement of its foreign-policy goals in the face of rising demands for other sorts of objectives is through diversionary tactics. By such a strategy, the government can turn the minds of its citizens away from unpopular programs that it is then free to pursue. But this sort of government strategy is likely to prove fruitful only for a limited period of time since public demands remain below the surface of politics and over a longer period are likely to become more vocal.

As was discussed in Chapter 3, diversionary tactics were an integral part of de Gaulle's concept of political leadership. These diversionary tactics consisted in the adroit use of elements of surprise in enunciating policies together with *grandes entreprises* designed to mobilize the French population behind its leadership. Surprise came through shifts in foreign policy that were timed for maximal effectiveness and that were unexpected either abroad or by the population of France. The timing of surprise in Gaullist foreign policy was based on elements of contingency in the political arena, and for de Gaulle it was the obligation of leadership to take advantage of them. The use of surprise and contingency as a political tactic was evident throughout de Gaulle's career both before and after 1958 and examples include: his return to power in 1958, his negotiating a settlement for the Algerian War in 1962, his veto of British entry into the Common Market in 1963, his reform of the international monetary system in 1965, his withdrawal of France from the military command structure of NATO in 1966, his recognition of Communist China, and his decision not to devalue the franc in 1968.

The targeting of *grandes entreprises* for the French population was similarly part of this set of diversionary tactics designed to enhance and exemplify de Gaulle's own autonomy from domestic and foreign constraints. The development of a nuclear striking force, the national economic plans, designs

185

for détente in Europe, the Concorde project, and the regional reforms of 1969 (the veto of which by the French electorate led de Gaulle to resign from office) were each described by de Gaulle as great undertakings or *ardentes obligations* of the French people.

The Gaullist style of leadership, described by Hoffmann as heroic leadership or as crisis leadership,[47] is part of the monarchic tradition of foreign policy in France. The policy of *grandeur*, reflective of the administrative tradition in France, was designed, so that foreign policy could be separated from the conduct of domestic affairs. In discussing this style, Hoffmann adopted certain notions developed in sociological studies of French society[48] and suggested that the French style of authority is characterized by alternations of routine and crisis authority. Routine authority is paralleled by the "stalemate society" and "stalemate government" that are produced by "the absence of face-to-face relations, the distance between strata, the conception of a higher authority both unsharing and bound by impersonal rules [that] condemn such authority to a mixture of abstraction and rigidity."[49] Routine authority is represented in foreign affairs by the "introversive" tradition, which had been criticized by de

[47] Stanley Hoffmann, "Heroic Leadership: The Case of Modern France," in *Political Leadership in Industrialized Societies*, ed. Lewis J. Edinger (New York: John Wiley & Sons, 1967), pp. 108–54. This essay represents an elaboration of thoughts on styles of French authority previously outlined in "Paradoxes of the French Political Community," in Stanley Hoffmann et al., *In Search of France* (Cambridge, Mass.: Harvard University Press, 1963), pp. 1–117.

[48] In particular, Hoffmann adopts themes and interpretations developed by Michel Crozier, *The Bureaucratic Phenomenon* (Chicago: University of Chicago Press, 1964); Jesse R. Pitts, "Continuity and Change in Bourgeois France," in *In Search of France*, pp. 235–403; and Laurence Wylie, *Village in the Vauclause* (Cambridge, Mass.: Harvard University Press, 1957). For a critique of this interpretation based on empirical data, see Fred I. Greenstein and Sidney G. Tarrow, "The Study of French Political Socialization: Toward the Revocation of Paradox," *World Politics*, xxii (1969): 95–138.

[49] Hoffmann, "Heroic Leadership," p. 116.

Gaulle and the other defenders of the monarchical tradition. Crisis leadership is represented by the heroic style of leadership, which

> on the one hand . . . represents the collapse of the norm, both in a substantive sense, for it constitutes a global injection of change in a previously immobile system, and in a procedural sense, for it corresponds to a collapse of the "delicate balance of terror" which exists in routine relations. . . .
>
> On the other hand, crisis authority performs a *function for* the system rather than a *change of* system. . . . The function it performs is double: crisis leadership is both the agent of social change *in* the system, and the preserver *of* the system against the mortal threat of either destruction by immobility or a change of system.[50]

Hoffmann sees a clear link between the heroic style of leadership in foreign and domestic affairs, and its monarchical habitat, represented by the wholesale impingement of personality on politics and by the exploitation of direct links between the leader and the populace, without any intermediary associational links. In foreign affairs, "heroic leadership means prowess; on the world stage, prowess and national self-assertion are twins. . . . Indeed, whether they originally tended to give precedence to foreign affairs or not, heroic leaders tend to find that a world stage of sovereign states provides the opportunities for prowess and national mobilization which the domestic scene often denies."[51]

One means by which the *grandes entreprises* of de Gaulle could be undertaken was the national referendum. Through this means, the leader could communicate directly with the population of France and thereby gain several ends at the same time. Bon has described it as follows: "The referendum ceremony not only has the function of periodically affirming the legitimacy of the head of state. It also enhances his freedom of action by putting other political forces out of the po-

[50] Ibid., pp. 116–17.   [51] Ibid., p. 139.

litical game. It isolates a privileged actor: his freedom of action is thus much greater than it would otherwise be."[52] The several referenda under the Fifth Republic thus were integrally part of the diversionary tactics of the Gaullist leadership. They served to both mobilize the public and to give the leader autonomy to pursue his goals unencumbered by divisional party politics. But they also placed a risk of failure on the government through a potential defeat.

De Gaulle held five referenda during his eleven years in office after 1958. One (September 29, 1958) was the Constitution of the Fifth Republic; two concerned the termination of the Algerian War (January 8, 1961 and April 8, 1962); the fourth pertained to the constitutional change that provided for the direct election of the President (October 28, 1962); and the last, coming after the events of May and the elections of June 1968, focused on the concept of political participation and incorporated regional reforms with a reform of the Senate (April 27, 1969). He received a mandate in each of the first four referenda, obtaining no less than 61.7 percent of the votes cast in any of them.[53] In the last referendum, however, de Gaulle's reforms were defeated and, since de Gaulle tied his own mandate to the fate of his reforms, the President resigned from office.

As in all electoral defeats, a variety of factors must be brought out to explain the majority vote against de Gaulle's regional reform proposal. The turn of public opinion against de Gaulle's proposed reforms occurred dramatically when on April 10 de Gaulle announced that he would resign if the referendum of April 27 was disapproved. The announcement had the effect of changing the stakes involved in

[52] Frédéric Bon, "Le referendum du 27 avril 1969: suicide politique ou necessité stratégique?" *Revue française de science politique*, xx (1970): 219.

[53] The percentage of votes cast receiving yes votes in the five referenda are: 1958, 79.2 percent; 1961, 75.3 percent; April 1962, 90.7 percent; October 1962, 61.7 percent; and 1969, 46.7 percent.

the referendum. In the following ten days, support for the referendum as measured in polls of opinion dropped from 55 percent to 47 percent of those intending to vote.[54] In fact, the French public had unenthusiastically supported the reform after it was announced. While a majority favored the slogan participation, which de Gaulle had wrested from the Left, and leaned toward the reform of regional administrative institutions, it was also negatively inclined toward a reform of the Senate. But when de Gaulle linked his own political fate to that of the referendum, he precipitated negative votes among several classes of voters, especially among small businessmen, professionals, white-collar workers, and civil servants and people between the ages of thirty-five and forty-nine.[55] These groups were no longer swayed by de Gaulle's referendum tactic of posing the alternative between himself and the emergence of social chaos. In fact, they now saw his policy as a *source* of disorder to be removed from the French political system. The members of the Center-Right in French politics also, apparently, foresaw the possibility of Gaullism without de Gaulle, that is, of social order, economic growth, and prosperity without the elements of *grandeur* associated with some of the expenditures on foreign aid and defense. Their discontent reflected a general dissatisfaction among the French electorate with the programs of de Gaulle's government, especially in domestic affairs. This malaise appeared not only in the events of May but also in opinion polls directly probing for it. For example, the marked hope for change on social questions is clearly reflected in the poll of May 13–14, 1969 the results of which appear in Table 9. The support for Gaullist foreign policy together with the discontent expressed with regard to domestic policies was an important indication of the major consequences of de Gaulle's priority on external af-

[54] Alain Lancelot and Pierre Weill, "L'Evolution politique des électeurs français de février à juin 1969," *Revue française de science politique*, xx (1970): 262.

[55] Ibid., pp. 258–60.

189

fairs. It also illustrated the degree to which de Gaulle's diversionary tactics became somewhat tiresome so long as domestic needs remained unsatisfied.

In summary, diversionary tactics, an integral part of the style of politics during the years when de Gaulle was President of the French Republic, had limited effectiveness. They could be used in 1961 and 1962 to mobilize the population to support the end of the Algerian War and could dazzle a society with the drama inherent in de Gaulle's international spectacle. But they could not indefinitely mobilize a population interested more in levels of income and the immediate material amenities of life than in the international glory of the French state. The politics of primacy worked in the early years of the Fifth Republic because of the contrast it presented with the instabilities and misfortunes of the Fourth Republic. Once order had been restored to social life in France, however, and once respect was again accorded

TABLE 9

Poll of May 13–14, 1969

Question: On each of the following points, do you believe that the policy of the Fifth Republic ought to be modified or that it ought to be continued as it is?

Believe that the policy of the Fifth Republic ought to be:	Social policy		Foreign-policy position toward		Freedoms		
	Wage policy	Social security	Communist countries	USA	Freedom of information on television	Powers of the administration	Role of parliament
Changed greatly	54 %	47 %	9 %	12 %	46 %	36 %	28 %
Changed somewhat	23	20	12	21	20	23	35
Continue as is	10	17	50	36	18	13	13
No opinion	13	16	29	31	16	28	24

Source: Alain Lancelot and Pierre Weill, "L'Evolution politique des électeurs français de février à juin 1969," *Revue française de science politique*, xx (1970): 262.

the French state, other issues assumed an increased importance. Diversionary tactics did not work in 1969 as they had previously. Apparently, the French public had grown tired of the dichotomy perpetuated by de Gaulle between himself and social chaos, wanted reforms that would lead to a quiet yet affluent life, and was not ready for yet another *grande entreprise.*

Manipulating Dissent

When governments are confronted by dissenting groups, they are likely to take steps to manipulate their opinions by changing them or by isolating them or, if necessary, by silencing them. Governmental efforts to manipulate dissenting opinions are likely to occur most frequently in democracies where the societies involved are highly fragmented and intensely divided on major issues. Such was the case of the Fifth Republic, especially in its first three to five years. As could be expected, governmental attempts to manipulate dissenting opinions, including those on foreign-policy issues, were rather extensive.

There were several categories of people who objected to the government's foreign policy even though the basic goals of the government's foreign policy were relatively popular. Although dissenters frequently fell into more than one of the categories listed below, the following bases for dissent can be isolated for analysis.

First, there were those for whom the institutions of the Fifth Republic were illegitimate. The Constitution of the Fifth Republic was approved by 66.4 percent of the registered voters (79.2 percent of the votes cast), yet a good many politicians who had played central roles in cabinets in the Fourth Republic did not at first accept the new regime.[56] They were

[56] Yet in the period between 1963 and 1965, a group of political scientists at Yale University surveyed the opinions of elite groups in France and Germany and found that only 53 percent in France were satisfied or moderately satisfied with their present governmental system versus 93 percent in Germany. See Karl Deutsch, *Arms Control and the Atlantic Alliance: Europe Faces Coming Policy Decisions* (New York: John Wiley & Sons, 1967), p. 101.

eager, therefore, to take issue with the policies of the new government in order to challenge its legitimacy either in Parliament or in political writings. They did this principally through parliamentary debate and motions of censure of the government or votes of confidence.[57] Of the fourteen votes of confidence or censure in the first National Assembly of the Fifth Republic, eight were on foreign-policy issues (Algeria and the deterrent force). The signatories to these antigovernmental motions generally came from members of the ruling parties of the Fourth Republic—Socialists, Radicals, and the Mouvement Républicain Populaire (MRP). These men were eager to discredit the presidential regime in France and to return to a regime of parties. These groups marshaled virtually all of the arguments against the government's defense policies during the debates over the First Program Law for military equipment in 1960. As a result of their opposition, Prime Minister Debré posed the question of the Program Law as a matter of confidence three times (in October, November, and December 1960). Each time the opponents to the regime also made the issue one of censure of the government. More than one third of the representatives in the Assembly voted for the censure motion on each occasion, but not once was the required absolute majority obtained.

When the Second Program Law was debated in December 1964, the issue of the legitimacy of the regime was less significant. The Algerian War had been settled and those members of the political Right and Left who had opposed the government for its handling of the war were not prone to take issue with it on every occasion. In addition, de Gaulle's majority in the Assembly had increased. The government therefore did not have to make the passage of legislation a matter of confidence and dissidents within the Assembly were unwilling to risk a motion of censure.[58]

[57] Williams, *The French Parliament*, p. 54.

[58] For descriptions of these two debates in the Assembly see Mendl, *Deterrence and Persuasion*, pp. 171 ff.; and, Roy C. Macridis, "The French Force de Frappe," in *Modern European Governments; Cases*

Second there were those who opposed the government's policy of defense autonomy consisting of Europeanists both in the Assembly and in the more general elite. Surveys of the French elite throughout the 1960s found that among them a European option was preferred to either an Atlantic option or a policy of independence and autonomy.[59] Deutsch and others analyzed the scale of preferences of the French elite groups in the mid-1960s ranging from the most to the least desired choice:

1. an independent European force (allied with the United States)
2. a Franco-British nuclear force (allied with the United States)
3. a multilateral force (MLF) within NATO if that body is reformed; otherwise,
4. an independent national nuclear force (allied with the United States) or
5. a national nuclear force totally independent of the United States.[60]

The Europeanists feared that an independent strategic force might be possible on the European level but was beyond the financial means of France alone and that the pursuit of an independent strategy would create severe imbalances in the general research and development efforts of France. Moreover, for ideological reasons, they preferred efforts to solidify European unity than those which would tend to divide the European states. These Europeanists were found by and large among those who were active politicians during the 1950s

---

in Comparative Policy Making, ed. Roy C. Macridis (Englewood Cliffs, N.J.: Prentice-Hall, 1968), pp. 68–91.

[59] In addition to Deutsch, *Arms Control and the Atlantic Alliance*, and Karl Deutsch et al., *France, Germany and the Western Alliance* (New York: Charles Scribner's, 1967), see Daniel Lerner and Morton Gorden, *Euratlantica: Changing Perspective of the European Elites* (Cambridge, Mass.: MIT Press, 1969), pp. 224–55.

[60] Deutsch, *France, Germany and the Western Alliance*, p. 112

and who therefore would have also preferred the French political institutions of the Fourth Republic to those of the Fifth.

Third, there were those who opposed the national striking force and criticized it on strategic grounds. Strategic arguments against the striking force centered around the disparity in size between France and the superpowers and the consequent higher level of vulnerability of France, the social and political system of which could effectively be destroyed by a single bomb exploded over Paris. The opposition also was doubtful of the capacity of the proposed French deterrent. Aron summarized that argument as follows:

> A nation regarded as small, such as France, could deter the Soviet Union from direct aggression if it had a minimal retaliatory capability. . . . But neither the first- nor the second-generation French deterrent will reach this level of efficacy. . . . No ally of the United States will be able to meet the conditions of potential balance between big and small powers by an independent effort in the next twenty years.[61]

Fourth, there were those, including many from the scientific and technological elite, who opposed the government's defense policies for economic reasons and who sought other uses of national resources. While supporters of the military programs argued that investment in the nuclear program and in armaments were essential as preparation for the general level of research and development in France, opponents felt that an imbalance would be created with a concentration on military uses of atomic energy. Still others felt that investment ought to have been concentrated in social areas, such as housing, rather than in the service of foreign policy.

Each of these arguments was marshaled by groups for different purposes. Interservice rivalry, for example, pitted some military people against others when it became apparent

[61] Aron, *The Great Debate*, p. 136.

that the nuclear striking force would consume the bulk of the military budget. Antigovernmental groups would accept any argument that would serve their ends. Those who supported efforts to create a nuclear force for European reasons rather than for the goal of autonomy were critical of the purposes to which the force would be directed and therefore also critical of the general foreign policy of the government. But, in spite of the opposition to the nuclear program as formulated by the government on the part of important groups in the French political and economic elite, public opinion was never really mobilized over the issue. While no clear majority of the French public ever supported the government's nuclear program, a substantial percentage did and this percentage in France during the 1960s was much higher than the percentage supporting a nuclear policy in Germany during the same period. Deutsch found, for example, that even among the French and German elite groups interviewed, 19 percent in France versus 0.0 percent in Germany felt that national nuclear arms were the best defense against aggression; 43 percent versus 15 percent thought that a national deterrent was required for national independence; 34 percent versus 4 percent regarded that it increased national prestige;[62] 46 percent versus 3 percent believed it to be worth the cost; 34 percent versus 31 percent expressed the opinion that such a deterrent would be credible to the nation's enemies.[63]

Since the public at large was split over the issue of a national nuclear force the government was not required to marshal its resources to silence dissent. It had the tacit support, moreover, of a large sector of the Parti communiste française (PCF). The party was against the development of the nuclear striking force but supported de Gaulle by and large on other aspects of his foreign policy. De Gaulle's efforts at national independence, after all, did contain many of the same foreign-policy goals that PCF advocated including the resistance to

[62] Yet 63 percent in France and 94 percent in Germany felt it would have no effect or a negative effect on national prestige.
[63] Deutsch, *Arms Control and the Atlantic Alliance*, pp. 128–130.

the United States in NATO, resistance to European integration, a détente with the Soviet Union aligned against a potentially resurgent Germany. De Gaulle's knowledge of this potential support from his domestic enemies on the Left was,
in fact, one central means by which he manipulated dissent
over his policies. With the support of the Left on foreign-
policy issues, he handcuffed his opposition. The PCF was
reluctant to align itself with other groups against the government for fear that it might lead to the replacement of
the Gaullist government by another, the foreign-policy goals
of which might be unacceptable.

The government also pursued a more active policy of
manipulating and silencing dissent ranging from the jailing
of thousands of actively and potentially violent dissidents who
posed an internal security threat during the Algerian War to
the influencing of public opinion through the control of the
public media. In the period after the settlement of the Algerian War, the government relied principally on the control
of public information as a means of manipulating dissent.[64]

Debré, one of the principal architects of the Fifth Republic, defined the official attitude of the regime with regard to
the use of public media (radio and television).

> The state has the obligation to intervene in order to defend
> at the same time both the individual and the nation. On the
> other hand, the basic facts of modern life give the public
> authority an obligation to explain to its citizens the reasons
> for its policies. The government in a democracy is the ex-
> pression of the majority which has delegated its power to
> assure the management of its business. In the end, some
> control is necessary.[65]

There had also been frequent governmental censorship of the
public media during the Fourth Republic, imposed essentially

[64] After the events of May, however, both de Gaulle's government
and the successor Pompidou government relied heavily on the use of
policy and brute force to silence dissent, especially among intellectuals.
[65] Michel Debré, *Au Service de la Nation* (Paris: Stock, 1963), p. 42.

during the wars in Indochina and Algeria. De Gaulle generalized the use of public broadcasting with a rather coherent policy of public manipulation that began when he assumed office
in 1958. In spite of promises to leave public broadcasting
autonomous, "the government exercised its powers of control," as Ordway has shown, "not only by exposing itself constantly before the cameras, but by tabooing certain sub-
jects . . . , firing newscasters and directors in the O.R.T.F.
[Office of French Radio and Television] and replacing them
with Gaullist sympathizers, and by instructing the upper
echelon of the O.R.T.F. to take controversial programs off
the air."[66]

The manipulation of opinion through the control of public
broadcasting facilities, although it was seen by the government as a legitimate activity, which it could pursue in order
to marshal support and control dissent, had the opposite effect. The government's control of the ORTF aroused opposition in the French Parliament, in private broadcasting, and
among the personnel working in the publicly owned facilities.
The opposition reached a peak just before May 1968 and
made this another issue in the antigovernmental riots that
spring. The month prior to those events (April 24) a motion
of censure was brought against the government that was concerned specifically with the political use of the media. That
motion received 236 votes of the 244 required for adoption.
The events of May, however, precipitated a major crisis in the
government's information policy. Ehrmann describes that
crisis as follows:

When television and radio crews wished to report first on
the student manifestations, then on the fighting in the
streets, on police methods, and on factories on strike, when
they insisted on presenting a debate about General de
Gaulle's televised speech, the government constantly inter-

[66] Eric Ordway, "The Political Aspects of Government Control of
Broadcasting As Practiced in Britain and France" (Princeton University, Unpublished Senior Thesis, 1971), p. 47.

ceded with the management of the O.R.T.F. and sought sanctions against individual employees. A general strike by many employees was the answer, paralyzing the operations of the O.R.T.F. during the height of the crisis. The strikers were not satisfied when the government offered improved pay and working conditions; they demanded a complete overhaul of the structure of the O.R.T.F. which in their eyes had remained a decisive instrument for the manipulation of public opinion. In typical language the Office became another "Bastille," which had to be stormed if freedom of expression was to prevail.[67]

As in the other tactics by which the government tried to assure the attainment of its goals, there was the gradual accretion of discontent on the part of the general public and special interest groups that finally exploded in May. The government's attempts to limit the spread of protest in May 1968 by minimally reporting the student violence in the Latin Quarter and by avoiding exposure of the tactics used by the police inspired the journalists at ORTF to organize their own protest against the government's misuse of information.[68] They protested the fact that independence guaranteed to the public media in the reorganization of the ORTF in 1964 was never obtained. The manipulation of opinion and the silencing of dissent like so many of the other tactics used by the government may have given the government a short-term freedom to pursue its foreign policy and other political objectives. But in the long run, the tactic backfired against the government, and, just as it increased its budgetary expenditures on items of public welfare, social services, and education after 1968, so too it made promises to assure the neutrality and freedom of the press in order to dispel discontent.

[67] Ehrmann, *Politics in France*, p. 137.
[68] See *L'Année politique* 1968 (Paris: Presses Universitaires de France, 1969), pp. 370–71.

International Burden Sharing

A final way in which governments may assure the achievement of their goals in the face of increased demands placed upon them is through cooperative ventures with other governments. The sharing of costs of armaments, for radar systems, or for the construction of missiles with other foreign governments pursuing similar goals was, of course, the option stressed by the Europeanists in France. Fearful that France could not afford to create an independent defense program that would provide a credible deterrent, they argued that the government ought to project its efforts to a wider political community. By and large this group was sympathetic with the efforts of de Gaulle's government to create a political and economic force independent of the United States and the Soviet Union. But they argued that this would be feasible only through the creation of a third force in Europe.

The government of de Gaulle did take several steps in this direction. The Fouchet Plan had been oriented toward the organization of the states of Europe in such a way that French foreign-policy goals could be implemented with the support of France's European neighbors but without the need to create an integrated political community. The Concorde supersonic airline project between France and Britain, the European Launcher Development Organization (ELDO) and the European Space Research Organization (ESRO) were broad efforts in which the French participated in order to reduce the costs of some items in their defense program. Of course, the three European Communities were organizations where French membership resulted in significant economic gains to France. In addition, French membership in NATO was a de facto form of burden sharing for over two decades. The very rationale for the alliance had been the provision of a collective defense mechanism that France or any other member felt it could not provide by itself.

International burden sharing, however, was completely

antithetical to the rationale of Gaullist foreign policy. The thrust of the defense programs outlined in the first two Program Laws for military equipment was the provision of the means for French withdrawal from the Western alliance and for the progressive unfolding of a neutralist defense posture based upon a credible deterrent against any enemy from any direction. Therefore efforts designed to bring about highly institutionalized or integrated efforts of defense burden sharing through any international forum were to be avoided at almost any cost if these efforts would reduce actual or potential defense autonomy to any degree.[69]

As was shown in Chapter 2, the efforts at French autonomy were buttressed by the changing configuration of international forces in the 1960s. The nuclear stalemate between the United States and the Soviet Union and efforts at détente in Europe had reduced significantly the danger of warfare in Europe. Since the risk of war was considerably reduced from that of the previous decade, the credibility of the French deterrent force was concomitantly enhanced. With the probability reduced that this deterrent force would ever have to be fully operationalized, its psychological value was simultaneously increased for it would be thought that its development in some measure helped to bring about the new international circumstances.

Events in 1968—both in France and in Europe—did much to dispel some of the illusion upon which the autonomous program was based. On the one hand, to be credible, the French program had to show some marked progress in developing an independent force. Domestic events that resulted in a transformation of French priorities as measured by governmental expenditures undercut confidence in that

[69] For an analysis of the progressive withdrawal by France from NATO and the potential withdrawal from the Alliance itself during the Gaullist years, see Edward A. Kolodziej, "France and NATO; Reflections on the Gaullist Era," in NATO in the Seventies, ed. Edwin H. Fedder, Monograph No. 1 (St. Louis, Missouri: Center for International Studies, February 1970), pp. 65–88.

force. On the other hand, international events, including the Soviet invasion of Czechoslovakia following the enunciation of the Brezhnev doctrine, showed that efforts at détente would for the short-term be relatively ineffective. Both sets of events increased for the French government the significance of efforts at international burden sharing. This was reflected both in NATO and in the relations between France and its European allies. In NATO, there was a resumption of French participation in military and naval exercises, albeit on a limited scale, as well as new bilateral arrangements with the United States. The European option was at the same time kept open under the belief that some day the American commitment to Europe, as symbolized by the deployment of U.S. troops, would be reduced. In either case the French actions were actually insignificant, but their potential for future international burden sharing was greater than their actual level.[70] And, they did point up the need for the French to consider the international option so long as fundamental defense goals were maintained and so long as the government acutely felt a domestic squeeze on its defense expenditures.

CONCLUSIONS

However anachronistic or idiosyncratic French defense policy might have been in the 1960s, it was constrained by the same limitations and fostered by the same mechanisms that could be found in other highly industrialized states. In fact, the extreme position of the French policy that attempted to provide a complete and autonomous defense establishment serves to reinforce rather than to falsify our generalizations concerning the dilemma between rising costs and demands, on the one hand, and the achievement of an increased panoply of governmental goals, on the other.

[70] For an analysis of the incentives and limits upon Franco-British joint defense efforts, see Michael J. Brenner, "Strategic Interdependence and the Politics of Inertia: Paradoxes of European Defense Cooperation," World Politics, XXIII (1971): 635–64.

The French case is ever the more significant insofar as it exemplifies the potential and limitations upon various governmental stratagems for resolving this basic dilemma. De Gaulle felt that the myth of *grandeur* would serve to make the French ignore domestic and private aspirations in favor of foreign-policy goals. The institutionalized mechanisms through the budgetary process and the insulation of the government from domestic demands that were designed to enhance the ability of the government to maintain the priority of defense over other social goals could not, however, in the end, forestall the crescendo of new social demands in France. A government more interested in its international role than in the achievement of domestic goals could not redirect the introversive tendencies of a modernized society. The attempt to achieve reflected glory on the international level sacrificed the legitimacy of the government's program domestically. The dilemma between the image of a state prepared to change the international system through autonomous actions and that of a government providing for the common welfare of its citizens could not be resolved over the long run.

Modernized societies are apparently unique in the degree to which their governments have assumed, as a response to increased politicization of their citizens, a wide spectrum of social goals. These goals have largely been domestic. They pertain to the increased well-being—spiritually, materially, and intellectually—of their citizens; they include the need to provide regulations controlling economic fluctuations and maintaining public order; and they can be achieved only at the sacrifice of other governmental goals, since the resources available to the state are inevitably limited. In a period when the costs of defense have increased disproportionately to other costs and when the outbreak of warfare becomes less probable, the curtailment of defense expenditures appears as a logical source of revenue that can be diverted to other governmental imperatives. In such circumstances the classical guns or butter issue is inevitably posed in politics. High cost expenditures on guns are likely to seem frivolous to some sectors in such societies. They are likely to appear baneful when the government marshals force to assure their achievement. As a result of a dilemma of resource allocation, governments are likely in the long run at least to submit to rising domestic demands. In such conditions, the pursuit of glory is likely to be short lived. When glory is tied to the autonomous pursuit of security, or indeed, the autonomous pursuit of other domestic or foreign goals, it is likely to prove counterproductive, if not quixotic.

FIVE

FOREIGN ECONOMIC POLICY
AND THE REFORM OF THE
INTERNATIONAL MONETARY SYSTEM

THE basic characteristics of French policy toward the other industrialized countries of the West from 1962 to 1969 can be illustrated by an examination of French proposals for a reform of the international monetary system. France's international monetary policy touched upon the various arenas in which France confronted the other highly modernized states. It was a basic instrument of the more general policy of independence and also crystallized the dilemma besetting such a policy because of the high degree of interdependence that characterizes the Western international economic system. In short, French foreign monetary policy can be viewed as a microcosm of French foreign policy toward the other industrialized states.

French foreign economic policy has been singled out for discussion for theoretical reasons. As suggested in Chapter 1, the politics of power and position have been superseded by the politics of wealth and welfare in highly modernized societies. Moreover, stalemate at the high-policy level has resulted in a shift of strategic interactions to low-policy areas. Both movements, characteristic of modernized societies, converged in French plans for a reform of the international monetary system and make an analysis of such plans all the more exemplary of the goals and dilemmas of recent French foreign policy.

Changes in the international monetary system in the 1960s are first briefly outlined. This section provides a background for the French proposals for reform. These proposals are described in a chronological account of events in the 1960s that is divided into three parts. These parts correspond to the three phases of foreign policy initiatives in the Gaullist years, which were outlined in Chapter 2.

The first phase (1958–1962) is viewed as preparation for a policy of independence. In the second phase (1962–1966) efforts at independence in monetary affairs are treated as part of a broadly based strategy for French autonomy. This strategy is shown to have its roots in the Gaullist interpretation of changes in the relationships among the Western societies. Finally, in the third phase (1966–1968), the increasing divergence between Gaullist ideals and actual practices is examined and is offered as an explanation for the ineffectiveness of French reform plans.

The Changing Dimensions of the International Monetary System

French foreign economic policy was directed in the 1960s toward the international monetary system as it evolved after the Bretton Woods Agreement of 1944. French policy efforts took the form of a call not just for a reform, but for a transformation of that system. The principal interlocutors with France in negotiations were representatives of Britain and the United States, although the French frequently found themselves at odds with their Common Market partners as well.

Throughout the debate the French found themselves in a position different from that of the United States, from the diagnosis of the ills plaguing the international monetary system to the remedies suggested for reform. This policy therefore took on the overtones of general French foreign policy, including the fight for independence and autonomy against the *soi-disant* American hegemony. In order to understand the basis of French perceptions in these matters as well as the general background of the politics of reform of the international monetary system, it is useful to outline some of the changes the system underwent in the 1960s.

The international monetary system that evolved after Bretton Woods was based upon the IMF, although ancillary arrangements and agreements modified it in the late 1950s and throughout the 1960s.[1] The fund was designed to avoid the anarchy of the international monetary system of the pre-World War II era. In that monetary system, exchange rates fluctuated within wide margins. In addition, national depreciations had become competitive, thus hindering the growth of high levels of trade. The postwar IMF system was designed to avoid major financial and monetary depreciations, to foster exchange stability, and to provide monetary reserves that would enable member states to overcome short-term balance-of-payments problems. Its aim, then, was not only to prevent economic anarchy but also to impede economic autarchy and nationalism. The principal basis of a new stability to be provided by the IMF was summarized recently by its French director, P.-P. Schweitzer, as follows: "The dream of Bretton Woods—or as many cynics were to say for more than a decade after the conference, the illusion of Bretton Woods—was the unrestricted convertibility for current transactions of at least the major currencies."[2]

With virtually fixed exchange rates, imbalances were generally financed by means short of devaluation or revaluation, principally by measures within the domestic economies. External measures involving changes in rates of exchange were to be permitted only in extreme cases. Any countries with a constant deficit would be allowed to devalue, while those with a constant surplus were pressured to revalue. It was felt that short-term deficits could be financed by borrowings from the IMF.

The IMF was designed to foster increases in trade and surpluses and thus had "the dual task of policing the rules and

[1] For a general survey of the historical development of the international monetary system, see Robert Triffin, *Our International Monetary System: Yesterday, Today and Tomorrow* (New York: Random House, 1966), pp. 3–45. A more detailed account is found in Richard N. Cooper, *The Economics of Interdependence* (New York: McGraw-Hill, 1968), pp. 24–55.

[2] Quoted in *The New York Times*, July 20, 1969, Section 3, p. 1.

of lending to member countries to cover temporary balance-of-payments deficits."[3] It was not seen as an agent for reconstruction after World War II and for lending as a means of covering deficits that arose from large flows of capital. On both counts, however, situations that were not foreseen in 1944 changed the original system. These changes in the international monetary system provided the framework of the debate between the Anglo-American countries and the French. The first such change involved European recovery and the dollar shortage that resulted in the generalization of the dollar exchange standard and the accumulation of dollars as monetary reserves with accompanying constant deficit for the United States. The second change pertained to the substantial increase in the mobility of capital from one country to another in search of investments and high short-term interest rates.

The first change, then, was the role that the dollar came to play in the postwar payments system. At the time of the establishment of the IMF, there had been a great imbalance between the monetary situation of the United States and that of the major countries of Western Europe. The United States at that time possessed the majority of the world's gold supply. Thus, in 1945, when the official holdings of all countries except those of the Communist bloc amounted to $33.3 billion worth of gold, the United States had $20.1 billion of gold in its reserves. In addition, the major European countries were in great need of reserves for purchases abroad for postwar reconstruction. In short, the United States had a dominant position in the international monetary system, and the major problem of the European countries in that system was one of liquidity to finance trade.

The IMF, therefore, could not be implemented until the completion of a transitional period that was marked by the "return to normalcy" and was defined by free exchange operations among the industrialized states. Such a situation could not be reached until Europe had recovered. Thus, the

[3] Cooper, *Economics of Interdependence*, p. 28.

IMF system was amended almost immediately after its inception by supplementary arrangements, which included the American loan to Britain in 1946, the Marshall Plan in 1947, and the subsequent formation of the OEEC. In addition, the European Payments Union (EPU) was formed in order to make payments within Europe multilateral while isolating the European monetary system from that of the rest of the world.

Not only were the Europeans dependent upon the United States in overcoming the dollar gap, but the United States found itself dependent upon Europe for its own security; therefore, U.S. policy-makers saw the need for securing European economic reconstruction. Thus, the initial stages of implementation of the postwar monetary system could be characterized as highly political. It was not only the economics of the situation but also the politics that served to modify the intended structures of the international monetary system.

The IMF was unable to enjoy its intended role until the transitional period of European recovery was completed. This took place in 1958 with the liquidation of the EPU and the creation of the European Monetary Agreement as well as with the initial implementation of the Common Market. By then all countries were committed to hold reserves not only in gold but also in dollars and sterling, as part of the gold exchange standard. The United States, for its part, was committed to maintain the price of gold at $35 per ounce. The whole system therefore became dependent upon confidence in the dollar; upon the ability of the United States to fulfill the liquidity needs of the Western world to finance growing levels of international trade by allowing dollars to be accumulated by central banks abroad; and upon the commitment to exchange dollars for gold.

The second set of changes in the international economic system refers specifically to the substantial increase in the mobility of capital during the 1960s. This increase in capital mobility along with the growth of dollar accumulations abroad served both to enhance and to restrict French maneuverability in negotiations for reform. This growth was, it will be recalled, part of a more basic set of structural changes in the economic system characterizing the industrial states that Cooper summarized under three categories:[4] First, the sensitivity of foreign trade to such domestic economic conditions as incomes, costs, and prices increased. Second, along with growing interdependence, there has been a tremendous increase in the mobility of production factors, especially of technology, business skills and long-term investment capital. Third, as a result of these changes, portfolio capital, made up of liquid funds, which seek short-term high interest yields, has increased in mobility.

Capital mobility was characterized by the six currency crises that occurred in the monetary system between November 1967, when the pound was devalued, and August 1969, when the franc was devalued.[5] The problem of liquid capital, very difficult to control through the mechanisms of a single market, is exemplified in the Eurodollar market. This market of free-floating capital, made up principally of the liquid assets of international banks and multinational corporations, expanded enormously in the late 1960s. From 1966, when it amounted to $13 billion, it expanded to $20 billion by the end of 1968.[6]

The liquidity needed to finance increases in international trade was one of the chief substantive issues of reform plans in the 1960s, and it was supplied principally by both increases

[4] Ibid., pp. 59–147.

[5] The other four crises were the disbanding of the gold pool of central bankers in March 1968; the run on the franc in May and June 1968; the imbroglio between the franc and mark in November 1968; and the flight of currency to Germany in May 1969.

[6] See Peter Dreyer, "Eurodollars," *European Community*, No. 120 (February 1969), pp. 3–5. The more technical aspects of the debate with regard to the origins and control of Eurodollars and Eurobonds are traced in Alexander K. Swoboda, *The Euro-Dollar Market: An Interpretation*, Essays in International Finance, No. 64 (Princeton, N.J.: International Finance Section, 1969); and in Fred H. Klopstock, *The Euro-Dollar Market: Some Unresolved Issues*, Essays in International Finance, No. 65 (Princeton, N.J.: International Finance Section, 1969).

in the gold reserves of the Western countries and dollar accumulations. Both sources of liquidity began to dwindle in the 1960s.

Gold, the basis of international liquidity, grew to have two important sources. In the first place, it could be obtained from new gold production, largely from South Africa. In the second place, it was provided by gold sales from the Soviet Union. The provision and use of gold from these two sources between 1960 and 1967 is summarized in Table 10.

In the postwar period, Western gold reserves first increased, then leveled off, and finally decreased as a result of speculation of devaluation of the dollar and because of increases in its industrial uses. Between 1948 and 1954, the gold component of reserves of Western countries increased by an average of $325 million per year. This figure doubled to an annual average of $560 million between 1954 and

TABLE 10

Origin and Use of Gold in the Western World, 1960–1967
(millions of dollars)

	1960	1961	1962	1963	1964	1965	1966	1967
Gold production	1,175	1,215	1,295	1,350	1,400	1,440	1,440	1,410
Soviet sales	200	300	200	550	450	550	—	—
Total	1,375	1,515	1,495	1,900	1,850	1,990	1,440	1,410
Increases in official gold	345	600	330	840	750	215	−50	−1,600
Other uses	1,030	915	1,165	1,060	1,100	1,685	1,490	3,010

Sources: Miroslav Kriz, *Gold: Barbarous Relic or Useful Instrument?* Essays in International Finance, No. 60 (Princeton, N.J.: International Finance Section, 1967), pp. 33–35; Bank for International Settlements, *Thirty-Fifth Annual Report* (Basle, 1965), rpt. in *Problèmes économiques*, No. 992 (August 31, 1965), p. 8; and Bank for International Settlements, *Thirty-Eighth Annual Report* (Basle, 1968), rpt. in *Problèmes économiques*, No. 1078 (August 29, 1968), p. 9.

1959.[7] By 1959, gold production had increased by 55 percent over its level in 1953, but demand had increased by 125 percent.[8] Between 1960 and 1969, there was a further increase in the demand for gold for nonfiduciary purposes. That increase came in part from speculators who saw financial windfalls in an increased price of gold. Speculative demand for gold rose throughout the decade as it became more and more apparent that the monetary system of Bretton Woods would have to be modified, if not overhauled. During the last of the series of monetary crises in the late 1960s, that of 1967–1968, total official gold holdings decreased by $2.4 billion by government gold sales largely to speculators.[9] Finally, in March 1968 the commitment of the United States to buy gold on the market for $35 per ounce was abandoned and the two-tier system was begun.

The second major source of liquidity, the dollar, could be supplied only so long as the United States could support a balance-of-payments deficit and still honor the commitment to buy gold at $35 per ounce. After 1958 the previously moderate American deficits assumed major proportions for the first time. By then, what had been a dollar shortage in Europe suddenly became transformed into a dollar glut. The United States lost $1.1 billion of gold in 1959 and $1.7 billion in 1960. At the same time, the United States put pressure on the European countries to hold more dollars than they wished. Between 1957 and 1963, U. S. gold holdings fell from $22.8 billion to $15.5 billion while official dollar holdings abroad rose from $9.4 billion to $18.2 billion. Dollar holdings by private parties almost doubled from $5.7 billion to $10.6 billion.

[7] *Problèmes économiques*, No. 1078 (August 29, 1968), p. 9.

[8] Ibid., p. 12.

[9] At the end of 1966, official gold holdings for IMF countries amounted to $40.9 billion. They decreased to $38.6 billion by the end of the second quarter of 1968, and then increased for the remainder of the year. By the beginning of 1969, they were up to $38.9 billion. *International Financial Statistics*, xxii (1969): 13.

As a result of the loss of confidence in the dollar as a reserve instrument and of structural changes in the international monetary system, there were two policy developments in the 1960s. On the one hand, there was a series of negotiations leading to a reform of the international monetary system. On the other hand, there was a series of *ad hoc* changes in that system that resulted from patchwork operations made necessary by the accelerated occurrences of crises sweeping the system. These arrangements principally involved the cooperation of the central banks of the leading industrial countries. As a result of these *ad hoc* arrangements, in addition to gold, reserve currencies, and IMF drawing rights, new reserve forms were created in the form of swap arrangements between central banks.[10]

The series of crises of the 1960s in the international monetary system, discussion for reform of the system, and *ad hoc* arrangements created to make the system endure all crises seem to reflect the growing interdependence of the Western economies as well as the lack of suitable institutions for controlling these interdependencies. Nonetheless, the discussions for reform have not been based generally on the effects of growing interdependence, but on either the political or economic implications of change in the international monetary system.

The general structure of the international monetary system has led to crises because of the interdependence of the Western economies and the lack of instrumentalities suitable to control the transnational reverberations of capital flows. Instead of having some form of transnational decision-making structure to control what are essentially transnational forces,

[10] The parallel between the negotiations for reform of the international monetary system and the *ad hoc* arrangements that were made to bolster reserves are summarized in "Etapes de la négociation monétaire internationale (1961–1968)," reprinted from *Banque* (November, 1968), in *Problèmes économiques*, No. 1090 (November 28, 1968), pp. 10–16; and in Samuel Schweizer, "Problèmes des liquidités internationales," *Problèmes économiques*, No. 1049 (February 8, 1968), pp. 2–12.

decision-making has been made by *ad hoc* management in the form of intergovernmental cooperation. At the same time, the commitment to fixed exchange rates has prevented gradual adjustments that would occur either through a more flexible exchange rate system or from more general periodic devaluations and revaluations.

France, like the other member countries of the IMF, has been committed to the maintenance of fixed exchange rates by the Bretton Woods Agreement. In addition, however, there is a need to maintain fixed exchange rates (with changes only under emergency conditions) because of the Common Market. This is so not only because the Common Market is a special economic subsystem of the international economic system in terms of trade and other exchanges but also because of the requisites of economic policy within a customs union. As discussed in Chapter 2, the logic of systemic interdependence within the European Communities has been that the destabilizing effects of the lowering of barriers to interchanges of all sorts and the concomitant increase in production factor mobility required the establishment of uniform, general policies, or the reraising of barriers and discriminations. The one major policy success for the EEC in its first decade of operation was the creation of an agricultural policy with a complicated price system establishing uniform prices for agricultural products. This price system, based on a set of "units of accounts" (equal to the dollar), was primarily responsible for the maintenance of fixed exchange rates in the EEC.

Although the Rome Treaty foresaw the need for eventual financial integration (Articles 104 and 105), little was done along those lines in the 1960s, except for the establishment of a European Monetary Committee as a consultative body "to promote the coordination of the policies of Member States in monetary matters to the extent necessary to ensure the operation of the Common Market" (Article 105).[11] The

[11] The Committee according to Article 105 was supposed "to keep under review the monetary and financial situation of the Member States

European Monetary Committee was little more than a forum until confronted by the price inflation crisis of 1963–1964. It was then that a series of recommendations were made on price stability to each of the six member countries.[12] The real work of the Committee began with the decisions of April 1964, but was hampered by the French position on gold and key currencies. However, in the wake of the currency crisis of 1967 and 1968, the Monetary Committee again became active and talk of financial integration reappeared.[13]

The combined impetus of the agricultural policy, the currency crises and customs union in Europe led to an agreement by the EEC Council in May 1968 on a set of procedures to be followed on agricultural policies if any country had to devalue or revalue. Further pressure for the formation of a common monetary policy resulted from the franc crisis of November 1968. The Commission then submitted a memorandum to the Council (December 5, 1968) on the need for "an investigation of the possibilities of intensifying monetary cooperation."[14] The major need was to prepare instruments to shift short-term capital from surplus to deficit countries via a reserve pool. Very little occurred along these lines before

---

and of the Community and also the general payments system of Member States and to report regularly thereon to the Council and to the Commission; [and] the drafting of comments at the request of the Council or the Commission or on its own initiative for submission to these institutions."

The Committee issues an annual report.

[12] For a review of these decisions, see Etienne-Said Kirschen, Henry Simon Bloch, and William B. Bassett, *Financial Integration in Western Europe* (New York: Columbia University Press, 1969), pp. 23ff.

[13] See the speech by European Commissioner Hans von der Groeben, *European Monetary Policy: Toward the Gradual Establishment of a European Monetary System* (Brussels: European Communities Commission, 1968).

[14] European Communities Commission, "Information Memo P-6" (February 1969), p. 1. See also *Commission Memorandum to the Council on the Co-ordination of Economic Policies and Monetary Cooperation within the Community* (Brussels: European Communities Commission, 1969).

the devaluation of the franc in the summer of 1969. However, commitment to fixed exchange rates as a basis of the contemporary international system was a problem.

Other characteristics of the international monetary system in the 1960s included the American commitment to maintain the price of gold and the holding of gold and dollars as reserves. However, there was no hierarchical structure of political authority that could maintain stability since it was contingent upon the harmonization of policies directed by nominally sovereign states. Together, these characteristics were bound to be destabilizing.[15] As Cassell has asserted,

> the inescapable fact from which all reformers of the international monetary system must start is the inherent inconsistency in the trinity of rigidly fixed exchange rates, inelastic reserves and independent national policies. It may be possible to keep any two of these, but only by the complete sacrifice of the third. And since freely floating exchange rates or completely elastic reserves . . . or completely subordinated domestic policies are the three untouchables of international finance, any acceptable reform can only be the result of compromise.[16]

Given these changes in international monetary affairs, de Gaulle found an opportunity to increase French freedom of action by criticizing the system and by taking actions which smacked of his vision of the inevitable.

INDEPENDENCE AND FRENCH INTERNATIONAL MONETARY POLICY

Like the other aspects of French foreign policy during the Gaullist years, French policy with regard to the international monetary system falls into three phases.

[15] See Francis Bator, "The Political Economics of International Money," *Foreign Affairs*, XLVII (1968): 51–67.

[16] Francis Cassell, *Gold or Credit? The Economics and Politics of International Money* (London: Pall Mall Press, 1965), p. 178.

Devaluation and Balance of Payments: 1958–1962

The first phase from 1958 to 1962 begins with the devaluation of the franc and the redressing of the French balance-of-payments situation. It parallels other events in the international monetary system when the American deficits rose to major proportions for the first time and when talk arose among American academics of the need for a reform of the international monetary system.[17]

The French devaluation of 15 percent of December 28, 1958 was carried out under de Gaulle's first Minister of Finance Antoine Pinay. The basis of the reform measures was prepared by a panel of experts headed by Jacques Rueff,[18] an opponent of Keynesian economic theory, who was scorned by fellow economists both in France and abroad.

Rueff's immediate aim in the 1958 devaluation was threefold. First, he wanted to bring the treasury out of financial difficulties encountered by the Algerian War. Second, he wished to prepare France for the freeing of exchange rates, the reconvertibility of European currencies, and the opening of the Common Market. Third, devaluation was designed to reinforce the value of the franc by restraining domestic demand for imports, and making exports cheaper, thereby reversing the French balance-of-payments deficits.[19]

[17] Among the academic works of this period, the most noteworthy is Robert Triffin, *Gold and the Dollar Crisis* (New Haven: Yale University Press, 1960).

[18] The best of Rueff's articles on international monetary affairs, extending over a thirty-five year period, are brought together in Jacques Rueff, *Le Lancinant Problème des balances des paiements* (Paris: Payot, 1965).

[19] Thus, devaluation was accompanied by a new economic policy designed to curtail consumption and increase investment. Subsidies were withdrawn, pensions reduced, and investment was increased by 25 percent. See de Gaulle's broadcast on financial and economic policy of December 28, 1958, *Major Addresses, Statements and Press Conferences of General Charles de Gaulle, May 19, 1958–January 31, 1964* (New York: Ambassade de France, Service de Presse et d'Information, 1964), pp. 30–33.

Underlying the Pinay-Rueff devaluation, however, were long-term interests that Rueff had espoused and in which de Gaulle saw important political implications. Rueff argued against the popular view that perennial French deficits in the 1950s could be ascribed to domestic French causes. Rather, he saw that these deficits were caused by inflation and increased purchasing power induced by the importation of dollars. He felt that with the use of traditional domestic instruments and an end to the dollar exchange standard French deficits could be reversed. He argued that the instabilities of the international monetary system during the 1960s were a necessary result of the American deficit and the dollar exchange standard which prevented general equilibrium, that the system ought not to be reformed but destroyed, and that the gold standard of pre-1914 Europe should be reinstated.[20]

What de Gaulle saw in Rueff's theories was an economic analysis that seemed to work. France's deficits were reversed and her reserves began to climb, and that implied an international political gain. Rueff's belief in a return to the gold standard was one that, in political terms, was the best situation for a country in a position of weakness against stronger states. The United States, according to this analysis, was benefiting from the dollar exchange standard by being exempted from the rules of international exchange and at the same time was exporting inflation to Europe. By returning to the gold standard, the United States would be prevented from enjoying this exceptional position, and France and the other European countries would gain if they could maintain surpluses in their balance of payments.[21]

[20] See J. Rueff, *Le Lancinant Problème*, pp. 13–47. See also Sidney E. Rolfe, with the assistance of Robert G. Hawkins, *Gold and World Power* (New York: Harper and Row, 1965), pp. 162–83. Rolfe too quickly equates the views of Rueff and de Gaulle on international monetary policy. For an insightful exposé of the ideas of the men who were de Gaulle's major financial advisers by the financial reporter for *Le Monde*, see Paul Fabra, "The Money Men of France," trans. Helen Katel, *Interplay*, 1:6 (1968): 37–40.

[21] Rueff's analysis of the international monetary system was essen-

Rueff's thesis thus had several principal political implications for de Gaulle. First, a reform along the lines envisaged by Rueff would result in the reemergence of a mercantilist zero-sum world where one country's gain was another country's loss. For France, with prospects of future balance-of-payments surpluses and a strong currency, any French gain would then be a loss for the United States. Second, there were sparks of Gaullist rivalry with the Anglo-American countries, which were seen as principal impediments to the reconstitution of great power status for France. The economic editor of the London *Times* later described French motives for a reform of the international monetary system:

> The mainspring of French policy is hostility to—or at least a keen sense of rivalry with—the United States, and to a much lesser extent with Britain, which is seen as a stalking (or perhaps Trojan) horse for American interference in Europe. The roots of this rivalry presumably go back at least to World War II. No proud nation can easily feel very warm toward its liberators. The situation is not helped by the United States having taken over France's so painfully abandoned role in Indochina.[22]

Finally, France would have been put in a strong financial position with respect to French client states in Africa, and this also supported de Gaulle's general foreign-policy posture.

As a result of the Algerian War, the impetus to reform was more latent than manifest in the first stage of French international monetary policy. De Gaulle still thought that the con-

---

tially the same as that of Robert Triffin. The two differed, however, on the question of liquidity and on the economic instruments they thought could secure liquidity. Rueff has felt that a return to the gold standard should be accompanied by a change in the gold price. Triffin, on the other hand, felt that the liquidity problem as well as the need for controlling the international monetary system could be handled by the creation of an international central bank with the capacity to issue currency.

[22] Peter Jay, "Why France Balks," *Interplay*, 1:5 (1967): 39.

tinuance of the cold war necessitated an alliance with the United States. Changes in the international monetary system would have been amenable to de Gaulle's general policy because they would have increased France's leverage over the United States in a general worldwide strategy, thus regaining its previous greatness. At the same time, therefore, measures were undertaken for strengthening the franc and for establishing a nuclear force, which would provide some control over U.S. defense policy with regard to European security.

Independence and Initiatives for Reform: 1962–1966

Extending from 1962 to 1966, the second phase of French international monetary policy was more active and complements the second phase of Gaullist foreign policy. During this phase, de Gaulle took general foreign-policy initiatives that were designed to assert France's independence from the alliance with the West. Here the antiintegrationist corollary of the policy of independence in NATO and the EEC was similarly reflected in antiintegrationist attitudes toward the international monetary system.

This phase of foreign policy in the Gaullist years is marked by vigorous efforts toward independence that were substantively different from those of the first phase in which independence was perceived by de Gaulle to involve a return to great power status. The demise of the French Community, which represented France's global interests, and the failure to achieve *contrôle* over NATO strategy by the creation of a tripartite directorate were followed by new initiatives that were based on a changed view of the structure of international society. De Gaulle began to feel that the cold war was ending with both the stability of the East-West balance of terror and the Sino-Soviet split. These changes, he felt, freed French diplomacy from the obligations of the alliance. With a nuclear force of its own, France too could achieve great power status in a reordered European setting under French leadership.

Similarly, in the international monetary field, de Gaulle perceived that changes were occurring in the postwar monetary situation. By guiding the direction of change, France, de Gaulle felt, could achieve both greater autonomy and more reflected glory. International economic relations thus assumed for de Gaulle all of the political implications of the high-policy defense area. By trying to re-create a situation in which increases in French power meant American power losses, French policy goals in the international monetary realm would coincide with those in other areas.

The French economist, Jacques Wolff, has summarized French diplomacy from 1962 to 1965 in monetary affairs as follows:

> These years were marked by a bold and growing harden-ing of the French thesis, especially during 1965. . . . The steps taken can be summarized as follows: the functioning of the international payments system was first criticized and its modification deemed necessary. Proposals for re-form dealing with international liquidity were presented and developed. The whole period is marked by a long con-troversy between France and the U.S.[23]

The second phase can be subdivided into two periods. In the first period, diagnosis of the disequilibria affecting the international monetary system was linked with a series of re-forms primarily involving economic motivation that were as-sociated with Finance Minister Valéry Giscard d'Estaing and his proposal for a Composite Reserve Unit (CRU) as a new basis for increasing and controlling the levels of international liquidity. The second phase began with de Gaulle's press con-ference of February 1965 that diagnosed the ills of the inter-national economic system in a way similar to the one articu-lated by Giscard with the exception that now the proposal for a reform was wholly political and implied a strict return to gold.

Between February 1965 and January 1966, during which Giscard remained Finance Minister, the French position

[23] Jacques Wolff, "La Diplomatie du franc (1962–1968), (1)," *Revue de science financière*, LX (1968): 787.

seemed to be based upon a contradiction that was apparently the result of de Gaulle's hesitation about running for a second term. It also stemmed from Debré's articulation of a policy different from that of Giscard and wholly consonant with de Gaulle's. The contradiction was resolved in January 1966 when Debré replaced Giscard as Finance Minister.[24]

The position of France on reform, between 1962 and de Gaulle's press conference of February 4, 1965, was articulated with growing momentum in the course of meetings of the IMF, the Group of Ten, and the Working Party Number Three of the OECD, was first outlined during September 1962 at the eighteenth meeting of the IMF in Washington, D.C., and was expressed more fervently at the annual IMF meetings of 1963 and 1964. In the Paris meeting of June 1964, the differences between the French and American positions were clearly delineated to the representatives charged with finding ways to improve the international monetary system. However, it was not until September 1964 during the Tokyo meeting of the IMF that they were publicized through Giscard's speech.

The dialogue during those years on methods for changing the international monetary system reflected policy disagreements between Britain and the United States, on the one side, and France and some other continental countries, on the other. The split was complicated by political implications of any change in the system established at Bretton Woods in 1944. Moreover, the discussion reflected not only the balance-of-payments problems of the United States and the

[24] There is a debate as to the reasons for the break between the second and third phase of French international monetary policy in the 1960s. According to Fabra, Giscard was free to articulate foreign monetary policy from 1962 to 1965. De Gaulle, according to Fabra, did not get interested in these affairs until early in 1965 when he saw the political implications involved in reform measures. See Fabra, "Money Men of France," p. 39.

According to another view, the change had more systemic causes. See Wolff, "La Diplomatie (1)," pp. 782–804, and "La Diplomatie du franc (2)," *Revue de science financière*, LXI (1969): 5–39.

United Kingdom but also awakened consciousness of the European countries to their monetary strengths. The controversy involved three economic questions and two political issues, which were interrelated and which became intertwined in the strategies of the Anglo-American and continental political and monetary authorities on reform.

First, the economic issues were related to the question of liquidity. The Anglo-American countries, hampered by deficits due to the role of the dollar and sterling in creating and sustaining world liquidity, were fearful that any resolution of their balance-of-payments problems would engender an acute and worldwide shortage of liquidity. The French argument, reflecting a more traditional conservative European outlook, suggested that the international economic system was suffering from an overabundance of liquidity, which implied inflation in Europe, and that the requisite of a sound and objective international monetary system was the elimination of American and British deficits.

Second, economic issues were concerned with means for creating liquidity. The official American and British proposals concentrated on improving the mechanisms of the IMF, the General Agreement on Borrowing and *ad hoc* swap arrangements. These arrangements reflected the post-Keynesian depreciation of gold as a rational basis for monetary reserves and international payments. The French, on the other hand, wished to eliminate vicissitudes of the system based on the creation of deficits for countries with key currencies, and wanted not only to return to a gold standard in the international monetary system but also to institute a rational objective system of sound international finance. Such a system would terminate the haphazard creation of liquidity and substitute for it certain well-defined rules of "proper behavior" and safeguards of national reserves. Reforms along these lines would eradicate the instability of a system allowing the two Anglo-Saxon countries to adhere to different "rules of the game" than the other participants.

Third, economic issues focused upon the habitual continental fear of inflation. While the Americans were concerned with the world's liquidity needs, French policy was preoccupied with dangers of European inflation that were felt to result from American deficits.[25] This fear of inflation explains much of the French proclivity for balance and equilibrium in international payments.

Two political questions reflected the desires of French policy-makers to make greater use of the power that accrued as a result of postwar economic recovery. On the one hand, there was an increasing desire to maximize freedom of action in all political realms that was reflected in a revolt against postwar Anglo-Saxon dominance in the West. This was exhibited in the desire to reduce the importance of the dollar and sterling in international monetary matters. On the other hand, there was a widespread suspicion of international organizations, including the IMF, where the industrialized countries could be outvoted by the Third World countries.

American and British diplomats paid lip service to the first demand of the French, but were reluctant to reduce the role of their currencies. They in fact rationalized the status of the dollar and the pound by claiming a universally recognized need for their currencies. At the same time, the Americans tended to identify their viewpoint with those of the developing countries and did not express disenchantment with organizations such as the IMF in which they could martial Third World support.

This latter difference of views was brought out in the greater willingness of the British and American governments to improve the adjustment mechanisms of the IMF by increasing quotas and drawing rights of members. The French, on the contrary, wished to magnify their own role in monetary affairs by moving the center of decision-making on reform from

[25] Inflationary tendencies in the EEC were seen as a result of American deficits in 1963. Although the European Monetary Committee of the European Community refuted this diagnosis in 1964 and linked the situation to predominantly internal phenomena, the French government has persistently argued against the potentially disequilibrating effects of a superabundance of dollars in Europe.

Washington and the IMF headquarters to the Bank for International Settlements (BIS) in Basle, and to crystallize the tendency begun with the formation of the Group of Ten in 1961 by increasing the role of the BIS and Working Party Number Three of the OECD. In these contexts, the French vote was more fully commensurate with the more recent importance of France and the other European countries in international monetary affairs.

The French view on the changes in the system by the mid-1960s was summarized in de Gaulle's press conference of February 4, 1965 as follows:

The conditions which formerly were able to give rise to the "gold exchange standard" have changed. The currencies of the Western European States are today restored, to the extent that the total gold reserves of the Six today equal those of the Americans. They would exceed them if the Six decided to convert all their dollar holdings into gold. This means that the custom of ascribing a superior value to the dollar as an international currency no longer rests on its initial foundation—I mean America's possession of the largest share of the world's gold. But, in addition, the fact that many States in principle accept dollars on the same basis as gold so as to offset, if need be, the deficits in their favor in the American balance of payments, leads the United States to indebt itself abroad at no cost. Indeed, what it owed abroad, it pays for, at least partially, with dollars which it alone can issue, instead of paying entirely with gold, which has a real value, which must be earned to be possessed, and which cannot be transferred to others without risks and sacrifices. This unilateral facility which is granted to America is serving to cloud the idea that the dollar is an impartial and international medium of exchange, when it is a means of credit belonging to one State.[26]

[26] Major Addresses, Statements and Press Conferences of General Charles de Gaulle, March 17, 1964–May 16, 1967 (New York: Am-

The political and economic viewpoints were tightly interwoven in Giscard's plan for a reform of the international
monetary system, which was the first French political challenge. While the British and American proposals for reform
during this period exhibit the political and economic preference for strengthening the system, the French were at
the vanguard of those who proposed a reversal of these
arrangements.

Giscard characterized the French attitude toward monetary
reform in a speech before the Maison de Droit in February,
1965, when he said, "France has money; therefore she must
have an international monetary policy."[27] An active policy was required for two reasons, one political and one
economic:

> The first is that such an attitude conforms to the idea which
> we have . . . of what must be the role of France in the
> world. France is not on the banks of the river of history.
> On the contrary, she is in midstream, where the fate of the
> world is gradually formed. It is thus perfectly normal that,
> like other countries, she should make observations, sugges-
> tions and proposals on the way in which this stream should
> be conducted and directed.
>
> The second reason . . . is that the present monetary sys-
> tem is in need of revision. However, those who would nor-
> mally claim the position of proposing this revision [the
> U.S.] given the importance of the responsibility which they
> have assumed in this matter and in the world, have ab-
> stained up to now from making proposals.[28]

---

bassade de France, Service de Presse et d'Information, 1967), p. 80.
In the same speech, de Gaulle prophetically states, "Given the worldwide upset that a crisis occurring in this domain would probably cause,
we have, indeed, every reason to hope that in time the means for
avoiding it will be taken" (p. 81).

[27] *Exposés de M. Valéry Giscard d'Estaing* (Paris: L'Economie,
1965), p. 15.

[28] Ibid., pp. 15–16.

Giscard foresaw four criteria for the workings of an adequate international monetary system. First, there had to be recognition of reciprocity of interests so that no individual country would receive an unfair advantage. Second, there had to be a mechanism for adjustment that would prevent any single country from prolonging indefinitely its debt payments. Third, sufficient but not too much liquidity was needed to meet the needs of growth in world trade without inducing inflation. Finally, the system had to be well established and instill universal confidence by means of an agreed-upon method of international discipline.[29]

The four criteria were to be fulfilled by specific principles of reform which could stop by means of "immediate measures and a 'return to discipline' the decadence of the world's international monetary system."[30] The requisite of any reform would, therefore, have to be the termination of American deficits and the ending of dollar accumulations in the reserves of other countries. Only those reserve currencies would be held that were agreed upon by international treaty, and any new reserve that might be needed would fall within the framework of a reformed system.

The upshot of Giscard's proposals was the return to a system based on gold. Gold was seen as essential to any rationally ordered monetary system because of the experience of the American deficits in the dollar exchange standard, because there was a "universal" psychological attachment to gold, and because the system of nation-states, without a central arbitrator or coercer, required something which transcended it. If, and only if, gold proved to be an insufficient source of liquidity, then a reserve unit ought to be created.

The most significant aspect of the French proposal for a composite reserve unit was its Rueffian character. It would

---

[29] These points were outlined in both positive and negative terms in Giscard's address at the Tokyo meeting of the IMF in September 1964. See *Exposés*, pp. 11–14. In positive terms, he outlined a proposal for reform; negatively, he saw each of these criteria unfilled in the gold exchange standard.

[30] Ibid., p. 22.

have been based on gold and established by and for the Ten. It was to be used only by the Ten and would have supplanted dollar and sterling reserves. It represented, therefore, a political attack on the universality of the IMF. It would have, in effect, reestablished a kind of European Payments Union for the members of the Ten. The CRU would have been deposited at the BIS and controlled by the Ten with only a formal liaison to the IMF.

CRU was to be created only when added liquidity was needed. Objective rules would be established on the amount needed in relation to a given expansion of trade, as well as on the system to be employed for its creation. Objectivity was needed in order to make the CRU durable in adding to or substituting for gold. Amounts to be used would be fixed to combat the natural tendencies of nations to increase liquidity to excess. For a CRU to be composed of *reserves veritables*, that is, to be as good as gold, it would have to consist of owned reserves; it would therefore contrast with IMF credits, which must be reimbursed; and its use would thereby have tended to reduce the Fund's credit-giving activity.

The initial French proposals for a CRU were criticized for ignoring the reserve requirements of the developing countries and for emphasizing the exclusivity of the club of industrial countries. To counter such complaints, the French at first argued that the problem of trade in the developing world was technically distinct from the creation of a CRU. However, aware of the political and psychological links between the two matters, the French suggested that a CRU be established in conjunction with the organization of worldwide primary product markets to guarantee exports from Third World countries.[31] Furthermore, they suggested the elimination of

[31] They carried the question into both the Kennedy Round and the Second UNCTAD conference and were unsuccessful in both cases. See Harry G. Johnson, "The Kennedy Round," *World Today*, XXIII (1967): 326–33. Also see the speech made by Michel Debré before the Second UNCTAD, February 5, 1968; Ambassade de France, Service de Presse et d'Information, *Speeches and Press Conferences*, No. 283.

obstacles to financial aid from the industrial countries to the Third World as well as the establishment of supplementary units of the CRU to aid the underdeveloped countries.

The virtues of the French plan for a CRU consisted in the equality it would have provided for the participating countries, the objective criteria it would have established, and the freedom it would have given to each country to use the CRU as it saw fit. French monetary action and criticism of the international monetary system had the further virtue of transforming a once taboo topic into the most heated issue of the decade. The French also showed some evidence of a certain flexibility, including the allowance for implementation of the CRU by stages; the retention of the dollar, sterling, and franc as reserves for those outside the Ten who might have wished to hold them; and the use of the old system as a base for building the new one rather than the introduction of a revolutionary and "theoretically perfect" system at once.

Flexibility in the French position, however, turned into ambiguity in 1965, during the second part of the second phase of French international monetary policy. De Gaulle's press conference of February, 1965 in a great many respects, contradicted Giscard's plans for a CRU. De Gaulle was now in favor of restoring gold standard as an immutable, eternal, and universal standard that would impose order on the system from outside. This policy was supported by the first French conversions of dollars into gold in the early part of 1965.[32]

[32] France had traditionally maintained a high percentage of its total reserves in gold rather than in foreign exchange. In 1957, when France's economic situation was weak, 90 percent of its reserves were in gold versus 50 percent in Germany, 100 percent in the United States, and 33 percent in Italy. The percentage had fallen to 72 percent in 1962, but reached 91 percent in 1966. In this sense French conversions were as much a return to normal financial policy as they were an attack on the dollar.

The level of French conversion can be seen in the increases both of gold and of total reserves. In 1962, of the $4 billion of French reserves, $2.6 billion was in gold. By 1967, the peak year of French reserves, total reserves reached almost $7 billion, $5.2 billion of which

In addition, the attack on the U.S.-dominated international monetary system was represented by the failure of France to vote on February 26, 1965 for a 25 percent increase in national contributions to the IMF. Giscard announced that the French delegate not only voted against the increase in quotas but also abstained on a vote on an increase in the quota proportions of sixteen countries. He said that France was against the quota increases because they changed the obligations inherent in the original Bretton Woods Agreement.[33]

Both the conversions of dollars into gold and the failure to vote for changes in IMF quotas were the result of other reasons. The principal one was that de Gaulle was unwilling to be a party to such changes in the international system which would serve to strengthen it, but preferred to see a change in the system rather than a reform in it. This position was interpreted by American officials as intransigence. American officials stated that if France were interested in changing the system, then France ought to accept reforms in it.[34]

Throughout the second phase the French elaboration of international monetary policy was based on an increasingly strengthened position not only relative to that of the United States but also to the balance between the United States and the other industrialized states—both in Europe and Asia

---

were composed of gold. *International Financial Statistics*, xxii (1969): 130.

[33] See Wolff, "La Diplomatie (1)," p. 791.

[34] One commentator on the politics of reform has interpreted de Gaulle's posture as more important formally than substantively. British economic analyst Francis Cassell feels that de Gaulle was more interested in the target of his action than in the economic logic of the gold standard: "Despite the many mystical references in his statement [of February, 1965] to the supremacy of gold, de Gaulle showed no inclination to follow that faith through to its logical conclusions. The suspicion must be that he was motivated less by a burning zeal to restore order to international money than by a shrewd calculation that here was an effective weapon for discomfiting Washington" (*Gold or Credit?*, p. 148).

(Japan). This change was not reflected, however, in the IMF quotas to which the EEC contributed 16 percent of total funds throughout the postwar period.[35] By mid-1967, however, the EEC combined reserves constituted 36.1 percent of the total member reserves.[36] Thus, after Baumgartner stage-managed the formation of the Group of Ten in 1961, France was faithfully backed by the German and Dutch central bankers in proposals to transfer monetary authority from Washington to Basle where European control was greater. Italy and Belgium also tended to support this position, albeit for reasons of EEC unity rather than for reasons of international position. Moreover, the specific French actions to force the United States to adjust its balance of payments deficits derived in good measure from France's balance of payments surplus. The surplus was maintained, in part, from the deflationary *plan de stabilisation* of 1963. It was derived also from capital transfers, for in no year in the 1960s did France run a surplus on trade.

French international monetary policy was supported by a domestic policy designed to make Paris a center of international finance that rivaled London. Among the means used to restructure French capital markets and to make Paris an international financial center was the creation of the Banque Nationale de Paris in 1966 by Finance Minister Debré. The Banque de Paris then became the largest bank in Europe with $6 billion in deposits.[37]

[35] Actually, with the increases in Fund membership, the combined share of the United States and Britain fell from 53 percent in 1947 to 33 percent in 1965. The EEC voting share remained at a level between 16 percent and 17 percent because of the increase in voting rights that they acquired as a group with the accession of Germany in 1952. See Cooper, *Economics of Interdependence*, p. 45.

[36] Fritz Machlup, *Remaking the International Monetary System: The Rio Agreement and Beyond* (Baltimore: The Johns Hopkins Press, 1968), p. 22.

[37] For a discussion of the strengths and weaknesses of French capital markets, see Holger L. Engberg, *French Money and Capital Markets*

By the end of 1965, then, the French position had become well known. De Gaulle and his financial advisors had seen that changes were, in the long run, inevitable in the international economic system. France with a balance-of-payments surplus was in a good position to influence the direction of change. France seemed to have the lone voice in calling for change in the system, especially insofar as the French position was based on both national interests and the need to redress in organizational form the changed status of the European and Anglo-American countries. But isolation had increased French prestige. Others, especially in the United States, looked upon the system less in terms of American imperialism than in terms of economic rationality and the virtues of a universally accepted reserve currency. The economic and political terms of the debate between France and the United States were well formulated. The appearance that France was moving from alignment to neutralism in the strategic field was paralleled by the movement toward independence in the monetary field.

Interdependence and the Eclipse of French Policy: 1966–1968

The third phase, which extends from 1966 to 1968, was characterized by an increasing divergence between the ideal system of international relations that de Gaulle was articulating and actual practices. It was a period when de Gaulle and his new Finance Minister Michel Debré were making efforts to increase French independence and autonomy in preparation

---

and Monetary Management, C. J. Devine Institute of Finance, *Bulletin,* Nos. 32–33 (New York: New York University Graduate School of Business Administration, 1965). The reforms carried out under Debré are outlined in Ferris, *Money Men of Europe,* pp. 103–25. See also Debré's speech of November 9, 1966 at the Conseil National du Crédit, where he outlined the new government credit policy. This speech is reprinted in *Problèmes économiques,* No. 992 (January 5, 1967), pp. 2–6.

for a post-de Gaulle era, and when the limits on independent French action in the monetary sphere, as in other spheres, were restrained by interdependence.

An increased hardening of the French policy on transformation of the international economy was accompanied by a decreased power base from which that position could be supported. Not only did the franc decrease in value, but also France was increasingly isolated from the other states on the issue of reform. The period ended with the creation of special drawing rights, with French acceptance of reform measures, with Germany replacing France as the country arguing for the most limited amount of drawing rights, and with the franc in crisis.

As the second phase was coming to a close, the French proposal for a CRU, identified with Giscard d'Estaing, had been discussed and evaluated by the Ossola study group. But the task of this study group was more or less academic. The British and American financial authorities had come out against the French proposal, and de Gaulle had virtually renounced it in his press conference of February 1965. At the same time, however, the Americans first outlined their proposals for reform, thus sabotaging the original French initiatives.

If the second phase was characterized by France on the offensive and the United States and Britain on the defensive, the third phase was marked by a reversal in roles with the United States increasingly taking the initiative. In July 1965 Henry Fowler announced an American program to redress the American balance-of-payments deficit, envisaging the elimination of the American deficit by the end of 1966. Simultaneously, Fowler suggested the need to create a new instrument of reserve to allow international liquidity to increase in the absence of new dollars, but his suggestion for an international conference was postponed because the European members of the Ten were fearful of any reform railroaded through the IMF where they were politically weak. By the end of the summer of 1965, however, agreement was reached for the establishment of separate and conjoint study groups of the Ten and the IMF Council.

Otto Emminger, a German central banker, replaced the American, Robert Roosa, as Chairman of the Ten in September 1965 and largely dominated negotiations on a reform for the next two years. Negotations within the Group of Ten were based on two antithetical positions, which have been described in the following terms. First, there was the position of the Americans, "who wanted to obtain, without delay, a new, specific device."[38] Second, the French "were looking for a vague plan and . . . worried about the announcement of any requisites or about defining procedures regarding a decision which would be sufficiently protective to avoid the imminent appearance of any new reserve."[39]

By the beginning of 1966, the French position was being formulated by de Gaulle and the new Finance Minister Debré, who had just made a political comeback and who was an ardent supporter of Gaullist foreign-policy goals. Debré took a more liberal position on American investments in France than had Giscard d'Estaing for two reasons. First, he saw that the policy had failed because American investments made in the Six outside of France meant a loss of potential employment and investment capital. Second, he wanted to keep open the possibility of accommodation with the United States in order to prevent the isolation of France.[40] He also wanted to provide France with the opportunity to replace Germany as the chief American interlocutor on the Continent.

Throughout 1966, the theme of French foreign policy was independence with its negative corollary of antiintegration. The end of the cold war and the creation of new situations in West and East Europe allowed France, in de Gaulle's mind, to take new initiatives that would free it from the alleged hegemony of the United States. Thus, the French position on

[38] "Etapes de la négociation," p. 14.
[39] Ibid.
[40] See Fabra, "Money Men of France," p. 39.

monetary reforms was tightly linked to the French withdrawal from NATO military command structure announced in March.[41]

Emminger's report, the general outline of which was made public in January 1966, was an effort at compromise between the French and the U.S. positions on four points. First, on the nature of the creation of additional instruments of reserve, the French thesis was accepted; a decision would be made by a small group of countries. Second, a compromise was reached on the implementation of decisions; unanimity was needed for the initial decision (the French position, so that France could maintain the veto), but only a majority was necessary for adjustment measures (the American position). Third, Emminger foresaw the use of both gold and new reserve units in settling balance-of-payments differences, although no country would be forced to accept that proportion in its reserves (compromise). Finally, Emminger proposed that the IMF would have some role in the negotiations as well.

After news of the Emminger report was released, the American project was presented in greater detail. This project foresaw the creation of a new reserve unit, not based entirely on gold, but to be as good as gold, and distributed initially according to IMF quotas. American policy sought a compromise that would be acceptable to the majority of the industrialized countries, so that it appeared that "it would be difficult for France not to take it into consideration without the

[41] De Gaulle never linked his monetary policy and defense policy in terms of independence, but in the fall of 1966 Couve de Murville clearly did so in an interview. In particular, he said that France was the only country to confront the United States in international monetary negotiations because France was "the only country to be able to demonstrate with sufficient independence her true sentiments" (*La Politique étrangère de la France en 1966*, Textes et documents, Notes et études documentaires, Nos. 3384–87, p. 164). In the same interview, the foreign minister brought together the themes of French withdrawal from NATO and French monetary policy in his declarations with regard to the role of France (ibid., pp. 169–70).

risk of isolating herself from her nine partners,"[42] especially since the American proposal resembled the earlier French plan for a CRU.

Fowler announced in early February that he foresaw that the new currency could be created within a two-year period and that a general agreement should be reached within the Group of Ten before any project would be submitted to the IMF. In contrast to this new American position, however, an interministerial council in France in late February reaffirmed its position that gold should be maintained as the only basis of the system and that there was enough liquidity in the world that obviated the creation of new reserve instruments.[43]

At the Group of Ten meeting in March 1966, confrontation between the United States and France was avoided by the formal procedure of examining additional proposals for reform. The French were reluctant to alienate five EEC partners, having just resolved with them the long seven-month crisis over agriculture and the structure of the Common Market. The March meeting of the Ten, however, seemed to portend deadlock. For it was feared that the real confrontation would take place when the final report was issued. If France would be isolated from its partners in the Common Market, then it would be excluded from participating in a reform of the system. On the other hand, if the other members of the Ten could not reach an agreement, the stalemate that France was seeking could be preserved.

After several months of evaluation, Debré tried to rally the Common Market partners behind the French position on a diagnosis of the ills of the system and on the validity of the reforms de Gaulle suggested. The Finance Ministers of the Ten then met in the Hague in preparation for the fall meeting of the IMF. The Hague meeting, an attempt at serious negotiation and agreement, ended with an even more striking contrast between the American and French positions and the isolation of Debré.

[42] Wolff, "La Diplomatie (2)," p. 8.
[43] Ibid., p. 9.

When the final Emminger report was issued and examined by the ministers and central bankers of the Ten, the attempted compromise found France in agreement on five of the seven points. These five points involved the diagnosis of the system. But Debré disagreed with the report on two points. First, he voted against the resolution that implied the need for new liquidity, fearing it would take the form of "paper gold." Second, he voted against a resolution that implied that the Ten and IMF administrators could continue their studies on conditions under which new reserves could be created.

The position taken by Debré was in many respects the reverse of the one taken by Giscard two years earlier. In the second phase of French international monetary policy, Giscard was lecturing the United States about the need to foresee what reforms would be necessary and to plan for a reconstitution of the system. The strength of his position was the relative neglect of plans for a reform by the United States which wanted to conserve its position in the system by defending the rational economic basis of the dollar exchange standard. Once the United States started pushing for reform, however, France was on the defensive, afraid that a reformed system would perpetuate American dominance, albeit under changed conditions. This fear was based on the understanding that any creation of new monetary reserves would allow the United States to continue to finance its balance-of-payments deficits by additional means.

The French position, however, began to change by late summer of 1966 and was most evident in Debré's speech at the annual meeting of the IMF on September 27, 1966. First, he analyzed the system and once again stressed the incongruity between the dollar exchange standard and the needs of the international community; the existing glut rather than scarcity of liquidity; and the inadequacy of artificially created liquidity for the less favored nations. Second, he recommended that certain actions for both the monetary system and the developing countries include not only the recognition of the central role of gold in the system but also the need to link reform of the system with reform of global primary product markets. This was an attempt to reconcile the French position with those of other European states as well as with the underdeveloped states in order to forge a common front in the IMF.

The French hoped to find an agreement among the Six at this time, not only because the American position had changed, thereby making negotiations more flexible than before, but also because the European partners of France were more willing to accommodate French demands. Strange summarized the situation in the fall of 1966 as follows:

The state of play at this level . . . would seem to reflect rather markedly two current political developments. One is the discovery by the United States of the limitations on her power to order the world according to the American interest, a discovery perhaps proceeding rather fast because her stance in the Vietnam war is increasingly dividing her from many of her natural allies. . . . Secondly, the slow crystallization of an opposing, collective European interest is being speeded up by the desire of the other members of the European Economic Community to humour France and to preserve the Community at all costs.[44]

During the rest of 1966, the French sought agreement with the Five EEC partners on ways to proceed on reform. Attempts were made at meetings of the Finance Ministers of the Common Market, the European Monetary Committee, the BIS, and the Group of Ten. The strategy to preserve the stalemate was a defensive one designed to postpone any reforms that would benefit the United States. The change from offense to defense had actually begun several months earlier in the Luxemburg meetings of the Common Market Foreign Ministers in early 1966, when the agricultural crisis was settled. The new policy orientation was the product of a

[44] Susan Strange, "The International Money Muddle," World Today, XXII (1966): 410–13.

policy formulated by Debré's associates, particularly Jean Dromer, who was an advisor to de Gaulle on economic affairs. Dromer was secretary general of a committee of civil servants in Brussels. In addition, Antoine Dupont-Fauville and René Larre concerted efforts with Debré to bring about agreement among the European countries on reform. Debré and his advisors made efforts in the winter of 1966–1967 to shift the European countries from the American position and toward a common position of creating new credit facilities for international payments rather than new reserve facilities. Simultaneously, Debré indicated that the French position was more flexible than it had appeared to be earlier. In particular, he recognized the need for studying an increase in the price of gold and the possibility of creating a new reserve instrument based on gold and reopened the question of creating CRU or an agency similar to it.[45]

Debré stressed that there was no urgency in the matter, but that a solution ought to be studied by a committee of experts representing the EEC. In effect, his suggestion regarding the change in gold price represented another attack on the dollar, for it would result in a gain for the European countries with their large gold stocks and a relative loss for the United States.[46]

The European position was worked out at a meeting of the Finance Ministers of the Six at The Hague in January, 1967 and at Munich in April. Debré's position on the change in the price of gold had proven unacceptable to the Five, especially Germany. But The Hague meeting ended in an important compromise. In the communiqué issued at the end of the meeting, the perfecting of international credit instruments was mentioned, but a revaluation of gold was not. The French thus sacrificed their position for agreement in the EEC. Debré

[45] See Michel Debré's interview in *Le Monde*, January 8, 1967, p. 11.
[46] At the same time, France had virtually stopped converting dollars into gold because of a peaking in the gold reserves of France and a diminution of dollars in French reserves needed for official settlements and central bank interventions.

also abandoned the French efforts to secure greater weight for the Ten in any revised system. That goal, which had been followed by both Baumgartner and Giscard d'Estaing, had never materialized. Instead, Debré suggested that the voting rights of the Six be increased in the IMF, assuring them 20 percent of the total, and therefore a collective veto on important issues.[47]

In return, however, important concessions were made to France upon which all of the Six agreed, and these were ratified at the Munich Conference in April.[48] The Finance Ministers agreed upon three points. First, new liquidity would be created in the form of automatic drawing rights on the IMF, which would be distributed according to quotas. Second, before these rights were created, the reserve countries had to eliminate their deficits and there had to be a collective agreement that a worldwide liquidity shortage existed. Third, any reform of the Bretton Woods system, which had been dominated since its inception by the Anglo-Saxon countries, would have to reflect the increased political importance of the European countries.

The agreement was, nonetheless, thought to be precarious. The Americans, especially, were skeptical that a lasting agreement among the Six had been reached. There was, in fact, some equivocation among them. The attempt by France to get an agreement of the Six achieved a shift in emphasis from plans for the creation of new reserve assets to much less ambitious proposals for extending credit. Still, the European position and American position were far apart, and it looked

[47] *L'Année politique*, 1968 (Paris: Presses Universitaires de France, 1969), pp. 145–46.

[48] Between The Hague and Munich meetings of the Finance Ministers of the Six, the Finance Ministers of the United States, Britain, France, Germany, and Italy met in London at the end of January. They agreed to joint efforts if any lack of liquidity arose which might lead to a slowdown in the expansion of world trade and induce recession. This agreement reflected a growing belief among these ministers of the need for a coordinated monetary policy, given the levels of interdependence of the Western economies.

as if the confrontation between France and the United States of the previous four years was evolving into a more muted, but equally irreconcilable confrontation between the United States and the Six. During June, for example, France withdrew from the cooperative arrangements of the gold pool, saying that the system was in crisis and that sales of gold to speculators would eventually have to end in order to prevent the system from collapsing. In 1967 a total of $1.6 billion was lost by Western reserves as a result of speculation.[49]

In the summer of 1967, after successive meetings of the IMF directors and the deputies of the Ten, the atmosphere seemed suddenly to have changed. An outline for reform was completed and approved in London in August by the Ministers and Governors of the Ten. A compromise text was approved by the Board of Governors of the IMF in September after which it was presented for ratification to the member countries at the IMF's annual meeting at Rio de Janeiro. The London and Rio compromises were based on three points. The European group in the IMF gained an important voice because approval of any new reforms was made contingent upon an 85 percent vote. Since the Six had over 17 percent in voting rights, they held a collective veto over new decisions. Second, any proposed change would be contingent upon the situation agreed upon by the Six at The Hague the previous January; that is, lack of liquidity, and an improvement in the American balance of payments. Third, the outline of a new instrument was presented under the name Special Drawing Rights (SDRs).[50]

Why, at the Rio conference, was there a sudden agreement on the procedures for a new instrument? The answer can be found in a convergence of events. First, the accumulated ef-

[49] *Problèmes économiques*, No. 1078 (August 29, 1968), pp. 8–15. In the previous year, only $50 million was lost, while in 1965 official reserves increased by $215 million.

[50] The general operation of the SDR system and its effects on the international monetary system are described in Machlup, *Remaking the International Monetary System*, pp. 13–41.

fects of four years of debate and the apparent reduction in available liquidity resulting from decreases in the supply of new gold or new dollars had convinced Debré and the French authorities that the disasters they had been predicting for years were more imminent than they had previously thought. This was especially so after French withdrawal from the gold pool, when lack of confidence in the system encouraged a high level of speculation. Second, and of importance in political terms, was the nature of the Rio compromise. As Machlup has written,

> the conflict between the U. S. and France over international monetary reforms was resolved, almost miraculously, by extraordinarily efficient mediators applying the recipe of avoiding all the words which the nations had written on their banners and for which they were battling. . . . Words not burdened with a history of controversy, not associated with recognizable ideologies, and not widely used in monetary theories, words, therefore, with still neutral and not always fixed connotations, were put in place of the old, battle-scarred and now banished words.[51]

By substituting words that could be interpreted ambiguously —in one way by Debré and in another way by the Americans—the Rio compromise could be acceptable to all parties. The new creation at Rio was a "facility," which the French could interpret as a "credit facility," and which the Americans could see as new reserve assets. In this way, the French and American representatives could interpret the new "facility" as they wished, either for home consumption or for purposes of face-saving. In addition, the ambiguity permitted further negotiation during the phase when the details of the outline would be supplied and reviewed by the Ten in March 1968 at Stockholm.

Debré, in his Rio speech, thus declared that the new SDRs were "in no way a revolutionary arrangement that would replace gold. If that was to be the condition of agreement, it is

[51] Ibid., p. 9.

quite clear that France would not have signed it. The plans call for the eventual creation of credit facilities. Such is the substance of the limited but important reform."[52] Debré acknowledged that the conditions for implementing SDRs were omitted from the outline, but he repeated his understanding that the three conditions agreed upon by the Six at The Hague still obtained. His remarks contrasted with those of other delegates, including British Chancellor of the Exchequer James Callaghan and American Secretary of the Treasury Henry Fowler, who felt that the SDRs were revolutionary and that they constituted reserve assets.[53]

It is still questionable, to some degree, whether the differences were only "semantic and theoretic," as Machlup has argued, or whether the matter reflected an attempt on Debré's part to maintain an ambiguous situation so that the opportunity would be preserved for France to reassert later an independent voice, either alone or together with the other Five in Europe. His movement toward an accommodation with the United States certainly seems to have reflected his growing consciousness of a potential economic threat from Germany in which French and American objectives coincided.

In any case, the situation in fall 1967, after the Rio conference, was different from the one in 1965 when de Gaulle pressured the United States to reform the system by selling dollars for gold. Between Rio and Stockholm, when the Finance Ministers of the Ten were scheduled to meet to approve more detailed plans on the SDRs, the first of the international monetary crises of 1967–1968 occurred. These were the devaluation of the British pound in November 1967 and the dollar crisis of March 1968. These crises revealed not only a shortage of reserves that the French and other European countries had denied during the previous years but also the difficulty of controlling what had

[52] Speech given by Michel Debré at the meeting of the International Monetary Fund in Rio de Janeiro, September 26, 1967, in *Problèmes économiques*, No. 1032 (October 12, 1967), p. 2.

[53] Machlup, *Remaking the International Monetary System*, p. 11.

been becoming highly mobile short-term capital in search of higher interest rates, or speculation money betting on changes in exchange rates.

The devaluation of sterling acknowledged that the pound was overvalued and that the resources at the disposal of the biggest reserve countries were not large enough to thwart speculation. In short, devaluation provided evidence for "speculators [that] they could win."[54] Profitability of speculation accelerated until March, when there was a $3 billion run on reserve gold, when gold reached the selling price of $44 per ounce in Paris, and when a meeting of the gold pool in Basle failed to restore confidence in the dollar.

As a result, just before the Stockholm meeting, the central bankers of the gold pool, which France left the previous summer, announced the two-price gold system and the end of central bank intervention in gold markets. This meant that the gold pool operation had terminated and that central banks would buy gold only from one another at the official price. At the same time, by refusing to sell gold on the market, the United States announced that it would freeze out any newly mined gold from the system. In a stroke of crisis decision-making, the dollar was reaffirmed as a standard, and the United States was no longer under great pressure to reduce its payments deficits.

The system had, in effect, moved through a crisis that hardened the dollar standard, and France was excluded from the decision because de Gaulle had taken France out of the gold pool the previous summer, albeit on the very grounds for which it collapsed. France was isolated by its unwillingness to cooperate and by the trends in changes in the system.

French isolation from other countries was, in fact, quickly apparent, by the nature of the decisions taken in this period of crisis. Between the Washington meeting of the gold pool and the Stockholm meeting of the Ten, the Finance Ministers of the Six met in Brussels on March 25. Debré indicated that important differences existed between France and the others,

[54] *The New York Times*, July 20, 1969, Section 3, p. 13.

especially Germany, over the acceleration of the implementation of the Kennedy Round that permitted the United States
to decrease its balance-of-payments deficits. In addition, he
indicated differences with regard to SDRs. These differences
were made more explicit at Stockholm, where the Ten were
meeting to accept the details elaborating the outlined plan accepted by the IMF at Rio.

The Stockholm meeting opened in a tense diplomatic atmosphere. First, there had been a crisis. The pound had been
devalued, the American balance-of-payments deficit reached
$4 billion in 1967; there were restrictions on dollar converti-
bility; and the gold pool had been dissolved. Second, Debré's
bargaining position had been whittled away. He had insisted
all along that France would be pleased to cooperate on a reform of the system, provided that SDRs had a solid fiduciary
base in gold and that the exorbitant privileges of the reserve
currency countries were eliminated. These objectives were not
placed on the agenda, and Debré insisted that a new IMF
meeting be held to discuss them. He also asserted that a loose
interpretation of SDRs, such as the United States was giving
at Stockholm, was a false and temporary solution.[55]

The United States, however, was in a strong bargaining
position. Germany and other countries found it more important to accept the U.S. interpretation to make it appear as
though a solution had been found at Stockholm, thereby
heading off new speculation. However, to open the opportunity for eventual French accession to the Stockholm agreement, the final report was ambiguous with regard to the need
for a conference before implementing the SDRs. In the end,
all but France agreed with the final communiqué. And, Debré
issued the following statement at the meeting, expressing the
reasons for which he took an independent view.

Two ideas have inspired my remarks throughout; the first
is, at least in our view, the grave divergencies between the

[55] For a sympathetic reading of Debré's actions at Stockholm, see
Robert Triffin, "De Gaulle at Stockholm: Villain, Hero or Sphinx?"
Interplay, 1:10 (1968): 15–17.

London resolutions ratified in Rio de Janeiro and the draft as it was presented to us, and even as it is after the few corrections that have been made. The Special Drawing Rights are no longer that form of supplementary credit which we had judged useful: they are, I fear, an expedient, unless they are the blueprint for a so-called currency. . . .

The second point of my remarks has been even more serious, if that is possible. The fundamental problems have not been tackled. . . . I have not been understood, at least not officially, and all happened around this table as though there has been no warning signals during the last six months. I regret this.[56]

Debré indicated at Stockholm that only a short time remained for making adequate reforms. He called for equality of treatment of all currencies and for raising basic questions. Giscard and Debré had consistently maintained that it was necessary to have a change of the monetary system and that the best way to proceed on change was to embarrass the United States as much as possible into accepting equitable reform without wrecking the status quo. Regardless of France's economic position, it was politically a very sound one. As London *Times* economic editor, Peter Jay, has said,

what, therefore, is basically at stake in these monetary arguments is not some synthetic fear of an economic takeover of Europe by American capital or a deep concern for the freedom fighter of Vietnam. Still less is it a fundamental belief in orthodox monetary theory for its own sake. . . . It would be a gross insult to French economists to suppose that they or the politicians whom they influence took

[56] Ambassade de France, Service de Presse et d'Information, No. 1060. Debré noted in the same statement that French cooperation would be forthcoming "when the real problems are tackled . . . the status of . . . those currencies called reserve currencies, in order that the discipline be the same for all, the standard of value which we must dare to name, gold, and its normal price." He said that since these main tasks were outside the scope of the Ten, France could not be associated with the Ten's communiqué of agreement.

seriously that sort of nonsense. These are merely the phrases that come to the lips of much-harassed French spokesmen who have to put some sort of economic or financial gloss on the basically political briefs to which they have to speak. What is at stake is French reluctance to accept indefinitely inferior status to the United States, let alone . . . Britain.[57]

The French position was weakened because of the international monetary system and the domestic events in France in the spring of 1968. By Stockholm, the French had abandoned negotiations even though the other European countries attempted to leave the back door open to her reentrance by claiming an unlimited right "allowing any country to limit its commitments by refusing to participate in a distribution of SDRs, which it felt untimely."[58] More important, the unforeseen effects of increasing momentum of crises made the SDR scheme acceptable in spite of the fact that the conditions set up at The Hague in January 1967 were not met. Interdependencies had risen to such a level that acceptance was imposed as a precondition of financial order. Most important, however, for undermining the French bargaining position was the effect of the domestic events of May and June that was completely unexpected by political authorities. The spontaneous uprisings of students and workers, which led to widespread strikes and disorders, and ended with large wage increases, had the effect of stimulating a run on the franc. By the end of 1968, $2.8 billion of the almost $7 billion of French reserves were lost and resulted in a curtailment of the criticism of the monetary system. As a recipient of aid by reciprocal arrangements with other countries, France through interdependencies gradually relied on the system that had been previously criticized from an independent position. Within the next few months, France received more than $1 billion in unofficial aid from foreign central banks. Moreover, the es-

[57] Jay, "Why France Balks," p. 40.
[58] "Etapes de la négociation monétaire," p. 16.

tablishment of exchange controls did not stop the flow of francs out of France and the franc zone by suitcases or by brokers.[59] Thus, given the level of interdependence, it was difficult, if not impossible, to control the exodus of francs without completely sealing French borders—even to communications which would have prevented selling by brokers.

In part, the sudden decline in the value of the franc represented the coming of a long-anticipated event. The strength of the franc had been eroding, and was bolstered up to some degree by interdependencies. The French negotiation position on reform was based on the power derived from France's overall payments surplus. The surplus was not on current account, but largely in short-term and long-term funds. Between 1962 and 1966, for example, $3.018 billion was invested in France from abroad.[60] If, during 1966, France had held back American investment, the surplus on capital account would have been substantially reduced. In addition, short-term currency came to France in pursuit of high interest rates. Throughout the 1967–1968 crises, there was an escalation of interest rates in each of the industrialized countries that served to send increasingly frequent and sharp fluctuations into the international capital markets.

Another factor in deflating the French position was the Soviet invasion of Prague in August 1968. The invasion had the effect at the high-policy level of depreciating the French diagnosis of changes in the international system. At the low-policy level, however, there was an increase in confidence in the United States, which was reflected in the increased flow of European money into America. This, in fact, resulted in an unanticipated short-term surplus in U.S. payments.

Speculation mounted on the franc throughout the fall of 1968 on the belief that the combination of a $4 billion annual

[59] *The Economist,* May 10, 1969, p. 64.

[60] Ambassade de France, Service de Presse et d'Information, No. 1045 (February 28, 1968). Of this, $800 million originated in the United States. The largest element—almost one third—came from Switzerland. Only $758 million came from the EEC countries.

German trade surplus and French deficits would result in an upward revaluation of the German mark and the devaluation of the franc. To find ways to stop speculation, the Finance Ministers of the Ten met in Bonn from November 20 to 22. The Germans, however, refused to revalue, partly for political reasons. The Christian Democratic government of Kurt Kiesinger feared that a revaluation would create an electoral disadvantage in September 1969. The French position was itself hardened by de Gaulle's brilliant, if Pyrrhic, defense of the franc.

On November 30, a week before the Bonn meeting, de Gaulle announced that there would be no devaluation of the franc. The result was not restored confidence in the franc, but an increased outflow of francs and the closing of the Bourse. By November 22, however, with everyone expecting a devaluation of the franc and with increased support from foreign central bankers, but without any commitment by the new Finance Minister Ortoli to devalue, de Gaulle decided to maintain the franc's rate of exchange. The monetary meeting was noteworthy for the rebirth of an economic alliance of Britain, France, and the United States against Germany and the undervalued mark. Germany had then replaced France as the prime interlocutor of the United States on monetary affairs, and the rebirth of this tripartite accord was based, in part, on the need of France to have support against the German negotiators, who had become the strongest in Europe. In addition, Nixon's more orthodox economic policies seemed amenable to de Gaulle. The United Kingdom for its part aligned with France for fear that a devaluation of the franc would lead to another run on sterling.

The franc was not devalued in November 1968 for political reasons. The effects of the domestic crisis of May and June 1968 were so great that they had severely limited the French policy of independence. Restrictions placed on the domestic economy with increased taxes and decreased spending in order to maintain currency stability revealed the sacrifice of the support of the high policy of independence. On November 20

248

Premier Couve de Murville announced a budget cut of 2 billion francs, and most of it was from the nuclear striking force.[61] The last remnant of the policy of independence was the franc, which de Gaulle was unwilling to sacrifice. His last-minute surprise refusal to devalue, he felt, would prevent the crisis and would allow him to save the franc and the basis of a future policy of independence.

De Gaulle's refusal to devalue, if it illustrated his emphasis on the morale of a nation in conducting foreign affairs, was economically irrational. In the end it did not stop a run on the franc and eventual devaluation. Moreover, it meant that there would have to be an austerity program at home that would harm both France and its trading partners. De Gaulle's reluctance to devalue, in addition, was based on a political myth rather than an economic fact. As Kenen said,

> governments believe that voters are more tolerant of high interest rates and taxes than of higher import prices. . . . They may very well be right—but the voters may be wrong.
>
> Too often, however, it is pure mythology, not rational political or economic arguments, that leads a country to defend the status quo. Few politicians, even statesmen, will willingly confess to failure, and that is how they and the public at large tend to view devaluations. In any event, economics certainly cannot explain de Gaulle. His contemptuous dismissal of devaluation is matched only by his general disdain for economists and for the facts of economic life. All acts are political, and unilateral devaluation is too conspicuous an act.[62]

The maintenance of the weak franc after November 1968 disclosed a latent aspect of French foreign policy after 1963, the sacrifice of domestic economic growth for foreign policy, and de Gaulle already had lost much domestic credibility.

[61] *Le Monde*, November 21, 1969, p. 1.
[62] Peter Kenen, "The General's Monetary Absurdity," *The New Leader*, December 16, 1968, p. 7.

By the summer of 1969, the American position on international reform had been virtually, if temporarily, victorious. On June 28, three months after de Gaulle's resignation, the French government joined other countries in accepting the SDRs. The attempt to make France a center of banking and commerce and to make the franc a strong currency had failed. Germany had replaced France as the spokesman of conservative European banking interests and was the main adversary of the United States over the number of units of SDRs to be issued. In effect, the reform of the system took place along lines desired by the United States and without the conditions that the European countries had set forth for such a reform—that is, without an end to the American payments deficits.

Conclusions

If the politics of monetary reform illustrated levels of interdependence among the industrialized countries, the manner in which France negotiated reform reflected the full force as well as the inconsistencies of French foreign policies in the 1960s. A policy of independence was translated into an attack on the international monetary system and several proposals for reforms, both of which would have bolstered France's international position. The attack on the dollar and the attempt to revive European power via joint European efforts in the end failed because of the changing monetary system. The dollar exchange standard was attacked for giving the United States unfair advantage; that is, for being the basis of a perceived American financial imperialism. France stressed a revised form of mercantilism in which a European or French victory would have meant an Anglo-American loss. But were there any winners at all in the reforms?

The main problem as perceived by France in its diplomacy was one of American dominance and lack of reciprocity. Political arguments were combined with economic arguments, especially with regard to liquidity and inflation. However, the crisis was brought about by a high degree of interdependence with short-term capital flowing rapidly from one country to another. This capital was owned mostly by international businesses, transnational structures that escaped the political controls of the states. These transnational flows of capital have triggered the crises and have resulted in a form of crisis decision-making in international monetary affairs that has become institutionalized.

The European states have tried to control these transnational activities within the context of the Common Market, but so far unsuccessfully. Efforts in the Monetary Committee of the EEC are still embryonic, and it is doubtful whether the problems can be solved even in this context. For the problem is essentially an Atlantic one—or, more properly, one which concerns the whole system of industrialized states. Efforts to look at this problem on an Atlantic level are likely to characterize Western diplomacy during the next ten years—for, if this problem is not solved, then the complete breakdown that de Gaulle had predicted for the international economy may come about, if for different reasons.

SIX

CRISIS DIPLOMACY: MANIPULATING
INTERDEPENDENCE IN THE EEC

DURING its first decade the EEC underwent a continued series of crises. In the development of communitywide policies— notably, the agricultural policy—the chief decision-making bodies of the EEC, the Commission and the Council, were forced to negotiate decisions in a crisis atmosphere almost annually. From time to time, but especially after the first French veto of the British application for membership in the EEC in 1963 and during the French boycott from June 1965 to January 1966, the EEC was thought by many to be under- going turning points the resolution of which was critical to its survival. By the end of its first decade, a series of currency crises resulting in the devaluation of the franc and revaluation of the mark posed for the EEC the question of whether it could pursue any of its common policies without planning for the eventuality of a common currency. So prevalent had crises become in the development of the European Communities that more than one observer described it as a political system which is in a permanent state of crisis,[1] and they have argued that the EEC has developed its own procedure—the mara- thon negotiating session—which is able to cope efficiently with the permanent crisis atmosphere.[2]

[1] See Frans A. M. Alting von Geusau, *Beyond the European Com- munity* (Leiden: A. W. Sijthoff, 1969), pp. 41–60 and idem, "Les Sessions marathon du Conseil des Ministres," in *La décision dans les Communautés Européennes*, ed. Pierre Gerbet and Daniel Pepy (Brus- sels: Presses Universitaires de Bruxelles, 1969), pp. 99–107; and, Leon Lindberg, "Integration as a Source of Stress on the European Com- munity System," *International Organization*, xx (1966): 233–65.

[2] Alting von Geusau describes the marathon as "a typical decision- making process for a system in permanent crisis. It develops under

Not only has the political system of the EEC been prone to crises, but the diplomacy of some of the member states, particularly France, has been based on the conscious precipitation of crises in order to extract from the other states benefits that would otherwise not have accrued. Thus, for example, the French threatened several times to withdraw from the EEC unless the CAP was settled in such a way that French farmers would receive benefits and that the position of the French vis-à-vis the Germans would be enhanced.

The manipulation of crises in the EEC, like the advent of unanticipated ones, seems to represent phenomena that could only arise in a highly interdependent system of relationships —a system where controls over unanticipated events seem to have been rendered ineffective. This chapter is concerned with the diplomacy of crisis in the relations between France and the other member countries of the EEC. In Chapters 2 and 5, some aspects of crisis diplomacy with regard to the French negotiating position in the reform of the international monetary system were discussed. In those chapters it was argued that crisis diplomacy in the predominantly economic relations among the advanced industrialized states could be predicted from the level of interdependence, which had grown among them by the early 1960s. In this chapter, the reasons for this situation as well as the limits and potential of crisis diplomacy will be explored. The details of any of these crises will not be expounded since most of them have already been

---

the pressure of time limits agreed upon beforehand, or imposed under a threat by one member state. Its style is one of intergovernmental negotiation on ministerial level with the participation of several ministers from each member state. The Commission takes part in the sessions as institutionalized mediator with the task of suggesting compromises and choosing the appropriate moment for tabling a package deal . . . . To avoid the risk of provoking an immediate crisis, ministers must reach a package on concrete arrangements and/or restrict themselves to vague declarations of intent and the fixing of new time limits. In this way, one marathon session tends to lead to another, thus keeping the system in a state of permanent crisis" (*Beyond the European Community*, p. 59).

detailed in other scholarly writings. Rather, more theoretical questions will be examined:

1. Why have crises become characteristic features of diplomacy in the EEC? How do these crises differ from the occurrence of crisis phenomena in other settings and in earlier periods? Is the occurrence of crises likely to remain a significant feature of intra-European politics and, indeed, of international politics, in the future?

2. How does the diplomacy of crisis management in economic affairs reflect the growth of interdependence among the industrialized states of the West? How do the various forms of interdependence widen the scope of issues which have entered Western diplomacy at various levels?

3. In what ways did French economic statecraft in the 1960s represent deliberate efforts to provoke and to manipulate crises for political gain? What factors have made crisis manipulation an effective form of statecraft? What sorts of constraints can limit the effectiveness of crisis manipulation? To what extent can French efforts at such manipulation be generalized as a salient form of contemporary statecraft?

Before analyzing these questions and crisis diplomacy in the European Communities, it is necessary first to define crisis; then to review some of the implications for crisis diplomacy inherent in the theoretical analysis of international interdependence outlined in Chapter 2; and finally, to examine French crisis manipulation.

Crisis—The Definitional Question

"Crisis" ordinarily carries with it the meaning inherent in its etymological origin. It is a Greek derived medical term that describes a decisive and sudden change in the human organism, a change likely to lead to either recovery or death. Political crises are frequently understood in precisely this sense. In normal usage, a political crisis refers to a a set of circumstances involving the survival of a political system under attack, or it refers to an intensive political interaction carrying implications for the stability of some pattern of interactions. Thus, a balance of power system may be undergoing a crisis when one state in that system becomes excessively powerful or weak and when consequently, the stability of the balance becomes problematic. When crises are understood in this sense, the analysis of crisis behavior is likely to be cast in some form of systemic framework whether such an analysis is predominantly political or predominantly economic.[3]

Theories cast in a systemic framework usually assume that crises can be understood in terms of conditions that give rise to disequilibria or to instabilities. Etiological analysis of crises and the various stages under which they go before they are resolved is also normally implied.[4] Such analyses have largely, however, failed to yield fruitful generalizations. Many reasons might be specified to explain this failing including the relative lack of quantifiable data. It seems more likely that these efforts were bound to be weak because of fundamental conceptual problems inherent in equilibrium and etiological analyses rather than because of any dearth of data. Analyses such as these place a central emphasis on behavioral traits

[3] For a well-argued example of a systemic analysis of crises involving the use of force, see Oran R. Young, *The Politics of Force* (Princeton, N.J.: Princeton University Press, 1968). An economically derived conceptualization of the same genre can be found in Robert A. Mundell, "The Crisis Problem," in Robert A. Mundell and Alexander K. Swoboda, eds., *Monetary Problems of the International Economy* (Chicago: University of Chicago Press, 1969), pp. 343–49. An analysis of the literature on crises in international politics can be found in Charles F. Hermann, "International Crisis as a Situational Variable," in James N. Rosenau, ed., *International Politics and Foreign Policy*, rev. ed. (New York: The Free Press, 1969), pp. 409–21.

[4] For examples of this pattern of analysis, see Charles A. McClelland, "The Acute International Crisis," *World Politics*, xiv (1961): 182–204; and idem, "Access to Berlin: The Quantity and Variety of Events, 1948–1963," in J. David Singer, ed., *Quantitative International Politics: Insights and Evidence* (New York: The Free Press, 1968), pp. 159–86.

that are purported to be commensurable in terms of changes in one or more systemic variables requisite to a system's "pattern-maintenance."[5] Mundell has identified these as changes in "boundary conditions" or in "control mechanisms."[6] Analyses formulated in such terms, however, inevitably turn the attention of an observer away from what seems to be the central political focus of crises—namely, the confrontation of the diverse and mutually incompatible objectives of the states involved in a crisis situation. Through the emphasis on behavior traits such as the intensity or duration of crises or on equilibrium conditions, the conflicting patterns of goals that are involved tend to be ignored.

It seems that it is generally more fruitful to think about political crises in terms of conflictual goal-oriented behavior. Such a conceptualization focuses upon those state objectives of which the probability of achievement could be translated into such terms associated with economic models as opportunity costs and possibility functions; it would also be more amenable to deductive analysis;[7] it would more clearly point out the interdependent relations between different governments in crisis situations; and, it would, therefore, lead to an analysis of the sources of crises that can be found in the growing interdependence of states.

Crisis will be defined as the *sudden emergence (whether or not anticipated) of a situation requiring a policy choice by one or more states within a relatively short period of time between mutually incompatible but highly valued objectives.* In a simplified model, a crisis can then be understood as a situation in which two highly valued and originally mutually compatible objectives—for example, the status quo in Berlin and the avoidance of war in Europe—seem to become incom-

---

[5] For a more complete but more sympathetic exposition of systemic analyses of crises, see Hermann, "International Crisis," pp. 411–13.

[6] Mundell, "The Crisis Problem," p. 343.

[7] For a general and deductively oriented treatment of conflict of objectives in a political context, see Robert Axelrod, *Conflict of Interest: A Theory of Divergent Goals with Applications to Politics* (Chicago: Markham, 1970).

patible and thus significantly pressure one state to make a choice. Under new circumstances, regardless of how they come about, in order to maintain peace in Europe, concessions must be made to the Soviet Union over Berlin; or, in order to maintain the status quo in Berlin, the risk of war in Europe is substantially increased. It is precisely this type of choice between highly valued but incompatible objectives that has characterized the relations among the member countries in the European Communities.

I have elsewhere argued that the politicization of economic interactions in international affairs is a relatively recent phenomenon that arose as a result of a significant change in the governance of societies as they became highly industrialized,[8] of the increased scope of responsibilities assumed by governments for those regulatory and welfarist purposes outlined in Chapter 1, and of a transformation in the structure of the national economy in industrialized states. This change in economic structure meant that individual states inevitably would pursue goals that would in themselves be incompatible. As Hirsch has argued with respect to international financial crises, "to a real degree, the pre-1914 standard avoided external financial crises at the expense of internal financial and economic instability. Of the modern triangle of conflicting economic objectives, stable exchanges—stable prices—domestic growth at full employment, the pre-1914 system aimed only at the first."[9] Under modernized conditions, all three are goals as governments have assumed increased responsibility for maintaining and creating minimum standards of welfare for their citizens; and, as a result of an effective relative decrease in the number of policy instruments available to governments, these goals have become impossible to achieve simultaneously. Economic relations have also become more

[8] See Edward L. Morse, "Crisis Diplomacy, International Interdependence, and the Politics of International Economic Relations," *World Politics*, xxiv (Supplement, 1972): 123–50.

[9] Fred Hirsch, *Money International: Economics and Politics of World Money* (Garden City, N.Y.: Doubleday, 1969), p. 56.

politicized because of the depreciation of power politics in the nuclear age and because, at least in the EEC, the politics of force based on military power has been renounced. As was argued in Chapter 2, one result of this is that plays for power and position among states occur principally in economic relations.

Most importantly, the forms of interdependence assumed in the EEC have politicized economic affairs and have made crises the characteristic international politics. The central hypothesis in this chapter, therefore, is that *as the advanced industrialized societies in the EEC have become significantly interdependent with one another, the objectives of the member states have become increasingly incompatible; and, this incompatibility has served to produce crises among them.*

INTERNATIONAL INTERDEPENDENCE AND CRISIS DIPLOMACY

Previously it has been argued that the linkage between growing interdependence and the increased incidence of crises stems from the diminished number of political instruments available to governments for regulating their economic and political affairs. This situation seems to me to be the crucial linkage between the growth of interdependence and crisis diplomacy.

Interdependence was originally defined in general terms as the outcome of specified actions taken by two or more parties when such actions are mutually contingent. It was argued that the contingency between such actions need not be perceived by the parties involved, but that when it is perceived and manipulated by them it involves strategic behavior or strategic interdependence. The contingency can best be understood not as characteristic of the entire range of actions pursued by these parties, but rather in terms of specific issue-areas of interaction. For example, two states may be more interdependent with respect to their security than with respect

258

to their trade. Further the contingency of action results essentially from the inability of statesmen to pursue autonomously the whole range of objectives associated with their statecraft because of the decreased number of policy instruments relative to policy objectives. This last point is a paradox of the growth of several phenomena associated with modernization. As governments have increased the number and scope of their domestic and foreign policies, their autonomy and therefore their ability to achieve these additional policy goals has been reduced by the concomitant growth in international interdependence. But, as a result of the same phenomena, their ability to manipulate the outcome of events in other societies also increases as a result of the increased contingency of their interactions.[10]

In Chapter 2, two different types of crisis situations specific to the levels of interdependence in the relations among the advanced industrialized states were identified. First, the increased incidence of *crisis management* in the economic relations characteristic of these states was noted. As a result of increasing levels of interdependence, an increased incidence of crises can be expected because of the speed of events occurring in one country inevitably spreads to others. Thus, linkages that have been established in the financial and commercial operations of these states have resulted in the spread of inflation and of monetary crises from one society to another. Second, an increased incidence of *crisis manipulation* was

[10] This is what Leon Lindberg means when he argues that "there is no paradox between the progress of economic integration in the Community and sharpening political disagreement; indeed, the success of economic integration can be a cause of political disagreement. The member states are engaged in the enterprise for widely different reasons, and their actions have been supported or instigated by elites seeking their own particular goals. Therefore, conflicts would seem endemic as the results of joint activity come to be felt and as the pro-integrationist consensus shifts" ("Decision Making and Integration in the European Community," *International Organization*, XIX [1965]: 80).

noted. This represents attempts to exploit interdependence through strategic behavior so as to extract from other states a higher level of benefits than would otherwise be possible.

Crisis management and crisis manipulation have both been characteristic of diplomacy in the EEC. The development of these phenomena in the European context ought readily to have been predicted from the levels of interdependence that have been obtained there. The opening up of the borders of the member states of the Communities to trade, to the flow of capital, and to the migration of workers meant that each of the member states had to relinquish some of the controls that it had over its own national economies and for the achievement of its own domestic social goals before implementation of the Rome Treaty. At the same time, the consequent growth in the contingency of goal achievement in any one state upon actions pursued in the others has meant that the probability has also increased that at least one state would use its ties to the others for its own ends. Thus, the incidence of *ad hoc* marathon decision-making sessions between the Council of Ministers and the European Commission should not have been a surprising development. The sudden and unanticipated emergence of problems of crisis proportions, especially in the monetary realm, requiring joint action by the several member states had to be a central focus of political life in the Communities so long as no supranational government existed. Similarly, the various attempts at manipulation —by France in the elaboration of the agricultural policy or by Germany and others in the GATT negotiations—should not have been startling. Decision-making in the EEC had inevitably to be crisis diplomacy so long as a high level of interdependence existed and so long as the governments of the member states were unwilling to relinquish a significant amount of political control to a supranational agency.

Crisis diplomacy has been further complicated by the simultaneous growth of interdependencies in a wide spectrum of issue-areas. In the European Communities, for example, the development of a common market in goods and services is linked to common policies in agriculture and transportation, to wage differentials in each of the states, to capital flows and financial markets, to taxation policies, and to virtually every important economic goal pursued by the member states. Disruptions in one field inevitably affect the stability of others. In addition, each of the member countries is a sovereign political entity pursuing its own objectives in policies toward third countries. Here, too, policies differ. Germany's objectives in its policy toward either the United States or the Soviet Union with regard to détente in Europe, the level of U.S. troop deployments, nuclear proliferation, and the set of policies which pertain to security, differ from those of France or Italy. These high-policy objectives are also linked to the predominantly economic objectives that the various states pursue in the European Communities. Thus, the pursuit of foreign-policy goals outside of the EEC has implications for what occurs within it and vice versa. This is why one observer of crises in the EEC has argued that the occurrence of crises has resulted from the penetration into the economic decision-making of the EEC of "Grand Politics."[11] Finally, crisis diplomacy has been entangled by the merging of foreign and domestic spheres of interaction, so that domestic crises generate significant foreign policy implications just as international crises have come to have manifold implications in the domestic sphere.

The increasing propensity for political events to spread through these three realms—the strategic, international economic, and the domestic sphere—is crucial for both crisis management and crisis manipulation. On the one hand, crisis management is concerned with isolating crises that may occur in any one sphere so that their implications for the other spheres can be minimized. Crisis manipulation, on the other hand, seeks to take advantage of the increased range of diplomatic issues that has resulted from the growth of international

[11] Alting von Geusau, *Beyond the European Community*, pp. 40ff.

interdependence. The importance of crisis manipulation, therefore, may be found in the growth of the range of issues, which have entered diplomacy at different levels since World War II, and in the kinds of different situations that are evoked in interdependent relationships. The range of manipulable issues may be reviewed as follows:[12]

1. An international crisis may be provoked by a government for predominantly domestic purposes, such as the crises in the European Communities in 1961 and 1964, which resulted in marathon negotiating sessions over the elaboration of the CAP. To be sure, the French government was pursuing foreign policy goals while pressuring the other governments in the EEC to negotiate before reaching deadlines. At the same time, however, the outcome of the negotiations was thought to be a significant boon to the agricultural sector of the French economy.

2. A government may provoke an international crisis primarily for external or foreign-policy purposes. This is the sort of crisis that the French government tried to manipulate in the international monetary sphere after 1965 by forcing the American government to come to terms with France in reforming the international monetary system. Such a reform was designed to enhance French autonomy and influence in this and other foreign-policy realms.

3. A crisis in the sphere of high policy may be provoked predominantly for purposes of high policy. This is the traditional sort of crisis manipulation found in international politics and is essentially a "manipulation of risk," to borrow Schelling's term. For example, "the Cuban crisis [October 1962] was a contest in risk taking, involving steps that would have made no sense if they led predictably and ineluctably to a major war, yet would also have made no sense if they were

[12] For an insightful discussion of the increased range of issues which have entered diplomacy, see Harold Sprout and Margaret Sprout, *Toward a Politics of the Planet Earth* (New York: Van Nostrand, 1971), pp. 401–26.

completely without danger."[13] Such crises are infrequent in international affairs in the nuclear age and were not provoked in Gaullist statecraft.

4. A high-policy crisis may be provoked by a government so that it may achieve predominantly low-policy goals. The politics of imperialism has frequently involved such crises when a great power has provoked a military confrontation with a small or weak power in order to achieve economic advantages. The Japanese take over a Manchukuo and the fostering of a Co-Prosperity sphere in East Asia represents high-policy action taken for low-policy purposes. This sort of crisis has also been relatively infrequent in the nuclear age for reasons specified in Chapter 1.

5. A crisis in a low-policy realm may be provoked by a government principally for high-policy purposes. This is one of the most interesting of all crisis phenomena and is particularly modern since it could occur only after economic interdependencies became significant. This is the principal aspect of the crisis of 1965 when the French boycotted the EEC ostensibly on the issue of financial arrangements for the CAP. The basic motivations of de Gaulle in that crisis involved high political issues including the structure of political organization in Western Europe and European policies toward the United States and Russia.

6. Finally, a low-policy crisis situation may be manipulated for low political, or economic reasons, as has already been discussed in example two above.

As statesmen have become aware of the increasing range of issues that have entered diplomacy at different levels, they have also become cognizant of the different sorts of interdependence, the so-called opportunities of interdependence, and the political problems associated with the political costs inherent in the growth of interdependence. Such problems demonstrate the ways in which each level of interdependence has

[13] Thomas C. Schelling, *Arms and Influence* (New Haven: Yale University Press, 1966), p. 96.

263

resulted in a more general political problem of controlling interdependence effects. Both sorts of problems are illustrated by French statecraft in the EEC in the 1960s and, especially, the subsequent French boycott of the EEC from July 1965 to February 1966.

THE OPPORTUNITIES OF INTERDEPENDENCE: FRANCE AND THE POLITICS OF CRISIS MANIPULATION

The tactical use of crises for political ends inevitably involves the forcing of a choice between incompatible and contradictory policy objectives upon others. This happens because the creation of a crisis changes the rules of a bargaining situation. It does so by making imminent a new possibility—that of a termination of a highly valued system of relationships. Thus, when the French threatened to leave the Common Market unless their goals were reached, they presented their partners the choice: accommodation or the breakdown of the EEC. Since the others were not willing either to have the system break down or to be viewed as responsible for such a rupture, they usually made efforts to accommodate. The tactical use of crises, therefore, involves a gradual change from a normal bargaining situation, a restriction of choice for the interlocutors of the crisis manipulator so that they no longer have the freedom to pursue their own objectives, and, a wager by the party inducing the crisis that the other participants believe that it is not bluffing.

As was argued earlier, crisis manipulation became significant in the EEC because of the interrelatedness of the political and economic issues involved as actions pursued on any one level became contingent upon actions pursued elsewhere. This interconnection of issues was readily apparent in the Common Market crisis from July 1965 to February 1966 begun by the French boycott of the EEC. The interrelatedness of the issues involved in that crisis together with the objectives pursued by the member states and the opportunities and limits of the French position will serve as specific examples of the above general postulates.

The French boycott during 1965 and 1966 started over a technical issue concerning the arrangements for financing the EEC's common agricultural fund, especially those provided by agreements in 1962 and 1964 to establish rules before June 30, 1965 for distributing money collected by the fund. This technical issue, which most observers of the Common Market agree could have been settled without a crisis,[14] provided the basis for a dispute over a set of disparate but parallel economic and political issues.

Most obviously a boycott of the EEC meant an attack on the viability of its political institutions since the EEC was prevented from making any significant political decisions for the duration of the crisis. In fact, the most direct target of the crisis was the structure of the EEC decision-making bodies and, particularly, the role of the Commission. In a press conference of September 9, 1965, de Gaulle clearly demonstrated that a crisis was inevitable so long as the logic of the integration process in Europe had meant a progressive increase in the decision-making domain of the European Commission. If de Gaulle's onslaught against the EEC was a defense of the sovereignty of the state, such an attack had to come eventually, since autonomy was progressively eroded by the growth of interdependence, and since the growth of the institutions of the Community was itself largely a response to French needs that had been articulated in the CAP. What de Gaulle wanted, in short, was both the CAP and a preservation of French autonomy in its own foreign and domestic policies. By mid-1965, however, that had become impossible and, forced with a choice, de Gaulle opted for the latter.

The French boycott had first appeared as a response to the tripartite proposal made by the European Commission

[14] France could have obtained satisfaction on the financing of the agricultural fund without sacrificing its position on the institutional framework of decision-making in the EEC.

concerning both the financing of agriculture and an increase in the powers of the EEC institutions. If those proposals had presented realistic options in March 1965, they would have changed radically the political structure of the EEC by giving the Commission its own resources and by bolstering the prestige and responsibilities of the European Parliament. But by late June 1965 no one thought seriously that these proposals were realistic and even the members of the Commission who had formulated them knew that a viable compromise could have been worked out without introducing a revolutionary transformation in the supranational institutions.[15] What de Gaulle had wanted, in part, was a pledge that no future Commission would make such a daring challenge to national autonomy.

The French boycott, therefore, represented a crisis over the direction in which the institutions of the EEC would evolve, and, at this primary level, the debate was posed in stark terms between a Europe governed by the member states and a Europe governed by the technocrats in Brussels. However much this may have been a false distinction imposed by de Gaulle for his own ends, the crisis affected other issues that had become linked to the technical issue over which the boycott ensued.

Another area affected by the French boycott in 1965 reflected the link between issues of predominantly low politics and those of high politics since de Gaulle felt that the development of a European framework for decision-making in that realm was at stake.

In discussing the meaning of the crisis, both Newhouse and Camps place emphasis on the high political stakes that de Gaulle felt were involved. For both of them, the crisis represented the interjection of fundamental strategic goals into EEC politics by French statecraft. Newhouse has argued as follows: "Reducing the scope of the Common Market was a project that de Gaulle had contemplated for years. As early

[15] See John Newhouse, *Collision in Brussels* (New York: W. W. Norton, 1967), p. 77.

as 1960, he had sent down word through his government that severe limits should be put on the Commissions of the three European Communities . . ."[16] He felt that conditions were opportune for doing so in 1965 because of the context of the general political relations between France and the other European countries especially, because of the conjunction of events including the proposals of the European Commission for reforming the EEC, the elaboration of the CAP, the foundering of Franco-German relations over foreign-policy issues; and de Gaulle's desire to broadly implement his policy of autonomy.

By the time the Commission made its sweeping proposals to the governments of the six member countries of the EEC, de Gaulle had realized that his plans for building a political coalition in Europe around the Franco-German friendship treaty could not be realized, since his plans had required an alignment of French and German foreign-policy objectives in Europe and toward both the Soviet Union and the United States. He had, in fact, planned to exchange a French nuclear guarantee to Germany for German economic support, both direct and indirect (via the Common Agricultural Fund) for harnessing France's nuclear establishment.[17] Although the MLF episode ended by December 1964, it not only resulted in de Gaulle's distrust of Erhard but also proved that at no time in the foreseeable future would the German government wish to dissociate itself from the American security guarantee as would have been required by the Gaullist notion of a political Europe. Thus, de Gaulle could not receive the quid pro quo from Germany and France had to pursue an autonomous course that might be risked by its own commitment to a fully developed common agricultural arrangement.

At the same time in early 1965, the second phase of Gaul-

[16] John Newhouse, *De Gaulle and the Anglo-Saxons* (New York: Viking, 1970), p. 279.

[17] Newhouse is more explicit on this point than is Camps, although both agree in their analyses that high strategy reasons lay behind the crisis.

list foreign policy, which was explicitly based on efforts at maintaining an autonomous position in practically all spheres, unfolded. Throughout 1965 de Gaulle hinted at a future crisis in NATO and launched an explicitly anti-American campaign on the reform of the international monetary system, beginning what Newhouse has called "the blossoming *rapprochement* with Moscow." That effort toward the East

> gave de Gaulle still greater freedom of movement; the role of an endlessly moving figure in the eternal ballet was now his. What did it matter if the performance merely pointed up the central theme without advancing it? Theater for theater's sake was the means of bringing his unruly and politically wayward people face to face with the splendor of their heritage. Tactically, the other performers must be alternately cajoled and menaced.[18]

Therefore, the low politics of economic diplomacy in the EEC were tied directly to de Gaulle's notions of both the future political structure of Europe and the tactics necessary for the diplomatic-strategic autonomy of the French state.

The economic negotiations involved in the formulation of the CAP were also directly tied to trade negotiations concurrently being pursued in the GATT in Geneva. The EEC had five years to negotiate the Kennedy Round before the 1962 U.S. Trade Expansion Act expired. Although a series of delays occurred over technical issues, serious ones were caused by the need of the Europeans to agree to a common agricultural policy before their negotiating position in the GATT could be clarified. The United States and other exporters of agricultural products wanted negotiations on industrial products to parallel those on agriculture. However, the French refused to negotiate a common trade policy until the CAP was fully worked out.[19] Specifically, the negotiating parties were

---

[18] Newhouse, *De Gaulle and the Anglo-Saxons*, p. 278.

[19] The complicated interlinking of positions in the GATT and the EEC have been spelled out in a series of books that have recently been published on the politics of trade negotiations in the 1960s. See, in

supposed to submit their main agricultural offers for negotiation on September 16, 1965. The French boycott meant that the EEC list could not be submitted until late summer in 1966, so that no serious trade negotiations could take place in the GATT until January 1967, six months before the Trade Expansion Act expired. When these negotiations did take place, they inevitably occurred in the atmosphere of marathon crisis similar to the one involved in the elaboration of the CAP.[20]

As a result of the link between the adoption of the CAP in the EEC and the GATT negotiations, politics in the EEC were dominated by these two substantive issues in the two years before the French boycott, especially because both issues, if resolved, would determine for the future, ties between France and Germany. As Coombes argued in his study of EEC decision-making processes,

the French (like the Commission) saw the Kennedy Round as an incentive to the Germans to agree to a common agricultural policy, which would contain a lower Community price for cereals than that which then prevailed in Germany itself and which would necessitate a substantial German cash contribution towards the cost of supporting European agriculture. Actually, it was felt that the French saw the adoption of such a policy as their sole remaining interest in the Community. In so far as this was true, the Kennedy Round was for them essentially a means to an end.[21]

particular, David Coombes, *Politics and Bureaucracy in the European Community; A Portrait of the Commission of the EEC* (London: George Allen and Unwin, 1970), pp. 166–210; Ernest H. Preeg, *Traders and Diplomats* (Washington, D.C.: The Brookings Institution, 1970), pp. 36–38; and John W. Evans, *The Kennedy Round in American Trade Policy; The Twilight of the GATT?* (Cambridge, Mass.: Harvard University Press, 1971), pp. 215–17.

[20] For a description of crisis diplomacy in the GATT and an elaboration of these points, see Preeg, *Traders and Diplomats*, pp. 178–95.

[21] Coombes, *Politics and Bureaucracy in the European Community*. p. 186.

In addition, because the GATT negotiations were directly linked to intra-EEC politics and were stalled by the French boycott, the French were particularly anxious to achieve certain goals in the Kennedy Round. They wanted to protect their own agricultural producers, especially wheat growers, within the EEC, and did not wish to allow the United States to advance in both agricultural and industrial sectors. But to prevent these gains, they had to martial the support of the five other partners in forming a common negotiating front in the GATT. They were able to do this only after they adopted a conciliatory mood with the termination of the boycott in the spring of 1966. The consequent success of the Six in preventing the United States from gaining advantage in the agricultural and industrial sectors was in no small measure a result of the French tactic; for, by 1967, the American negotiators were eager to come to an agreement in the GATT negotiations even without achieving the success they had once hoped for in agricultural goods.

The crisis in 1965 and 1966 linked foreign and domestic policies in France as well as in the other EEC member states. The positions taken by the various governments before or during the crisis were in an important way determined by domestic interests. In France, de Gaulle's move to precipitate the crisis was clearly motivated predominantly by strategic interests. As Newhouse has argued, de Gaulle probably timed the crisis partly because he felt that in June 1965 domestic pressures did not restrict his policy. Newhouse maintains that

"very possibly, he [de Gaulle] decided finally to have his showdown with the Community on or shortly after June 18. It was on this day that the effort of France's Gaston Defferre to put together a center-left political federation based mainly on the MRP and Socialist parties collapsed, thus apparently eliminating the only possibility of serious political opposition to de Gaulle in the December elections."[22]

[22] Newhouse, *Collision in Brussels*, p. 121.

The unanticipated change of opinion among French peasants and farmers against the government's posture during the crisis, and the mobilization of anti-Gaullist support by the two opposition candidates in the elections of December 1965 limited de Gaulle's mobility.[23] In fact, the slight victory won by de Gaulle after his humiliating inability to achieve a majority on the first ballot has been seen by many commentators as a major reason for which de Gaulle decided to return to serious negotiations early in 1966.

The positions of the other five were similarly, if less dramatically, linked to domestic political issues during the crises.[24] Before the crises broke out, the German government had wanted French support in the GATT negotiations in return for the financial price it was paying on the CAP. This was because the Christian Democratic government was facing elections in September 1965 and needed to assure important domestic interest groups that they would benefit from one, if not both, sets of negotiations. The Italian government wanted to modify the financial arrangements that had been agreed to in 1962 because Italy had, in the intervening years, become a net agricultural importer rather than exporter and found the short-term costs of the CAP too high.

The attempt to manipulate a crisis in the EEC in the last half of 1965 illustrates, then, the manifold ways in which actions in both domestic and international spheres have become linked through the web of international interdependencies. In the countries of Western Europe the foreign-policy positions of each state with respect to the CAP were linked to important domestic interest groups, and the CAP itself was a requirement for the Six if they wished to form a common external policy for a common negotiating position in the

[23] For details, see Hanns Peter Muth, *French Agriculture and the Political Integration of Western Europe* (Leiden: A. W. Sijthoff, 1970), pp. 214–48.

[24] The national positions on the financial arrangements for CAP are detailed in Hélène Delorme, "L'Adoption du prix unique des céréales," in *La Décision*, ed. Gerber and Pepy, pp. 269–96.

GATT. Through the interjection of high-policy goals, de Gaulle was able to take advantage of the contingency of actions which had developed among these different spheres.

De Gaulle's attempt at crisis manipulation, like his international monetary position, represented an insight into international developments that statesmen in neighboring countries were unwilling or unable to make. At the same time, however, de Gaulle's efforts at crisis manipulation depended upon a persistent inability of the Five to formulate a common negotiating position. In fact, he reasonably believed that any one of them would be willing to come to separate terms with him, particularly Germany since its position on the structure of the EEC, after all, was basically as antiintegrationist as was France's. De Gaulle's sweeping political attack on the Five and the Commission in his news conference of September 9, however, together with the other attacks made in October by Couve de Murville before the National Assembly united the Five under German leadership. In fact the continued unity of the Five, which demonstrated their desire to prevent the EEC from breaking up or changing its structure in accordance with French will, demonstrated, as Camps argued, that "the French no longer had the power to paralyze the Community by remaining outside. The period of stalemate was drawing to a close and signs were multiplying that if they continued to boycott the Brussels meetings the Five would shortly begin taking decisions on their own."[25] The French would, de Gaulle realized, be in danger of losing more under those circumstances than they would gain by continuing the boycott. At stake were not only the future of the CAP and the GATT negotiating position but also the possibility that in France's absence the other members of the EEC would renew membership negotiations with Britain—a prospect that would have at the time even more diminished the chances for de Gaulle to obtain the kind of political organization he sought in Europe.

[25] Miriam Camps, *European Unification in the Sixties* (New York: McGraw-Hill, 1966), p. 122.

Crisis manipulation, then, seems to be an affair with short-term benefits that can work only when some of the manipulated parties can reap some gains. This happened when France precipitated crises leading to marathon negotiating sessions on the structure of the CAP in 1962, 1963, and 1964. In each of those crises, the main target of the French attack was German unwillingness to pay the bulk of the common effort, and the French received the support of some of the other member countries as well as of the Commission who saw in the elaboration of the CAP an augmentation of their political role in Europe. In the 1965 crisis, the French, although they were unable to divide the Five, and were without the Commission's support, could not honor their threat to leave the EEC since the system of relations had grown so interdependent that it would have been too costly to do so.

Even with the failure of crisis manipulation in 1965, the French tactical use of crises does demonstrate that they can be potentially useful. The French were by and large successful crisis manipulators in the short run for several reasons. First, Gaullist foreign policy more than that of any of the other Six or of the United States was relatively insulated from domestic pressures, given the constitutional framework of the Fifth Republic and the reserved power of the President. The domestic autonomy until the spring of 1968 enabled de Gaulle to implement a rational strategy relatively free of domestic pressures for so-called consummatory external purposes. Second, the French had the support of the EEC Commission in most of the crises which they had tried to induce. The EEC Commission had, after all, a stake in the development of a common agricultural policy which was at least equal to that of France. Third, interdependent relationships usually enable one state to have an incentive to manipulate crises in order to obtain increased benefits. Since there inevitably are trade-offs in these relationships, the leadership of any one state, however large or small, can always threaten "agonizing reappraisals" of policy that are designed to precipitate some change while threatening to destroy some common activity. Such a policy, however, cannot be attempted too frequently both because of domestic reactions[26] (for example, in the spring of 1968 workers joined in a student-led protest in order to extract benefits withheld by the government so that it could spend more on defense and maintain a policy of independence) and because of the potential reactions of other international participants.[27]

The Costs of Interdependence and Prudential Statecraft

The French efforts at crisis manipulation in the EEC or in the international monetary system illustrate both the opportunities available for crisis manipulation and the heavy costs they carry as a result of the increased vulnerability that accompanies interstate interdependence. This increased vulnerability was brought home to the French when their government was forced to devalue the franc in 1969. For, just as the common negotiating position of the Six in the Kennedy Round hinged upon the elaboration of a common agricultural policy, the CAP itself depended upon the maintenance of fixed exchange rates among the Common Market partners. The currency crises, which had been developing over a year-long period, and the French devaluation in August 1969 forced the

[26] The role of domestic factors in crises cannot presently be precisely determined. Governments can manipulate domestic opinion to a degree, especially in the short run, but the extent of manipulability is dependent upon many factors, including the political importance of the issues involved. Moreover, once a type of interdependence is identified between some domestic and external factors, a government may provoke an institutional crisis in order to achieve predominantly domestic ends. This is often the case, for example, when a government's legitimacy is at stake.

[27] A fourth reason, independent of the French case, involves the bargaining position of small or weak parties over larger or stronger parties in situations where the weaker party may in fact blackmail the stronger one by making extravagant demands, the position of the stronger party is usually devalued.

entire CAP to be suspended temporarily[28] because the complicated price mechanisms involved in targeting prices in the CAP were linked to a unit of account then equal to the dollar. The common policy assumed the existence of the equivalent of fixed exchange rates or a common currency among the Six. Once the franc was devalued, the fixed base upon which the agricultural policy was built was shattered. The devaluation and the CAP arrangements were incompatible, thereby requiring a renegotiation of the policy, the creation of which had been a central focus of French diplomacy the previous decade.

The incidence of crises in the political and economic affairs of the Western industrialized states has reflected the increased scope and significance of international interdependencies. Although the result of a series of simultaneously converging factors, interdependencies especially stemmed from two sets of factors: (1) the increased sensitivity to external phenomena in societies that have become highly industrialized and at the same time have witnessed a radical centralization in their own internal organization; and (2) the conscious efforts on the part of decision-makers, especially in the industrialized states, to lower the barriers to international interchanges.

These interdependencies, if they have generally been accompanied by both benefits and costs to the citizens and governments of the societies involved, have facilitated an increased awareness on the part of individuals in these societies of peoples and habits of other cultures and societies, and have brought new opportunities for satisfying material wants themselves, a part of the expectations of individuals in all societies affected by the processes of modernization, have also brought new problems—problems associated not only with the regulation of interdependencies and the crises associated with them but also with the loss of political autonomy. For, interdepend-

[28] The same situation existed in the currency crisis of 1971.

ence has decreased the freedom of governments to act to achieve their own domestic social goals or international goals, or even to regulate their interdependent relationships.

Interdependent relationships in economic affairs have been politicized not only for reasons already specified but also because they present to governments possibilities for manipulation that are less costly than manipulation of military and security matters. Unlike security affairs where the stakes have been traditionally perceived as higher than those in economic affairs, governments have begun to use their newly perceived leverage over other societies to create a variety of effects, including some aimed directly at their own societies.

Crises have occurred in international economic relationships in part as a result of these new opportunities for political pay-offs, but they would have occurred even had there been no de Gaulle on the scene to see the possibilities inherent in them, because in the contemporary international system, new forms of interdependence have arisen without the appropriate mechanisms needed to control them. Crises have arisen because national goals tend to conflict, especially as international interdependence has increased the intercourse among societies. So long as there is no integrated supranational government, transnational or interdependent interactions serve as breakdowns of control over the foreign activities of citizens by governments. As transnational interactions increase, the possibilities of affecting decision-making in a purely national setting become less likely. And, so long as governments will not relinquish their sovereign rights to autonomy, control remains even more difficult.

Increased control through new institutional arrangements is largely a function of knowledge of interdependence and its various effects. This sort of knowledge is not yet at hand so that the practical effects of theories of interdependence are now quite limited. Officials responsible for formulating and implementing governmental policies cannot, of course, postpone their actions until new knowledge of interdependence is available. They must act to meet crises and to head off potential disruptions caused by international interdependence, but they need not face situations of uncertainty in a complete theoretical void.

Some of the actions that governments might consider undertaking in order to curtail the destabilizing effects of interdependence might be deduced from theoretical assumptions such as those outlined above. The central focus of those assumptions pertained to the relationship between policy objectives or targets, and policy instruments needed to attain them. Interdependence, it was suggested, results in a significant loss of policy instruments relative to policy targets at a time when the number and types of policy objectives have substantially increased. Two major types of choices are then available and the major political decisions to be made involve the appropriate mix of the two. On the one hand, new efforts can be made, such as the creation of SDRs in the International Monetary Fund in the 1960s, or the implementation of more common policies (e.g., in monetary affairs) in the EEC, in order to marshal new policy instruments for the attainment of existing objectives. Since these new tools are likely to result from multinational diplomacy and to involve some loss of national autonomy, they ought to be created from a perspective that takes into account their long-term benefits and costs. On the other hand, a new prudential statecraft is sought to establish priorities among existing objectives so that governmental control at the national level can be reasserted. This may involve the reimposition of barriers to international interchange as governments adjust to the quick rate at which such barriers have been removed in recent years (e.g., quotas imposed on particular items in order to protect domestic industry or import controls along the lines of those imposed by the British in the 1960s in order to head off the collapse of sterling).

Since policy regulation of this sort must be directed toward a wide range of issues related to both international and domestic affairs, and to both economic and security matters, success will depend upon the coordination of various kinds of efforts *within* governments. From the theoretical perspective discussed above, it can be deduced that planning efforts are requisite to the reassertion of central national political control over the destiny of the industrialized societies. Their exact nature will depend upon issues confronting governments since our ability to theorize is not yet well enough advanced to isolate the relationships among particular variables. To date, theory has advanced only far enough to offer a new *perspective* on international affairs. It is from that perspective that crisis diplomacy seems to be most satisfactorily explained. Likewise from the perspective of international interdependence certain policy decisions can be made, depending on the values of the decision-makers in office, to maintain the status quo, to take steps toward increased international integration with greater stability, greater wealth, and less national control, or to reassert autonomy and to incur the losses, in national wealth, which such a move might entail.

SEVEN

DOMESTIC EXIGENCIES AND
INTERNATIONAL CONSTRAINTS

Planification Française and European Integration

The consequences of growing international interdependence have been no less dramatic on domestic politics than they have been on international relations. While governments in modernized societies have assumed an increasing array of responsibilities in providing social services, ordering economic growth, redistributing wealth, and fostering welfare, their abilities to meet these new goals have become increasingly a function of activities in international society. As was postulated in Chapters 1 and 2, increases in international systemic interdependence have broken down the distinctions between foreign and domestic policies by increasing the sensitivity of domestic affairs to external events and by decreasing the number of policy instruments available for controlling both kinds of policies. As a result, interdependence has limited autonomy in both external and internal affairs.

The antithesis between national domestic objectives and international constraints was particularly striking in France where the institutionalization of national planning after World War II had been one of the highlights of recent history. Such a national programme appeared to offer an effective set of instruments for directing a wide spectrum of general social and economic objectives, was seen as an advantage of modernization and centralization in France, and systematized all governmental domestic activities, both in the long and short run. Through the instruments of planning the government could balance development in those areas of France most peripheral to the capital with that of the new industrialized regions in order to ensure steady and equal growth.

Open-ended and not "imperative" national planning had also been praised as demonstrating a unique form of national decision-making that combined the benefits of both capitalism and communism without the social and political costs of either. The plan thus complemented the nationalism and autonomy of de Gaulle's foreign policy, and appeared to be the capstone of modern French democracy, giving the government the means of reaching national objectives without undue incursions upon domestic freedom.

When planning had reached its maturity in the late 1950s and early 1960s, the EEC was established. This deliberate creation of international interdependence in a restrictive area had known consequences for domestic planning. As the small group of French planners foresaw, the breakdown of barriers to trade among member states meant that planning would have to be projected in some form onto the European plane or it would quickly wither as an effective domestic-policy measure. This first reaction of French planners should have been entirely predictable, and in addition to economic goals, there were other ideological orientations that led them to foster European planning. Educated into what was earlier called the baroque rationalist tradition, the so-called technocratic frame of mind, they were oriented to feeling that the international environment—in this case the EEC—could be cast into a French mold. French planning could be rescued by creating a European plan with which it would be compatible.

The French technocratic plan for Europe that was domestically beneficial for France faced three obstacles between 1962 and 1964. First, planning was not compatible with the desires of the other members of the EEC and was especially anathema to the Germans, who only slowly grew to accept a diluted *programmation* for Europe. Second, even if *planification*, as it was developed in France, had been accepted, the Brussels bureaucracy lacked the staff, financial credits, and other instruments needed to implement it. Third, the creation of a European plan conflicted directly with de Gaulle's intentions.

For de Gaulle integrationist goals were anathema. He would not tolerate any *apatrides* as supranational functionaries. Indeed, de Gaulle refused to see what was new about the changed European context—that domestic and foreign activities were becoming intermeshed and that interdependence existed at levels which were high enough to prevent autonomous action either at home or abroad. What he did see— colored by his political vision of the permanence of the nation-state and of independence for national leadership from domestic affairs—was the enormous political potential of a social and economic plan. For de Gaulle the plan thus came to represent decision-making structures by which France could be modernized in order to increase autonomy and independence in foreign affairs. If the plan could equip France with large-scale modern industries in nuclear energy, computers, aircraft, etc., he felt that the material base of French independence from America, and indeed of French neutralism, could be secured.[1]

Gaullist policy with respect to the plan and the general relationship between foreign and domestic affairs thus suffered from serious delusions. It was based on the classical style of monarchist foreign policy—the separation of foreign and domestic affairs, the primacy of foreign policy, and the efficacy of control over domestic society. The plan, he thought, could be implemented domestically because domestic and foreign affairs were unrelated; and it could also serve primarily external ends. On both counts, he was proved wrong—for reasons which have to do both with growing interdependence among the European states and with changes in domestic French decision-making. Both sets of conditions merged in the mid-1960s when the Fifth Plan was being formulated and implemented. Although these factors are closely interwoven, they are easily separable for analysis, and a study of the Fifth

[1] An additional motivation of de Gaulle in this respect was the need to prepare French industry for full competition from Germany with the implementation of a customs union in Europe after July 1968.

Plan is designed to explain both domestic and foreign affairs.

Planning in France has been both a political method for decision-making in social and economic affairs and a set of instruments for implementing governmental objectives across a broad front. Economic planning is usually thought of as a development or offshoot of modernization, a product of the Age of Collectivism with political implications for parliamentary democracy. Like other products of collectivism, it is said to erode parliamentary decision-making and to represent one set of conditions that has served to increase the powers of administrations over those of representative institutions. Although this situation usually exists in countries where the theory of parliamentary democracy developed in the age of *laissez-faire* economics, France has a history of government control of the economy that may be traced to Colbert.[2] In the economic realm, then, decision-making in France as a process of direct confrontation between the state's administrative apparatus and organized interest groups antedates collectivism, while it emerged with such phenomena as welfarism and anti-cartel policies elsewhere.

The direct confrontation between state and interest groups arose early in France not only because of the long established administrative tradition but also because of the peculiar French cultural trait of the baroque-rationalist heritage. Rather than accept the chaos that might result from the free interplay of economic forces, French statesmen have long believed that the human factor must be introduced to orient economic trends, be it for purposes of domestic or foreign policy. Thus, economic planning is the most startling example of the apotheosis of rationalism in France and is an offshoot of *mercantilisme à la français*. Rather than refer to planning in purely economic terms, former Planning Commissioner Pierre Massé, for example, speaks of it in the most baroque lan-

---

[2] See the two important studies by John U. Nef, *Industry and Government in France and England, 1540–1640* (Ithaca, N.Y.: Cornell University Press, 1964); idem, *The Conquest of the Material World* (Chicago: University of Chicago Press, 1964).

guage as "the interpretation of human activity as a calculated adventure, as a struggle between fate and 'anti-fate.' "[3]

PLANNING AS A FORM OF DIRECT CONFRONTATION

When economic planning was introduced in France in 1946, it lay entirely within the province of the administration and beyond the purview of Parliament. Its purposes were entirely domestic and involved the rebuilding of the French economy to the level of 1929 by aiding the basic industries in their postwar recovery. Although armed with fiscal and monetary inducements to industry, the newly created planning commission, the Commissariat Général au Plan (CGP) faced several hurdles before it could draw up a plan. First, given the traditional atmosphere of secrecy with which businesses operated, not least of all because they did not wish the government to know their real incomes for tax purposes, no national accounting or statistical collecting system existed. Second, given the postwar reaction to the German war machine, there was a general unwillingness to give too much economic power to the state.

In the face of these and other obstacles, the first Planning Commissioner, Jean Monnet, coined the phrase *économie concertée* and established the atmosphere in which planning later operated. The plan was announced as a great endeavor of the whole society for "the concerting of all economic and social forces of the nation."[4] It was the idea of Monnet and the other members of the CGP that if the plan were a joint effort of all the economic interest groups and representatives of the state, information could be provided for the state to compensate for the lack of an agency gathering statistics. Moreover, they also felt that if the various economic groups could join together to establish targets for the plan, they

[3] Pierre Massé, *Le Plan ou l'anti-hasard* (Paris: Editions Gallimard, 1965), p. 8.

[4] Bernard Cazes, *La Planification en France et le IVe plan* (Paris: Editions de l'épargne, 1962), p. 62.

283

would be much more likely to follow their own fixed goals. A direct confrontation therefore occurred between representatives of the state and of economic interest groups, and was easily popularized because in many respects it institutionalized a long-standing informal feud between the groups.

From Monnet's concept a mythology arose about planning in France. French planning became known as *indicatif* rather than *impératif* since combined economic groups pooled information forecasting productivity, wages, and income that the government would then utilize to orient its own fiscal and monetary policies for the duration of the planning period. By the time Massé was directing the preparation of the Fifth Plan in 1965, the idea of an *économie concertée* had become widely accepted as a national effort that was democratic in spirit and function because it was formulated by the cooperation of all of the socioeconomic groups of the country together with the government. It was, moreover, promoted by businessmen and civil servants as the only democratic means of formulating a technical economic plan because Parliament could not provide the proper forum for the confrontation of socioeconomic interests.

Monnet also created an institutional framework in which a direct confrontation between the various interest groups and civil servants could take place, namely, the Modernization Committees. These committees were appointed in the initial stages of the plans and were composed of thirty to fifty members selected by the government on the basis of a recommendation of the planning commissioner from three major socioeconomic groups: heads of business corporations and leaders of management organizations; representatives of the major trade union confederations; and civil servants, government officials, and experts representing the various ministries involved in the formulation or implementation of the plan. In addition, a few representatives of other groups, agricultural and independent experts, were included.

Initially, the Modernization Committees drew up preliminary forecast sketches providing the government with information from which plans could be formulated. Later, they met again to study critically the possibilities of implementing the orientations and targets which had been correlated by the CGP and Cabinet. The Modernization Committees were functionally of two types. The majority were vertical in that they studied various sectors of the economy such as steel, coal, transportation. Others were horizontal and cut across all production sectors in such areas as manpower and research. It was within the Modernization Committees that the *concertation* occurred in the form of a "constant exchange of information in order to achieve an harmonious action."[5] The Modernization Committees were thus the most essential element in the whole French planning mechanism. They not only provided information upon which plans could be formulated but also constituted the political structures by which all socioeconomic groups planned the economic activity for the next four- or five-year period.

If the idea of an *économie concertée* was implemented by the Modernization Committees, it remained a hortatory and normative concept, which could never be fully implemented, but which would provide the mystique in which the prestige of planning could grow. The failure of all socioeconomic groups to cooperate had long been recognized by the left-wing critics of the plan who wished to replace the administrative structure of planning with a decision-making process in either Parliament or the Conseil Economique et Social (CES).[6] However, for a variety of factors discussed below, including, above all, the unprecedented growth of the French economy in the 1950s, the mythology surrounding French planning continued to grow and to obscure, on the one hand, the real confrontation that took place, and on the other hand, the part that planning played in economic growth.

Planning never resulted from a *concertation* of all socio-

[5] P. Leroy-Jay, "Coordinating the Stimulating French Industry Planning," *Conference Board Record*, 1 (1964): 60–63.

[6] See, for example, Pierre Mendès-France, *La République moderne* (Paris: Gallimard, 1965), pp. 155ff.

economic groups. The common interest of industrial and ministerial representatives on the Modernization Committees overshadowed the union representatives' role. Ideological and political cleavages among union leaders further hampered their efficiency and usefulness in any of the various planning groups. Perroux found, for example, that "however great the formal participation of the world of labor may be in working out, in controlling and in implementing the Plan, the 'democratization' of the Plan is hindered by a social structure and by mental habits which are wholly unfavorable to it."[7] Businessmen tended to cooperate with the civil servants in formulating production targets because they were able to avoid risks and to ensure their investment decisions.[8] The civil servants, for their part, cooperated with businessmen because they wanted information on production and investment which only business could provide, and because they wished to increase productivity to expand the economy so that social goals could be obtained.

Moreover, the mystification, interjected into the technical problem of planning, obscured the elaboration and implementation of a plan requiring separate discussions among various interest groups. Monnet's idea was that if businessmen, union leaders, and civil servants cooperated in the formulation of a plan, compliance of all parties would be facilitated. This idea proved utopian. Since plans were voluntary rather than required and since the various ministries lacked control over even the nationalized sectors, targets remained hortatory, even if they were often reached. Mendès-France recognized this when he formulated a reform of the economic structure which would have required that nationalized companies follow the plans. He felt that public corporations "have too often followed their own interests, sometimes with good results, but without adhering to the Plan."[9]

[7] François Perroux, *The Fourth French Plan*, trans. Vera Lutz (London: National Institute of Economic and Social Research, 1965), p. 58.
[8] See Mendès-France, *République moderne*, p. 58.
[9] Ibid., pp. 146ff.

The plans, then, were placed in a seemingly rationalized and institutionalized structure that hid the real alliances and operational coalitions. Although businessmen and civil servants generally aligned themselves against the unions, there were also coalitions among them. Typically, representatives of the planning commission who participated on the modernization committees were expansionist in outlook and aligned themselves with representatives of large businesses, who had similar views. Finance ministry representatives were typically stability-oriented and tended to align with representatives of smaller businesses, who were less willing than their bigger colleagues to take risks. In reality, then, the plans did not result from a *concertation* of economic forces, nor from a direct confrontation of interest groups and civil servants. The mystification of plans persisted, however, in spite of efforts on the part of union leaders and certain civil servants to demystify it.

A vigorous expanding economy produced the illusion that planning was primarily responsible for France's new economic order. Moreover, the mythology of planning popularized the notion that French *indicatif* planning not only used sophisticated techniques for controlling and orienting economic activities, but also was processed within a democratic order, parallel to the representative body, which provided a direct confrontation between the state and interest groups outside the control of the legislature. Just as the efficacy of planning was an illusion, so was its democratic framework, which Bauchet recognized in the conclusion of his classical study of French planning.[10]

By the time the Fourth Plan was implemented in 1962, French planning had reached its apogee both in prestige and effectiveness. By then statistical gathering had become greatly facilitated by the willingness of businesses to furnish previously hidden data to the government, and a mature national accounting procedure had been developed. The plan was heralded by civil servants in the planning commissions as the

[10] Pierre Bauchet, *Economic Planning: The French Experience* (New York: Frederick A. Praeger, 1964), p. 249.

foundation of French postwar economic expansion and as evidence of the technical proficiency, which economists had developed for controlling economic growth in a mature capitalist economy. Their views seemed justified by several factors.

First, the development in planning had been accompanied by a period of economic growth unprecedented in France; industrial production had grown 250 percent between 1946 and 1962.[11] However, in reality, it was difficult, if not impossible, to separate the role of economic planning from other factors encouraging growth.[12] Recovery from the wartime devastation was responsible for much of the initial growth, and it was fostered by Marshall Plan aid and the prosperity induced by industrial orders in the Korean War. Then, just as the economy began to slow down at the end of the 1950s, the currency devaluation of 1958 and the subsequent implementation of the Rome Treaty gave productivity a new impetus. But all of these factors were hidden beneath the surface of the mystique of planning whose prestige had grown out of proportion.

Second, planning's contribution to economic growth was the result of the so-called conspiracy-to-plan on the part of businessmen and the *hauts cadres* of the civil service. Shonfield attributes planning to their alliance:

Since the government had a substantial part of the nation's economic activity under its direct control and exerted an indirect, though powerful, influence on a great deal more, it was not too difficult to convince private business that its decisions would be more intelligently made, over a wider range of industry, if they were made in unison with the public authorities. Similarly, many of the objectives of the public sector depended for their fulfillment on the cooperation of privately owned business. Both sides had an interest

[11] *United Nations Statistical Yearbook*, 1963, p. 98.
[12] For an elaboration of these other factors, see Charles P. Kindleberger, "The Postwar Resurgence of the French Economy," in Stanley Hoffmann et al., *In Search of France* (Cambridge, Mass.: Harvard University Press, 1963), pp. 118–58.

in limiting the element of unpredictability in their operations.[13]

The alliance was abetted because businessmen and high civil servants belonged to the same socioeconomic class and often knew each other well. They both graduated from the *grandes écoles* and never lost the *esprit du corps* that persists among their alumni.[14] Moreover, their relationship was made even closer with the accelerating rate of *pantouflage* during the 1950s (the name given the recruitment by businesses of directors and managers from the civil service corps). By 1964, for example, more than 20 percent of the alumni of the Ecole Nationale d'Administration (ENA) had moved from the civil service into directorships of industrial firms and banks.[15]

Finally, the elaboration of four plans had been accompanied by the development of refined and complicated techniques for orienting and controlling the economy. The very institutionalization of a planning mechanism had resulted, moreover, in a rather large bureaucratic structure whose personnel had a vested interest in planning. Their constant propagandizing on behalf of *indicatif* planning was reechoed by journalistic reports received by a population that had no reason to disbelieve them.

THE CRISIS IN FRENCH PLANNING

Planning had originally been constructed as a purely administrative task. The initial plan, the aim of which was the implementation of a coherent postwar recovery program in a period when economic resources were scarce, had reinforced

[13] Andrew Shonfield, *Modern Capitalism: The Changing Balance of Public and Private Power* (London: Oxford University Press, 1965), pp. 128ff.

[14] For detailed analyses of the relationships between the *cadres* of the civil service and directors of large businesses, see Nicole Delefortie-Soubeyroux, *Les Dirigeants de l'industrie française* (Paris: A. Colin, 1961).

[15] "Une Promotion de l'E.N.A.," *Entreprise*, June 22, 1963, p. 50.

this belief. Furthermore, the confrontation of socioeconomic groups in the Modernization Committees seemed an adequate means of gaining the approval of the groups concerned. Because increased productivity meant increased profits and wages, management, unions, and civil servants all gained. However, as planning became institutionalized, and after postwar recovery was completed, the goals of planning had changed. More and more the government came to see planning as a tool not only for economic development but also for facilitating structural changes in the economy. These changes naturally had political implications.

The transformation in the ends of planning was made more obvious by the change of regime from the Fourth to the Fifth Republic. Gaullist Cabinets began to fashion a plan for domestic and international political ends. At the same time, the political and socioeconomic forces affected by planning began to rebel against the administrative framework in which it was cast and to advocate a democratization of planning. Such a change would have transferred the confrontation from the Modernization Committees to the CES and to Parliament. Four distinct groups, in fact, advocated this transformation, each for different purposes: these were the trade unions, the clubs, the CES and parliamentary leaders themselves.

The trade union leaders were the first to react to the purely administrative procedure of planning, for they had been largely ignored in the Modernization Committees. As Table 11 indicates, the number of union officials participating in the modernization councils increased from the Second to the Fourth Plans, but the trade unionists were still overshadowed by the representatives of management and the civil service. When the Modernization Committees were appointed for the Fifth Plan, union representation was doubled, but by then, for a number of reasons to be examined below, the whole process of planning had changed, so that this increased union representation was meaningless.

The various union groups were the first to organize conferences for the purpose of discussing reforms which could democratize planning. A conference in June 1959, sponsored by the Catholic Confédération Française des Travailleurs Chrétiens (CFTC), issued a report entitled *Pour une Planification démocratique* that called for the establishment of workers' councils and reforms at the level of the firm and the region as the basis of democratization.

Union officials argued that they were unjustly treated because business representatives and civil servants misinterpreted their goals as revolutionary. In an important conference on the decision-making structure of planning sponsored by the Fondation Nationale des Sciences Politiques, Marcel Gonin, Secretary-General of the CGTC, declared that the Left was no longer animated by the myth of the strike and that it was ready to participate politically in the formulation of plans. He asserted that even they would take into consideration short-term antiinflationary goals.[16]

The political clubs were, in general, sympathetic to the reforms submitted by union leaders and leftist parties, and they

TABLE 11

Representation in the Modernization Committees

Group	First	Second	Third	Fourth
Labor union officials	77 (16%)	34 (6%)	52 (7%)	114 (11%)
Farmers and farm managers	19 (4%)	21 (3%)	22 (3%)	20 (1%)
Heads of corporations	108 (22%)	137 (23%)	119 (17%)	198 (20%)
Civil servants	118 (24%)	184 (30%)	201 (29%)	202 (20%)
Management officials	59 (11%)	95 (16%)	140 (20%)	239 (24%)
Other experts	113 (23%)	133 (22%)	170 (24%)	233 (24%)
Total	494	604	704	1006

Source: Ambassade de France, *France and Economic Planning* (New York: 1963), p. 6.

[16] See Marcel Gonin in *Colloque sur la planification comme processus de décisions*, Cahiers de la Fondation Nationale des Sciences Politiques, No. 140 (Paris: FNSP, 1965), pp. 90–91.

felt that if Parliament were involved in the planning process there would develop a politicization of economic-policy issues, which were technical and which should be determined by experts. At the same time, they feared that in areas where real political decisions were needed, such as the general orientation of the plan in terms of economic growth, incomes policy, and structural reforms, parliamentary control would be impossible, if only because Parliament would be limited to debating proposals made by the Cabinet. In general, the clubs actually feared that either as an administrative decision-making process, or as a democratic process involving a Parliament where the Gaullists were in a majority, such a plan would become a significant plank in the electoral platform of de Gaulle in 1965.

The CES, like the trade unions, was juridically linked to the planning process from the beginning, but was ignored during the informal bargaining processes among business interests and civil servants. Although the CES was constitutionally required to be consulted, the First Plan was promulgated by decree without the advice of the CES. By 1951 a law was passed, requiring that the CES make annual reports and recommendations on the implementation of the plan. Yet the role of the CES remained limited. When the Fourth Plan was under preparation, the CES finally began to play a more important role. This happened not only because of pressure from the membership of the Investments and Planning Section but also because Massé saw in the CES an ally to be used against the Ministry of Finance in advocating expansionist policies.[17] Giscard d'Estaing had been fighting to cut the CGP's 5 percent growth forecast. Massé, trying to find support, then submitted the proposed plan to the CES, giving it plenty of time to consider the growth rate. The Investment and Planning Section criticized the plan, as Massé knew it

[17] The clash between Giscard and Massé and their divergent policy positions are documented in Richard B. Duboff, "The Decline of Economic Planning in France," *Western Political Quarterly*, xxi (1968): 98–109.

would, suggesting a 6 percent rather than a 4.5 percent yearly growth target. Since members of the CES were heavily represented on the General Economic and Financial Committee, the Modernizaton Committee that synthesized the work of all the others, they finally were able to influence the government to adopt a 5.5 percent yearly growth target for the Fourth Plan in spite of the protests of the conservative representatives of the Ministry of Finance.

The increased activity of the CES in planning so disturbed Parliament that it enacted the Law of August 4, 1962 not only approving the Fourth Plan but also requiring the consultation of Parliament in the initial stages of future planning. This law represented to the deputies and clubs the real democratization of the planning process and a step away from the centralized administrative decision-making procedure of the Gaullist regime. But the participation of Parliament in the planning procedure also represented an important transformation in the philosophy of planning in France.

Originally, planning was represented as a process in which all the economic and social forces of the country were integrated for the national interest. If Parliament were involved, it was feared that deputies would change their minds too quickly and disrupt the organic nature of the plans. When Parliament did vote on the plans, it was only a symbol of the approval of an orientation and did not involve debates over substance. Even in the Fourth Plan, Parliament saw it only after it had been formulated and the vote on it was only a kind of sanction of the national will. The participation of Parliament after the Fourth Plan, however, gave recognition that planning had become a political act, requiring the sanction of political representative institutions.

Three external factors helped in the implementation of a democratized plan. First, the split between Massé and Giscard d'Estaing reinforced the argument of those in Parliament wishing to see it recoup some of its lost prestige by participating in the plan. Both Massé and Giscard felt that they

293

could gain the support of Parliament in their argument against the other. Giscard felt that the Gaullist majority would be conservative in monetary policy and advocate a reduced goal for economic expansion, while Massé felt that if Parliament could participate actively in the planning process the plan would reflect the interest of the French nation in expansion.

Second, a change in the planning process necessitated a change in the structure of the confrontation and of the decision-making process involved in the plan. Economic objectives no longer aimed only at an increase in productivity; they also encompassed structural changes in the economy that required political decisions. The politicization of the Plan thus resulted because structural objectives ran counter to the short-term interests of both business and union representatives in the Modernization Committees. Furthermore, these structural changes were linked with objectives concerning national security and independence that required parliamentary approval in that they were political rather than economic choices. And they were linked with regional planning objectives that also ran counter to the short-term interests of various socioeconomic groups.

Third, it must be recalled that the implementation of the plan occurred in the final phases of the Algerian settlement. When Giscard promised Parliament that it could have an important and effective role in the elaboration of future plans in a speech before Parliament in June 1962 he therefore must have had the approval of de Gaulle, who was not at the time reluctant to increase the stature of Parliament as one more means of gaining a consensus for the Algerian settlement. This was all the more important since the Gaullist majority was tenuous in 1962. Having lost the support of the political Right by the independence of Algeria, de Gaulle found it necessary to secure support from the Left.

On June 23 with the promise of future participation in the early stages of planning, the Assembly overwhelmingly approved, by a vote of 410 to 98, the bill to which was appended the text of the Fourth Plan. The bill, approved by the Senate in July and implemented on August 4, contained the following provision as Article Two:

> The government shall submit to Parliament a bill regarding a report on the principal choices involved in the preparation of the plan before the Planning Commission is given directives. These choices should relate to regional planning, as well as to economic expansion, the breakdown of GNP with regard to investment and consumption, the desired structure of consumption, the direction of social policy and regional policy.[18]

Parliamentary leaders understood that by this law the CES and Parliament in the future would not be presented with an already established plan in which nothing basic could be changed, but that both groups would be able to choose from among the larger options the basic hypotheses upon which the plan would be elaborated. Only then would the *Commissions de Modernisation* be able to establish the details of the plan that would conform to the choices made by the national representative bodies. However, this optimistic attitude toward a democratization could never occur both because of changes in alliances among interest groups concerning planning decisions and because of other changes in the formal and informal decision-making processes associated with the plan.

Although a national accounting system had been developed by 1962, which would provide greater coherence than ever before for planning, a variety of other developments occurred that resulted in a decrease in the control of planners over the economy. That this crisis was recognized is attested to by the ease with which the democratization of planning was accepted and by the orientation report on the Fourth Plan, the first ten pages of which detailed a justification of

[18] Law No. 62–900. See *Journal officiel, lois et décrets* (August 6 and 7, 1962), p. 7810.

the plan. Eight separate elements can be singled out of the interrelated phenomena that by 1962 had eroded French *indicatif* planning.

First, there were certain contradictions regarding planning inherent in the Gaullist regime. It was only after the change from the Fourth to the Fifth Republic that French governments had been entirely mobilized behind the planning procedure. Thus, in the middle of the Third Plan in 1960, the Cabinet decided to implement a *plan interimaire* to diminish the gap between original goals and the results brought about by the devaluation of 1958 and the Algerian War. Furthermore, beginning with the Fourth Plan, the budget became part of the plan in order to ensure its coherence. But this commitment to planning was undercut by several factors summarized by Boissonat as follows:

> First, this regime, which aimed to strengthen the authority of the state, ended by emptying the organs of the administration of their power, and, to a certain degree, of their responsibilities, to the benefit of a patriarchal power that could not do everything. . . .
>
> Gaullism, in the second place, places emphasis on the grandeur of France in its military and diplomatic efforts, for which it seeks out the support of opinion by promising the French that this will not prevent them from living peaceably. . . .[19]

Second, and related to the first factor, is the contradiction that existed because of the prestige that planning had in France and the consequent unwillingness on the part of planners to abandon outmoded elements. Only in 1965 could it be publicly declared that "it was in France itself that planning seemed to be brought into question, and above all by the State, which now acted in such a way as to seem to renounce that which it had idealized."[20] But the government continued

[19] Jean Boissonat, "Le Ve Plan et la crise de la planification française," *Esprit*, February 1965, pp. 403–04.

[20] Michel Garibal, "Le Gouvernement veut-il encore un plan?" *Revue politique et parlementaire*, No. 760 (1965): 19.

to support planning because of its prestige. It was, after all, created by de Gaulle in the postwar period, and was envied and copied by other Western states, including Britain. Moreover, de Gaulle insisted upon the necessity of planning in 1962 partly to distract the population from the bitter loss of Algeria and to direct its attention to the future rather than the glorious past. Thus, de Gaulle referred to the plan as *la grande affaire* and *l'ardente obligation* of the nation, enhanced by its already great prestige at a time when its usefulness was being seriously questioned.

Third, the very success of planning in increasing the productivity of French business corporations revitalized a capitalist spirit and this in turn, ended the need to provide a conspiracy-to-plan between French businessmen and civil servants. The *patronat* had developed a new expansionist attitude almost diametrically opposed to its protectionist heritage. The development of large business corporations from mergers was accompanied by a rehabilitation of the profit motive and a call by both the *jeunes patrons* and the Conseil National du Patronat Français (CNPF) for a *renaissance des libertés* of the entrepreneurial class.[21] Calls for freedom of action could only mean an end to the submission of business to state controls and the termination of the close working relationship among businessmen and civil servants in the Modernization Committees. In short, the very logic of the planning endeavor developed a distinctly antiplanning bias among business executives.

Fourth, the fiscal and monetary requirements of long-term planning increasingly lost their priority and gave way to the exigencies of short-term antiinflationary policies. A year after the Fourth Plan was implemented, a *plan de stabilisation* was substituted for it, cutting down investments and preventing expansion. The increased priority of short-term fiscal policy was not only antiinflationary, however, but was also tied to the Gaullist international monetary policy aimed at maintain-

[21] These arguments are summarized in Pierre de Calan, *Renaissance des libertés* (Paris: Plon, 1963).

ing a strong currency and weakening the international role of the dollar.

Fifth, there were changes in the objectives of planning that could not be realized by the type of confrontation that had been institutionalized by Monnet. The plans aimed at structural changes rather than productivity goals. Rather than targeting a number of units of a product to be manufactured, the plans began to target the optimum size and capacity of industries. Other objectives were made in the light of a policy of independence in world affairs. Neither of these types of goals were amenable to integration within socioeconomic groups that stood against them.

Sixth, the plans began to foster regional development to counteract the strangulation of the economy by overconcentration in the Paris basin. In January 1963 the president appointed a *Commission Nationale à l'Aménagement du Territoire* (CNAT, National Committee for Integrated Development), which was associated with the CGP. Subsequently, a battery of administative reforms was introduced to develop a regional rather than national economic decision-making structure. France was divided into twenty districts in addition to Paris in which regional action was to occur. These districts were headed by a regional prefect who was made the direct representative of each ministry over all the ministerial services and who headed an interministerial mission of civil servants acting as his Cabinet.

Since planning was aimed at structural changes that would take place on a regional level, Regional Committees took over the function once performed by the Modernization Committees. The old Monnet confrontation formula was thus transferred from the level of economic sectors to that of the regions. The purpose of concerted regional action was to provide a center for pooling of information and a framework fostering the carryover from elaboration to implementation of regional plans. Just as no national accounting or statistical system existed when the *économie concertée* was introduced via the Modernization Committees, no regional statistical data service was then available. The Regional Expansion Development Committees were to serve as information pools from which plans could be made, just as the Modernization Committees served the sectors in the postwar period.

The regionalization of the plan, which transferred the confrontation from the Modernization Committees to the Regional Expansion Committees, necessitated a *débudgetisation*, which crippled the CGP by abolishing its control over economic inducements for businesses. Under the new budgetary process, the regional prefect would take charge of channeling investments so that businessmen would no longer come to the CGP or Finance Ministry to get their funds, but would go to the regional prefect. Thus, while the plan could become more sophisticated in its elaboration, it was stifled in its implementation.

Seventh, the changes in the objectives of planning and concomitant change in the planning process had changed the role of the CGP from a coordinator of long-range planning to a center of day-to-day economic decision-making. That the CGP would assume this role was a natural outgrowth of its central position under the Prime Minister and as coordinator of the various ministries in economic matters. But it was also both a result of and a further impetus to short-term economic policy-making. The short-run policies long advocated by the Finance Ministry have become necessary by the urgency of controlling inflationary pressures to keep France in a competitive position in the Common Market. Furthermore, the Modernization Committees, which were in the domain of the CGP, had lost their importance and gave way to the Regional Economic Development Committees acting under the supervision of the regional prefects. The CGP, as a result, lost its primary function, but gained new importance.

Eighth, the efforts to regionalize the plan as well as the administrative reforms discussed above were affected by the implementation of the Rome Treaty and the establishment of the Common Market.

The implementation of the Rome Treaty, producing sys-

temic interdependencies among the economies of the EEC
countries, in itself, would have made planning impossible
along the lines created by Monnet. The rules governing trade
and competition under the Rome Treaty introduced unknown
factors into the forecast calculus and took from the French
government the monetary and fiscal control that it could previously use to orient the economy to meet the goals of the
plan.[22] The lowering of tariff barriers and of labor frontiers
necessitated by the Common Market made it impossible for
the planning commissioners to predict the growth of trade or
the increase in labor power that would result. Without hard
data for either factor, predictions on economic growth became highly tenuous. At the same time, the EEC required the
maintenance of fixed exchange rates with the other European
currencies, thus taking from the government the important
monetary instrument that could have been used in trade. And
the introduction of similar value-added taxes and the limitation placed on government subsidies and investments in private corporations removed some fiscal controls. French planners had two reactions to the dilemma brought about by the
Common Market. The first reaction was to transfer *planification française* from the French state to the EEC.[23] The second was the regionalization of the planning.

First, initiatives were made in the EEC in 1962 and 1963,
and became a *cause célèbre*. They provoked a bitter controversy, especially between the French, who saw it as a necessity, and the Germans, who regarded it as anathema. The
French planners had a great influence on the European Commission, which, in drafting its action program for the second
stage of implementation of the Rome Treaty, foresaw the

[22] For a full discussion, see Malcolm C. MacLennan, "The Com-
mon Market and French Planning," *Journal of Common Market
Studies*, iii (1964): 23–46. See also Bela Balassa, "Whither French
Planning?" *Quarterly Journal of Economics*, lxxix (1965): 537–54.

[23] See Etienne Hirsch, "French Planning and its European Application," *Journal of Common Market Studies*, i, (1962): 125ff.

need for a middle-range plan similar to the French one.[24] When discussions on the action program reached the European Parliament, there arose a debate between two Germans, President of the European Commission Hallstein and German Economic Minister Erhard.[25] Marjolin, the European Commissioner from France who was responsible for planning, and Hallstein had asserted that a modern economy required a policy of active intervention and that the general welfare article of the Rome Treaty (Article 2) implied a need to go beyond anticyclical policy through the agreement upon long-range communitywide targets. Erhard, however, a neo-liberal economist, felt that central planning was contrary to the spirit not only of the Rome Treaty but also of the German federal political system. A compromise was eventually reached, which was more semantic than structural. Instead of being called a plan, the EEC's medium-term economic policy was called a programme. One reason for the eventual agreement was that the Germans gradually saw the need for planning and to accept broad economic planning in Germany.[26]

The first French efforts had a good theoretical base in the need for planning derived from interdependence in a common market. In the first place, there was a need to draw up either a general planning policy for the European Communities or

[24] EEC Commission, *Memorandum de la Commission sur le programme d'action de la Communauté pendant la deuxième étage* (October 24, 1962). Obviously the Commission took the opportunity to strengthen potentially the community's institutions, which was made possible by a European plan.

[25] European Parliament, *Débats, session, 1962–1963*, November 19–23, 1962, pp. 51–56.

[26] Reasons for the change included the need to control inflation in Germany and to find a way to increase productivity once large scale immigration from East Germany ended. See Geoffrey Denton, *Planning in the EEC: The Medium-Term Economic Policy Programme of the European Economic Community*, European Series No. 5 (London: Chatham House, 1967), pp. 17–18.

a general point of view under which particular national policies could be harmonized, for reasons similar to those in a national community. In addition, however, there was a special need foreseen in a common market because of the effects of such a market on existing regional disparities.[27] According to theory, economic development is an uneven process that favors certain regions endowed with natural resources, manpower, communications and transportation.[28] Further industrial growth, as provided by increased trade in a common market, works to the advantage of those central regions that have already developed economic overhead facilities and interindustry relationships. In the absence of diseconomies of agglomeration, underdeveloped areas tend to lose ground to the dynamic and developed centers. The dangers resulting from such disequilibria are twofold in the context of the EEC. On the macro-plane, the underdeveloped areas became economic burdens on the dynamic centers and tend to slow the overall growth of the Community. On the social plane, the relative worsening of the economic conditions in certain areas are contrary to the welfare objectives of the various member states as well as of the Rome Treaty.[29]

[27] Herbert Giersch first noted this theoretical probability. See his "Economic Union between Nations and the Location of Industries," *Review of Economic Studies*, No. 2 (1949–1950), pp. 87–98. François Perroux's models are based on an elaboration of Giersch in *L'Europe sans rivages* (Paris: Presses Universitaires de France, 1954), pp. 274ff. Even economists who disagree with this notion as an imperative do not rule out its danger. They generally tend to argue for the coordination of national regional policies. See, for example, Paul Romus, *Expansion économique régionale et communauté européenne* (Leiden: Sijthoff, 1958).

[28] For an analysis of the merits and deficiencies of this model, see Bela Balassa, *Theory of Economic Integration* (Homewood, Ill.: Richard D. Irwin, 1961), pp. 121–210.

[29] These issues were further elaborated upon in EEC Commission *Rapports de groupes d'experts sur la politique régionale dans la C.E.E.* (Brussels: EEC, 1964). See also Jean Rey, "The Economic Community's Role in Mediterranean Europe," *Journal of International Affairs*, XIX (1965): 163ff.

The European plan was necessarily weak, however, for three reasons. First, the other European states in the EEC were unwilling to accept the kinds of economic controls that French planning necessitated. Second, even if they had been willing to accept the idea of middle-range planning, no European civil service existed to implement a European plan. Moreover, the French government would have been the last to countenance the control of its economy by a European civil service of *apatrides*. Finally, the EEC, even with a European Investment Bank, did not have at its disposal the required resources for investment purposes. The result, on the European level, was an ineffectual *politique au moyen terme* implemented in 1966 but lacking the spirit and force of the French *économie concertée*.

The second reaction of the French planners was the regionalization of the plan discussed above, which saved it but meant the demise of the CGP as the central economic decision-making body in France. In fact, it was the change in a decision-making structure for French planning that occasioned the transformation of the CGP into a central advisory body for governmental, day-to-day decisions in economic and social matters. In short, for reasons derived from interdependence within the EEC from changes in foreign policy under de Gaulle, and from changes in domestic decision-making, planning as it had been formulated in France in the 1950s passed out of existence in the 1960s.

The eight factors singled out above reinforced each other and interacted to bring an end to the type of planning to which French economic policy-makers had grown accustomed. They were not entirely perceived until after the Fifth Plan was elaborated because the new effort to democratize the plan camouflaged the crisis stage that planning had entered. The full extent of the demise of planning did not become apparent until the laborious process of formulating the Fifth Plan was underway. And, when that did take place, it quickly became apparent that de Gaulle was attempting to use the plan less for the purpose of orienting domestic social goals than for harnessing the domestic economy for external purposes.

THE FORMULATION OF THE FIFTH PLAN:
THE ECONOMY AND FOREIGN POLICY

Like previous plans, the Fifth Plan was to be elaborated in two stages. During the first stage, the growth targets would be selected, and during the second, the details of the plan would be elucidated and approved by the various socioeconomic and political groups.

Superficially, the chief innovation of the Fifth Plan was the introduction of parliamentary participation in both stages of its development. During the debate on the Fourth Plan in the spring of 1962, Parliament passed a bill that democratized the planning process by bringing about CES and parliamentary participation in its early stages. Only after Parliament had passed a bill approving a report on the major options to be considered in a plan could the modernization committees fill in the details, working on the choices made by the legislative body. This first stage was to be implemented in the fall of 1964 in three phases. First, the CGP together with the statistical office of the Ministry of Finance was to present a report enumerating several options upon which the representative bodies would debate. Second, the CES was to study the options and send its recommendations to the CGP, which would then revise them. Finally, the Investments and Economic Planning Committee of the National Assembly was to examine the options and send recommendations to the Assembly which would pass a bill selecting the basic options upon which the plan would be elaborated in the second stage.

Meanwhile, however, a new innovation was introduced which gave the Fifth Plan a framework different from that of other plans. Before the Fourth Plan was formulated, the CGP drew up a ten-year prospectus on economic growth, which listed the basic goals at which the plan would aim. This time, however, the "Groupe 1985" was appointed by the

304

Premier in 1962 to formulate a twenty-year projection of growth outlining long-range productivity and social targets. It was felt that a forecast that projected into the next generation would reveal an economic structure entirely different from the one existing in the early 1960s.

The report of the "Groupe 1985" was submitted in its final version to the Premier on September 10, 1964. Unlike the group that produced the decade forecast for the Fourth Plan, this group did not come under the supervision of the CGP, but rather under the CNAT. Working for a two-year period in various groups on the regional level, the CNAT provided the real center for the integration of socioeconomic forces. And this confrontation occurred *before* the formal structure and mechanisms for formulating the Fifth Plan were set in motion. The central position of the CNAT in the formulation of this report is noteworthy, for it represents the changing integration of interest groups from the CGP's modernization committees to the CNAT's regional economic development committees.

It was only as a result of the report, called "Horizon '85," that Massé's group could complete its report to the CES on the options of the Fifth Plan. This was done on September 23, when it was immediately obvious that the Fifth Plan fit perfectly into the framework created by "Horizon '85." The draft immediately evoked two basic questions which were central to the discussion of the CES: Is a plan useful? Is planning any longer possible?

The *projet d'options* presented to the CES was based on three factors. First, it took account of the increase in the active population based on natural demographic growth, immigration (70,000 per year), and an exodus from rural to urban areas (110,000 per year). Second, it outlined certain *impératifs* including full employment, the maintenance of economic growth, and increases in social overhead capital including schools, roads, hospitals, and housing. Third, it took into account the final opening of frontiers in the EEC and the world, and the consequent need of maintaining a commercial balance and a competitive position. In addition, the forecast accounted for two elements fixed by the government independent of the prospects for economic growth: (1) the total of military expenditures as a percentage of the GNP equal to that of 1964; and (2) aid to underdeveloped countries, fixed at 1.5 percent of the GNP. Thus, the plan was to be used as a device to assure the government freedom to implement its foreign-policy goals.

As a result, the report of the CGP outlined five groups of options to be discussed by the CES and Parliament. But no choice was actually allowed, for the so-called options were interdependent hypotheses based on a fixed rate of growth projected at 5 percent per year. The CGP argued that if the growth rate were lower, the social and economic targets would be unobtainable; and if they were higher, an insufficiency of manpower and an investment bottleneck would result. This single hypothesis was unexpected and disrupted the planning procedures. When Parliament passed the 1962 bill, it had fully expected to be presented with a series of projections among which it would select one. This was to have been the innovation on the democratization of planning.

The Section du Plan of the Council gave its report to the plenary session on October 27 and 28. This was the so-called Chardonnet Report, named after the *rapporteur*, that represented neither approval nor a rejection of the plan. Rather, it was a competent analysis containing serious doubts on the possibility of realizing the basic options of the Massé report. In addition, it clearly rejected the social options which the government had presented. The Council approved the Chardonnet Report with a vote of 88 to 27 with 53 abstentions. However, in 1961 the Fourth Plan was approved by a vote of 130 to 15 with 42 abstentions.

Briefly, the Chardonnet Report noted that the projected 5 percent yearly growth would be impossible to obtain given the stabilization policies of the government—policies invoked for foreign-policy purposes. It hoped that the government was not merely issuing pious wishes in its belief that the self-financing of industries would reach the 70 percent level, especially given the absence of available investment funds. Moreover, it indicated that the government had presented a bulletin of electoral propaganda for the 1965 presidential elections rather than an economic plan.

The report severely criticized the social aspects of the plan for which semiausterity was advocated, objecting to the maintenance of the work week and age of retirement; the expected rises in gas, electrical, and transport costs; and a minimal increase in consumption. Such measures were clearly against the interests of consumers and designed to support a foreign policy.

Massé, who appeared before the Council during the debates, promised that these suggestions would be taken into consideration when the government *projet d'options* was presented to Parliament. In fact, however, the report, which the CGP published on November 4, only slightly modified the report it had sent to the CES.[30]

After the plan reached Parliament, Louis Vallon, *rapporteur* of the Assembly's Budget Committee, issued a report to the plenary session on the first day of debate. The report lauded the government bill, but had serious reservations on the means by which the government could implement its targets. The report had been approved by the committee by the vote of 14 to 3 (PCF) with 5 abstentions from the Center.[31] The Assembly began to debate the Fifth Plan on November 24 and continued the debates for three days. The basic issues were the same as those brought up in the CES. As Drouin editorialized in *Le Monde*, "It would be risky, however, to feed upon too many illusions. The margin of choice left to the deputies has been highly limited."[32] Parliament had, in short, been left in the same position that it found itself when it debated the Fourth Plan. It had practically no choice to make other than to accept or reject the Fifth Plan altogether.

[30] *Le Monde*, November 6, 1964, p. 11.
[31] *Le Monde*, November 19, 1964, p. 22.
[32] *Le Monde*, November 25, 1964, p. 1.

On the second day of debate Premier Pompidou spoke at length on what he hoped would issue from the debates on the Fifth Plan, a new form of decision-making based on

the fundamental collaboration between the executive and legislative branches. . . .

In effect, the plan is not, in our eyes, a technical document formulated by specialists. It is the proof of our will not to abandon ourselves to events, to abnegate the law of *laisser-faire*, which is in these matters the sister of fate, allied to fortune and accomplice of injustice. It is a task of the political authorities to take charge of economic life, to give it our mark, the mark of our reason and spirit. It is also the demonstration of the will of France to live and grow, to lift itself up to the most severe international competition, to assure, domestically, the most harmonious development of its regions, the equalization of individual opportunities, and the bringing together of conditions. It is, and it will be, in the last analysis, the affirmation that Frenchmen want to become masters of their future and to construct a future of prosperity and social justice.[33]

He clearly defined the role of the plan as the Cabinet perceived it. Aimed at economic expansion and stability, it would result in the modernization of industries and would consequently strengthen the French economy so that it could remain independent of the economies of other states. The contradiction between this goal and the obligations and goals of the Rome Treaty did not escape editorial or parliamentary attention. Nor did the fact that the government now saw the plan as a central instrument of its foreign policy.

The most lively interchange occurred on the final day of debate between Deferre and Debré. Their dialogue was obviously more political than constructive. This was the first time since Debré was reelected that he took a major legislative role. He was seeking the attention to announce his candidacy

[33] *Débats parlementaires*, November 26, 1964, pp. 558ff.

for Premiership after the 1965 election. Deferre was at the time a potential socialist candidate for the Presidency. Debré constructively pleaded for acceptance of the plan and, eloquently defending the social and economic choices, emphasized the first priority should be given to military expenditures and foreign aid.[34] Deferre, however, denounced the danger of industrial colonization by the United States, the excessive military expenditures of the government, and the small appropriations in the plan allotted for housing, schools, hospitals, and other social measures. The debate, in short, was over the question of whether the Fifth Plan ought to be used predominantly for either external or domestic purposes.

The government had performed a *tour de main* by deciding upon an econonic policy designed to bolster French economic independence without any confrontation of political or economic groups. Parliament was presented a *projet de loi* on basic options that, in fact, contained no options at all. And the government's majority passed the bill with no difficulty. If the opposition groups in the Assembly complained that there was no real democratization in the elaboration of the plan, Pompidou countered their argument saying that the plan was not a political tool.

After the Parliament "selected" the basic options for the plan, the task remained of specifying the detail. In the spring of 1965 as in the past, Modernization Committees were appointed to examine the possibilities of implementing the plan in the various sectors of the economy. The traditional confrontation of socioeconomic forces was established and again the appearance persisted that the elaboration was proceeding normally. The regional confrontation, it is to be remembered, had already taken place in the outlining of "Horizon '85." However, there were increasingly apparent certain indications that the basic options of the plan were, in fact, dictated by Gaullist designs for France's future. In a press conference on February 4, 1965, de Gaulle declared that the plan would

[34] *Débats parlementaires*, November 27, 1964, pp. 5624–74.

be used as an instrument for implementing all French domestic policy in the desire to create a society that was neither capitalist nor totalitarian.[35] This was, in fact, one foreign-policy slogan of the government in its effort to create a third force. Later that spring, Pompidou, on television, enunciated the plan, saying that first priority must be given to investments in industry and agriculture for the purpose of modernizing the economy, and that sacrifices for the interest of the nation would be required of all consumers.[36]

Two days after the Cabinet accepted his report, Massé issued the final synthesis of the plan at a press conference on July 30. It was then obvious that the plan had been created independent of the confrontation in the Modernization Committees. For the committees not only had not yet formulated their reports, but were still conducting their inquiries on the basic options. Massé, in an act of bad faith, congratulated the Modernization Committees, still meeting, for their work.[37]

Finally, at his press conference of September 9, de Gaulle confirmed that the Fifth Plan was formulated with certain foreign-policy goals in mind and that it would be an important plank in the platform of the Union pour la Nouvelle République (UNR) whether he or another Gaullist sought the Presidency in December. He devoted the first part of the press conference to the plan, eloquently demonstrating that it was a Gaullist creation and that it was under a Gaullist regime in which the plan had been fully democratized.

> There has undoubtedly been decisive progress made in planning such as we adopted and instituted it at the time of the Liberation, in the wretched state in which we then found ourselves, which was then fairly neglected during the time when our economic life depended to a great extent on loans from abroad, and which was finally put into effect

[35] *Major Addresses, Statements and Press Conferences of General Charles de Gaulle, March 17, 1964–May 16, 1967* (New York: Ambassade de France, Service de Presse et d'Information, 1967), p. 92.

[36] Ibid., p. 77.

[37] *Le Monde*, July 21, 1965, p. 2.

and honored since we regained our independence in this field as in the others.[38]

The plan was to be transformed into a blueprint for revitalizing the economic potential of the state and to put France into the economic front rank of nations. It was to prepare France for the expanding competition not only within the EEC but also with the most highly industrialized countries:

As the threat of general war ceases to smother the world and brutal conquest to tempt the strongest, progress will become a world-wide aspiration. Science, technology and industry will open up to each developed country the opportunity to strengthen this hope and to spread it. The speed of communications and the multiplicity of contacts among peoples will create in all a growing desire to deal with one another. Thus, competition will more and more be the springboard of a legitimate ambition. That is why France wants to have the means for this.[39]

The plan, which Massé presented to the CES, was hardly different from the *projet d'options* presented the previous year. The examination by the Section du Plan was thorough and lasted from August 31 to September 17. Finally, Chardonnet issued another highly critical report, which was approved almost unanimously by the members of the committee. He condemned the plan on three grounds. First, he pointed out that the plan would be implemented in the midst of terrible uncertainties, including the future of the EEC. He questioned the value of the forecasts in agriculture, commerce, productivity, and price levels, and suggested that the plan remain dormant until after the Common Market crisis was resolved. Second, he objected to the manner in which the plan was elaborated, especially its formulation before the reports of the modernization committees were known. Third, he criticized the fiscal and social content of the plan as un-

[38] *Major Addresses, de Gaulle, March 17, 1964–May 16, 1967,* p. 92.
[39] Ibid., p. 94.

realistic and contradictory because not enough funds were available for either social reforms or investments, let alone both.[40]

Chardonnet then asked that the government severely modify the plan before it presented it to Parliament and that it resolve technical inconsistencies and propose adequate monies for social goals. The Chardonnet Report was then sent to the membership for discussion at the plenary session (September 18–30). Jeanneney, a former Minister of Industry, offered a counterproposal less critical than Chardonnet's and approved by the government. He suggested only a partial reexamination by the government of certain points of detail, but his proposal was rejected on September 29 by a vote of 115 to 41 with 26 abstentions.[41] The same day Massé told the CES that the government would not leave the EEC, which was enough encouragement to obtain the support of the members of the *patronat* for the government's bill. Finally, on September 30, the CES accepted the Chardonnet criticism by rejecting the plan by 112 to 1 with 68 abstentions.[42] In summary, the CES reviewed the plan of the Massé commission, registered formally its disagreement with the whole of the content of the Plan in financial and social spheres and demanded that the government change it before submitting it to the National Assembly.

The government virtually ignored the Chardonnet Report. At the Council of Ministers meeting on October 7, the Cabinet approved Massé's report of July 26 with modifications involving only *précisions* and *éclaircissements*, thus denying the requests of the CES, which had asked the government to change the text before submitting it to Parliament.

The Finance Committee of the Assembly was presented the text of the plan by Pompidou and Massé on October 19. Pompidou insisted that all the necessary consultations had been carried out in accordance with the options selected by

[40] *L'Année politique*, 1965, pp. 139–44.
[41] *Le Monde*, October 1, 1965, p. 20.
[42] *Le Monde*, October 2, 1965, p. 21.

the Parliament. He said that the plan was coherent and that it would be implemented within the framework provided by the expansion of trade in the Common Market. The following day, Chardonnet appeared before the committee and repeated the criticisms he made in his report to the CES. Rather than answer his criticisms, the deputies of the majority only responded with optimism. When Vallon reported the Committee's recommendations to Parliament he gave a simple approval of the government's proposal, barely veiling his criticism of the manner in which the plan was elaborated. On November 5, after debate, Pompidou accepted two minor modifications on the regional aspects of the plan and the Assembly accepted the government's bill by a vote of 283 to 184 with 9 abstentions. Those voting against the bill included all Socialists, Communists, and a majority of Independents and Center Democrats.

The government had, in effect, stifled the debate by mustering its majority. Unlike the debate of 1964, no cogent criticisms were launched. The representatives of the opposition realized that the government had used the democratization of the planning process as a means of preventing any confrontation of either socioeconomic or political representatives in the elaboration of the plan. Instead, it resembled a governmental decree. The government was able to deflect the criticism of the manner of elaboration as well as of the content of the plan because the oncoming presidential campaign was in the center of the nation's political concerns. In fact, on November 6, the day after the Assembly passed the government's bill, de Gaulle announced that he would run for the Presidency in December.

Conclusions

This case study of the elaboration of the Fifth Plan has shown the domestic decision-making that resulted from the conjunction of external and internal influences. Externally, the opening of French borders to the Common Market has increased the sensitivity of the French economy to external events and has made the implementation of 1950s-style planning extremely difficult to implement. Internally, the domestic political and economic system had changed so that the goals and means of planning had to adapt to new circumstances. Whereas the initial plans for modernization and development had established a formal confrontation of traditional socioeconomic forces, which together ideally harmonized their efforts to make forecasts and goals for the economy, the very success of planning, together with external factors derived from international interdependence, brought an end to the situation that had made the confrontation possible. Instead, the process of planning was changed so as to include the formal political bodies of the representative institutions.

But the so-called democratization of the plan resulted in the total politicization of planning as a political tool of the executive branch. Clearly, the plan was formulated solely in the framework of a Gaullist image of the requisites of independence. The omission of the confrontation among the socioeconomic or political interests of the state was reflected in a cogent criticism of the plan on the arbitrary manner in which it was elaborated, the contradictory objectives that it contained and the inadequate means it foresaw to implement its goals. The plan thus came to represent the mobilization of the domestic economy in the service of foreign policy.[43] Even here, however, given the subsequent history of the Fifth Republic, the role of the plan seems to have been aborted both by the diminishing role of France in the late 1960s and the revolt of domestic interests against the mobilization of domestic society for external ends.

[43] See Robert Gilpin, *France in the Age of the Scientific State* (Princeton, N.J.: Princeton University Press, 1968), pp. 218–52.

EIGHT

CONCLUSIONS

THE patterns of French foreign policy in the 1960s exhibit an acute counterpoint between idiosyncratic objectives and the constraints imposed upon their attainment by the growth of new forms of international interdependence. This interplay is, however, by no means a characteristic peculiar to France's external relations. Rather, as a result of the trenchant definition of nationalist objectives in Gaullist thought, the French case crystallizes what has become a general problem in the conduct of foreign policy for the highly modernized societies —namely, how to attain objectives that have become imperative and to preserve historically derived cultural values in the face of domestic and international pressures that impede the rational control of public policy.

French foreign policy has been examined in a few selected areas, including defense autonomy, the reform of the international monetary system, and crisis manipulation in the EEC, in order to illustrate this universal problem. By emphasizing those aspects of recent French foreign policy that have more general implications, it has highlighted conditions common to France and other highly modernized societies as well.

The French case has been invoked as a test of a partial theory of foreign policy as well as for illustrative purposes. A single case test is, of course, not entirely a satisfactory device. Ideally, the set of problems adumbrated by the theoretical analysis should be examined in other highly modernized societies, and, they should be contrasted with relatively non-modernized societies of both the present and past. But the French case does present a good test precisely because the rhetoric of its foreign policy so markedly emphasized a particularistic approach to external relations that superficially seems to contradict the general theoretical framework of the book. This is one of the advantages of a theoretical study based on a single case. So long as the case is well selected, it can provide a test that can be used with a high degree of confidence. The selection of that case involves the precise delineation of a larger universe to which the generalizations are meant to apply. It also means that the sampling from that universe ought to be based upon apparently counterfactual evidence as a means of providing critical validation. And, it requires that the theory subjected to testing must be logically coherent. If these criteria are applied, a single case test should be as significant as a multicase analysis, at least as a preliminary check.[1]

This study, then, has been concerned with French foreign policy and with a broad set of problems that have become increasingly central to the statecraft of the industrialized states. The duality between a particular case study and the wider universe to which it belongs inevitably introduces a fundamental tension into a study such as this. There is always the risk that the individual case will be treated inadequately and that the model will suffer in the quality of its elaboration and application. The ambivalence in treatment is inherent in the kind of analysis to which French foreign policy is submitted, and is made all the more apparent by the difficulties encountered in reconciling particular and general aspects of explanation. If, however, the problems delineated in this book are as significant as the analysis indicates, such tensions ought to be accepted insofar as the juxtapositions are illuminating.

The degree to which nation-state values were the primary concern of Gaullist statecraft, especially after 1962, has pointed up vividly the ways interdependence among societies has eroded national autonomy in international affairs. What had been latent elsewhere in the world was made fully manifest by de Gaulle's France. The impulses toward independence in international affairs, regardless of their origins, have

---

[1] I am indebted to my colleague Harry Eckstein for his own analysis of single case studies for many of these arguments.

remained a fundamental factor in international life. However, the numbers and types of conditions that can be handled in the nation-state context have been changed. This is as true for a state of great scale, such as the United States, as it is for one of small scale, such as Luxemburg.

National autonomy has both domestic and external aspects. Domestically, national autonomy implies the independence of political authorities from their constituencies as a requisite for maneuverability abroad. The independence of political leadership from domestic politics was the central theme around which de Gaulle molded the constitution of the Fifth Republic. This theme reflected the monarchic tradition of foreign policy that was central to Gaullist thought. Political leadership, for de Gaulle, was based on the ability of the leader to act strategically abroad, to take surprise initiatives, and, above all, to maintain a constant offensive in interactions with the leaderships of other states.

When de Gaulle found that both his and France's political independence became difficult to maintain, he was faced with two general options. These two options represent the limits of the spectrum of options open to the leadership of any highly modernized state. He could, on the one hand, have surrendered executive autonomy to the demands arising from domestic society and tried to balance one against the other to achieve compromise solutions. Or he could have mobilized the whole of domestic society for the achievement of external goals.

Neither solution can be solely maintained in the long run. The first option opens the state to encroachments from abroad that might prevent the attainment of fundamental domestic goals. The second, which is based on the politicization of the electorate, creates new demands on a government that would likely have a predominantly domestic orientation.

De Gaulle chose the latter option in 1962. This meant that if he was to achieve his external goals, he had to do so quickly. Otherwise the momentum that was built up by politicization would overcome the autonomy of the executive. There is good reason to believe that de Gaulle understood this, and therefore took initiatives in NATO and the EEC, toward Eastern Europe and in the international monetary system to establish the basis of a more viable long-term independence. But politicization occurred sooner than de Gaulle had anticipated. The events of May and June 1968 initiated demands that de Gaulle had tried to restrain during the previous decade, especially those for welfare and social service expenditures since they undermined the domestic aspect of the policy of independence.

Either option points up one of the salient features of all highly modernized states—the erosion of the distinction between foreign and domestic affairs. Since this distinction cannot be made over the long run—even over a period of a few years—in any modernized society, the maintenance of a rational foreign policy, with all of the denotations of a formal definition of rationality, is very difficult. As long-range and consistent policies become less salient features of modernized states, *ad hoc* relationships are likely to become increasingly important.

If the domestic-foreign distinction is eroded significantly with increased levels of modernization, the distinctions that have traditionally separated individual states, or societies, from each other are also diminished. As modernization proceeds, the levels and types of interdependencies among societies inexorably increase. De Gaulle understood this in the context of systemic interdependence, and in both domestic and international relationships de Gaulle wanted to define a central position for France that reflected his image of it, before interdependencies were so high that they impeded greater maneuverability. Again, events overcame the Gaullist strategy. The series of crises in the international monetary system, including the one precipitated by the events of May 1968 aborted the French position for monetary reform as well as the conditions for an independent nuclear force. Interdependence, in short, increases both the unanticipated consequences of policy and the degree to which autonomy can be maintained.

The manner in which interdependence was confronted in French policy is suggestive of the way it may be met in the foreign policies of other similar states. This is true in both the extreme of independence as an ideal or goal and that of crisis as an effect or outcome. Modernization has eroded both the independence of the political executive in domestic affairs, and the autonomy of a state in international affairs. Interdependence at the international level has not been accompanied by the institutionalization of transnational political institutions. Instead, the nation-states must confront the problems that arise from transnational society.

Increased levels of interdependence imply the increased institutionalization of structures of transnational society. Without hierarchical political institutions, cooperation or policy harmonization among states has become the norm rather than the exception. In everyday policy-making, it has become impossible for any state to achieve its objectives in isolation. Even the most common objectives require some form of international collaboration, especially those pertaining to wealth or welfare.

The circumstances involved in daily decision-making apply in crisis decision-making. Interdependence in the absence of transnational political institutions has meant that there is an increasing probability that crises originating in any one part of international society will affect people elsewhere. In order to prevent crises from going awry, cooperation in *ad hoc* decision-making at the international level has become more and more significant.

Again, the French case has been instructive. In seeking to secure a central position for France in the EEC where systemic interdependence had become fundamental, de Gaulle saw the implications of crisis decision-making. But the success of this kind of politics in agriculture veiled the dangers of crisis decision-making when the crises were less manipulated than unanticipated. As the handling of unanticipated crises, as explained in Chapters 2 and 6, will assume a greater importance in the diplomacy among the modernized states in the next decade, institutionalization of decision-making similar to that in the ten major reserve currency countries can be expected.

Both the politicization of society and the growth of systemic interdependence are specifically pertinent to economic policies since high levels of modernization have been accompanied by a concern for wealth and its more equitable distribution. Economic aspects of statecraft in forms other than traditional mercantilistic ones were also significant in France under de Gaulle. The imperative of assuring national well-being, which results from politicization, and the opportunities for increasing it through international interdependencies have resulted in the transference of politics from issues that are transcendental to those that are empirical. The political and economic aspects of the relationships among the highly modernized societies have been merged; political acts are now seen as economic and vice versa.

A final aspect of French statecraft that represents a more generalized phenomenon is the appearance of mutability. The ideal of Gaullist foreign policy was, in institutional terms, the establishment of a political apparatus that would permit relative permanence and continuity in foreign policy. Yet in confronting interdependence with its sudden crises and unanticipated events, attempts to define or implement any sort of permanent order were constantly voided. Even if an independent executive were organized around a structure enhancing flexibility, the dissolution of the distinction between foreign and domestic affairs creates such constraints that policy becomes highly inflexible, at least in the long run.

Continual movement, unanticipated crises, and the paradoxical inhibition of flexibility are also developments of modernization. Modernized societies and the relationships among them are undergoing continuous and rapid transformations, characterized by constant breakdowns and creations, which respectively restrict and aid international institutionalization. On the one hand, transnational activities are largely responsible for the currency crises that have plagued the industrialized states in recent years. In this context, changes in exchange rates are inevitable, even in the EEC where they hinder the maintenance of the CAP. With the establishment of uniform prices for agricultural products, currency realignments were ruled out. When currency realignments took place, as in 1969 and 1971, the result was a temporary breakdown of a communitywide agricultural policy. At the same time, however, needs for new forms of institutionalization have arisen. The problems that were involved in the currency crises of the late 1960s have yet to be solved. Multinational corporations and their role in the increased mobility of capital have largely escaped the controls that exist under the political framework of national governments. New initiatives for controlling them by widening the scope of international cooperation have begun in the EEC. Since the problem is essentially one that affects the whole system of highly industrialized states, institutionalization is required.

The continual breakdowns in and creations of new institutions in the relations of modernized societies also raises the question of whether interdependencies have risen too quickly among the industrialized states to be managed in their present form. There is no general law that describes the growth of interdependence internationally as an inexorable phenomenon. As long as the national framework for decision-making exists, it is likely that national decision-making, such as the French devaluation of August 1969, can be used to restrain the growth of interdependence and even to reverse them for short periods. Both choices, that of restraining interdependence or that of making great leaps forward, carry heavy political costs in freedom or wealth. The balance between costs and benefits, however, is not likely to be reached on a wholly rational basis; international independence erodes rational strategy too severely. More likely, it will occur via *ad hoc* decisions made to meet new crisis situations. Even with a theoretical understanding of the contemporary situation, controls are too insufficient to permit rational strategy in low-policy affairs.

The turn of events taken in the relationships between France and the other modernized states are summed up in a paradox that is the most general implication of this study of the foreign policies of France in the 1960s. This is the paradox of high modernization as now known. Modernization has had a double effect on international relationships. It has hardened the psychological barriers between peoples and apotheosized the nation-state. The political sense of "belonging" and the structures of political mobilization have remained confined within the context of the nation-state. But with increased modernization, the actual processes of interactions have been at levels that transcend the individual political community. The dual reality of transnational interdependence and national sovereignty is the central feature of international politics today. The Gaullist experiment in facing interdependence has been completed. It demonstrates both the importance of crisis decision-making and also the need for ideas that soften psychological barriers among different nationalities. Its implications for the future of international affairs in the West are momentous.

INDEX

administrative tradition, 19f
agricultural policy, 77, 82
Ailleret, C., 94
Albrecht-Carrié, R., 144n
Algerian War, 77, 93; effects on
    French foreign policy, 106
alliance and interdependence,
    126f
Allison, G. T., 36n
allocation of resources, 156–200
Alting von Geusau, F.A.M.,
    19n, 252n, 261
Ambler, J. S., 153n
Amme, C. H., 93n
ancien régime, 133–36
Andrews, W. G., 93n, 107n, 109n
Antiphon, R., 159n
Ardagh, J., 112n, 166n
army, reorganization, 154f; and
    society, 153. *See also*
    defense policy
Aron, R., 23n, 139n, 151n, 194n
Arrow, K., 58n
autarchy, 76
autonomy, bases of, 151f, 200;
    domestic demands and, 148;
    foreign economic policy
    and, 205; as goal of foreign
    policy, 149; illusion of, 106,
    112f; and independence,
    16, 95; limitations on,
    125f, 128, 200; requisites of,
    118; unintended
    consequences, 112f.
    See also collective goods,
    C. de Gaulle, and
    interdependence
Avril, P., 19n
Axelrod, R., 256n

Baillou, J., 35n, 37n
balance of power tradition,
    130, 140–44
Balassa, B., 73n, 75n, 300n, 302n
Bank for International
    Settlements, 224
Banque Nationale de Paris, 230
Barraclough, G., 99, 144n
Barthélémy, J., 9n
Bassett, W., 214n
Bator, F., 215n
Bauchet, P., 287n
Baumgartner, W., 230, 239
Baumol, W. J., 89n
behavior, rational, 57f, 66, 89f
Black, C. E., 11n, 12n, 98n
Bloch, H. S., 214n
Boissonat, J., 171n, 296n
Bon, F., 188n
Brenner, M. J., 201n
Bretton Woods Conference, 206
Brezhnev Doctrine, 201
Brown, B., 107n, 110n
Buchan, A., 43n, 95n
budgetary process, 177–80
burden sharing, *see* North
    Atlantic Treaty Organization
bureaucratic politics and foreign
    policy, *see* foreign policy

Calan, P. de, 297n
Callaghan, J., 242
Calleo, D. P., 59n
Cambon, J., 9n, 140
Cameron, E. R., 144n
Camps, M., 83n, 266, 272n
capital, mobility of, 208f
Carr, E. H., 157n
Carré, J. J., 170n

European Econ. Com. (*cont.*)
objectives, 30, 35; regional
planning, 300–303;
value-added tax, 78–81.
See also, crisis, functionalism,
C. de Gaulle, international
integration, planning, and
Treaty of Rome
European Investment Bank, 303
European Launcher Development
Organization (ELDO), 199
European Monetary Agreement,
208
European Payments Union,
208, 227
European recovery and
convertibility of currencies,
208
European Space Research
Organization (ESRO), 199
Evans, J. W., 269n
events of May 1968, 95: effects
on defense budget, 183;
effects on foreign policy,
156, 248, 318; French
educational reform and,
166; French foreign
monetary policy and, 246f;
governmental priorities and,
176; information policy and,
197f; legitimacy of the
Fifth Republic and, 167

Fabra, Paul, 217n, 221n, 233n
Feis, H., 126n
Ferris, P., 231n
Ferry, J., 140
Fifth Plan, *see* planning
Fifth Republic: Constitution,
107f; Constitution and
foreign policy, 17–19;
legitimacy of, 167, 191–93.
See also, C. de Gaulle

force de frappe, 94, 154, 181:
cost, 183; domestic politics
and, 33; opposition to,
193–95; popularity, 175.
See also, defense policy,
foreign policy, C. de Gaulle
Force Nucléaire Stratégique, see
force de frappe
*Forces de Défense Opérationnelle
du Territoire* (DOT), 154
Forces d'intervention, 154
foreign aid, 160–63
foreign policy: autonomy and,
16–18, 94, 106, 112f, 117,
149–52, 167; bureaucratic
politics and, 36f; censorship
and, 196; case studies,
315–22; consistency of, 41f;
contents, 25; control of,
38f, 68; defined, 13–15;
dimensions of, 24f;
diversionary tactics, 185,
188–91; domestic social
demands and, 32–35;
economic policy, 72; effects
on domestic policy, 22f;
governmental organization
and, 36–38; instruments,
68; limitations, 125f;
merging with domestic
policy, 57; objectives, 67;
objectives and modernization,
25–35, 45; outcomes, 25;
primacy of, 14–19, 148;
processes, 25, 36f. *See also*
autonomy, crisis, defense
policy, dilemma of rising
demands and insufficient
resources, economic growth,
events of May 1968, *force
de frappe*, C. de Gaulle
geography, *grandeur*, high
politics, interdependence,

326

Passeron, A., 77
Pavitt, K., 172n, 173n
Paxton, J., 78n, 83n
Pelletier, P., 35n, 37n
perception and policy, 100
Perroux, F., 286, 302n
Peterson, W. C., 166n
Pickles, D., 107n, 108n
Pigou, A. C., 88
Pinay, A., and devaluation of
    1958, 216f
Pinder, J., 52n, 59n, 78n, 59n, 80
Pitts, J. S., 186n
plan de stabilisation (1963),
    121, 174
planning, 42, 80, 279–314; and
    CES, 292; changes in goals,
    290; crisis in, 289–304;
    democratic institutions and,
    282; democratization of,
    293–304; effects of Treaty
    of Rome, 299–303; Fifth
    Plan, 281–84; 304–14;
    Fourth Plan, 292–96;
    Gaullism and, 297;
    Modernization Committees,
    284–96; Parliament and,
    292–314; political clubs and,
    291f; as a political
    instrument, 282; success,
    288f; technocracy and, 282;
    trade unions and, 290f
policy instruments and
    objectives, 40f, 258f, 277
policy-making and direct
    confrontation, 109
politicization of economic affairs,
    102, 257f
Pompidou, G., 109n, 308–313
Preeg, E. H., 269n
private consumption, 171
Pryor, F. L., 91n, 152n
public goods, *see* collective goods

Quester, G. H., 142n

Ranke, L. von, 14
Ranney, A., 24n
rationalism in France, 133
referenda, 188f; of 1962, 108;
    of 1969, 38; and presidential
    leadership, 187f
research and development,
    172–74
reserves, monetary, *see* liquidity
Rey, J., 302
Richelieu, Cardinal, 141
Rolfe, S., 217n
Rome Treaty, *see* Treaty of Rome
Romus, P., 302n
Roosa, R., 233
Roosevelt, F. D., 152
Rosenau, J. N., 7n
Rossi-Doria, M., 81n
Rueff, J., 216n, 217n; and
    devaluation of 1958, 174,
    216f; and international
    monetary reform, 218
Russett, B. M., 10n, 53

Sanguinetti, A., 33n
savings and investment, 171
Scheinman, L., 93n
Schelling, T. C., 262, 263n
Schuman Plan, 127
Schuman, R., 128n
Schweitzer, P.-P., 206
Schweizer, S., 212n
Sedan, 141
Serfaty, S., 61n
Shonfield, A., 289n
Silberner, E., 30n
Silj, A., 59n
Simon, H., 35n
Special Drawing Rights (SDR),
    277, 240–50
speculation, 243
Spengler, J. J., 138–40

Books Written Under the Auspices
of the Center of International Studies
Princeton University

Gabriel A. Almond, *The Appeals of Communism* (Princeton University Press 1954)

William W. Kaufmann, ed., *Military Policy and National Security* (Princeton University Press 1956)

Klaus Knorr, *The War Potential of Nations* (Princeton University Press 1956)

Lucian W. Pye, *Guerrilla Communism in Malaya* (Princeton University Press 1956)

Charles De Visscher, *Theory and Reality in Public International Law*, trans. by P. E. Corbett (Princeton University Press 1957; rev. ed. 1968)

Bernard C. Cohen, *The Political Process and Foreign Policy: The Making of the Japanese Peace Settlement* (Princeton University Press 1957)

Myron Weiner, *Party Politics in India: The Development of a Multi-Party System* (Princeton University Press 1957)

Percy E. Corbett, *Law in Diplomacy* (Princeton University Press 1959)

Rolf Sannwald and Jacques Stohler, *Economic Integration: Theoretical Assumptions and Consequences of European Unification*, trans. by Herman Karreman (Princeton University Press 1959)

Klaus Knorr, ed., *NATO and American Security* (Princeton University Press 1959)

Gabriel A. Almond and James S. Coleman, eds., *The Politics of the Developing Areas* (Princeton University Press 1960)

Herman Kahn, *On Thermonuclear War* (Princeton University Press 1960)

Sidney Verba, *Small Groups and Political Behavior: A Study of Leadership* (Princeton University Press 1961)

Robert J. C. Butow, *Tojo and the Coming of the War* (Princeton University Press 1961)

Glenn H. Snyder, *Deterrence and Defense: Toward a Theory of National Security* (Princeton University Press 1961)

Klaus Knorr and Sidney Verba, eds., *The International System: Theoretical Essays* (Princeton University Press 1961)

Peter Paret and John W. Shy, *Guerrillas in the 1960's* (Praeger 1962)

George Modelski, *A Theory of Foreign Policy* (Praeger 1962)

Klaus Knorr and Thornton Read, eds., *Limited Strategic War* (Praeger 1963)

Frederick S. Dunn, *Peace-Making and the Settlement with Japan* (Princeton University Press 1963)

333

Arthur L. Burns and Nina Heathcote, *Peace-Keeping by United Nations Forces* (Praeger 1963)

Richard A. Falk, *Law, Morality, and War in the Contemporary World* (Praeger 1963)

James N. Rosenau, *National Leadership and Foreign Policy: A Case Study in the Mobilization of Public Support* (Princeton University Press 1963)

Gabriel A. Almond and Sidney Verba, *The Civic Culture: Political Attitudes and Democracy in Five Nations* (Princeton University Press 1963)

Bernard C. Cohen, *The Press and Foreign Policy* (Princeton University Press 1963)

Richard L. Sklar, *Nigerian Political Parties: Power in an Emergent African Nation* (Princeton University Press 1963)

Peter Paret, *French Revolutionary Warfare from Indochina to Algeria: The Analysis of a Political and Military Doctrine* (Praeger 1964)

Harry Eckstein, ed., *Internal War: Problems and Approaches* (Free Press 1964)

Cyril E. Black and Thomas P. Thornton, eds., *Communism and Revolution: The Strategic Uses of Political Violence* (Princeton University Press 1964)

Miriam Camps, *Britain and the European Community 1955–1963* (Princeton University Press 1964)

Thomas P. Thornton, ed., *The Third World in Soviet Perspective: Studies by Soviet Writers on the Developing Areas* (Princeton University Press 1964)

James N. Rosenau, ed., *International Aspects of Civil Strife* (Princeton University Press 1964)

Sidney I. Ploss, *Conflict and Decision-Making in Soviet Russia: A Case Study of Agricultural Policy, 1953–1963* (Princeton University Press 1965)

Richard A. Falk and Richard J. Barnet, eds., *Security in Disarmament* (Princeton University Press 1965)

Karl von Vorys, *Political Development in Pakistan* (Princeton University Press 1965)

Harold and Margaret Sprout, *The Ecological Perspective on Human Affairs, With Special Reference to International Politics* (Princeton University Press 1965)

Klaus Knorr, *On the Uses of Military Power in the Nuclear Age* (Princeton University Press 1966)

Harry Eckstein, *Division and Cohesion in Democracy: A Study of Norway* (Princeton University Press 1966)

Cyril E. Black, *The Dynamics of Modernization: A Study in Comparative History* (Harper and Row 1966)

Peter Kunstadter, ed., *Southeast Asian Tribes, Minorities, and Nations* (Princeton University Press 1967)

E. Victor Wolfenstein, *The Revolutionary Personality: Lenin, Trotsky, Gandhi* (Princeton University Press 1967)

Leon Gordenker, *The UN Secretary-General and the Maintenance of Peace* (Columbia University Press 1967)

Oran R. Young, *The Intermediaries: Third Parties in International Crises* (Princeton University Press 1967)

James N. Rosenau, ed., *Domestic Sources of Foreign Policy* (Free Press 1967)

Richard F. Hamilton, *Affluence and the French Worker in the Fourth Republic* (Princeton University Press 1967)

Linda B. Miller, *World Order and Local Disorder: The United Nations and Internal Conflicts* (Princeton University Press 1967)

Henry Bienen, *Tanzania: Party Transformation and Economic Development* (Princeton University Press 1967)

Wolfram F. Hanrieder, *West German Foreign Policy, 1949–1963: International Pressures and Domestic Response* (Stanford University Press 1967)

Richard H. Ullman, *Britain and the Russian Civil War: November 1918–February 1920* (Princeton University Press 1968)

Robert Gilpin, *France in the Age of the Scientific State* (Princeton University Press 1968)

William B. Bader, *The United States and the Spread of Nuclear Weapons* (Pegasus 1968)

Richard A. Falk, *Legal Order in a Violent World* (Princeton University Press 1968)

Cyril E. Black, Richard A. Falk, Klaus Knorr and Oran R. Young, *Neutralization and World Politics* (Princeton University Press 1968)

Oran R. Young, *The Politics of Force: Bargaining During International Crises* (Princeton University Press 1969)

Klaus Knorr and James N. Rosenau, eds., *Contending Approaches to International Politics* (Princeton University Press 1969)

James N. Rosenau, ed., *Linkage Politics: Essays on the Convergence of National and International Systems* (Free Press 1969)

John T. McAlister, Jr., *Viet Nam: The Origins of Revolution* (Knopf 1969)

Jean Edward Smith, *Germany Beyond the Wall: People, Politics and Prosperity* (Little, Brown 1969)

James Barros, *Betrayal from Within: Joseph Avenol, Secretary-General of the League of Nations, 1933–1940* (Yale University Press 1969)

Charles Hermann, *Crises in Foreign Policy: A Simulation Analysis* (Bobbs-Merrill 1969)

Robert C. Tucker, *The Marxian Revolutionary Idea: Essays on Marxist Thought and Its Impact on Radical Movements* (W. W. Norton 1969)

Harvey Waterman, *Political Change in Contemporary France: The Politics of an Industrial Democracy* (Charles E. Merrill 1969)

Cyril E. Black and Richard A. Falk, eds., *The Future of the International Legal Order*. Vol. I: *Trends and Patterns* (Princeton University Press 1969)

Ted Robert Gurr, *Why Men Rebel* (Princeton University Press 1969)

C. Sylvester Whitaker, *The Politics of Tradition: Continuity and Change in Northern Nigeria 1946–1966* (Princeton University Press 1970)

Richard A. Falk, *The Status of Law in International Society* (Princeton University Press 1970)

Klaus Knorr, *Military Power and Potential* (D. C. Heath 1970)

Cyril E. Black and Richard A. Falk, eds., *The Future of the International Legal Order*. Vol. II: *Wealth and Resources* (Princeton University Press 1970)

Leon Gordenker, ed., *The United Nations in International Politics* (Princeton University Press 1971)

Cyril E. Black and Richard A. Falk, eds., *The Future of the International Legal Order*. Vol. III: *Conflict Management* (Princeton University Press 1971)

Francine R. Frankel, *India's Green Revolution: Political Costs of Economic Growth* (Princeton University Press 1971)

Harold and Margaret Sprout, *Toward a Politics of the Planet Earth* (Van Nostrand Reinhold 1971)

Cyril E. Black and Richard A. Falk, eds., *The Future of the International Legal Order*. Vol. IV: *The Structure of the International Environment* (Princeton University Press 1972)

Gerald Garvey, *Energy, Ecology, Economy* (W. W. Norton 1972)

Richard Ullman, *The Anglo-Soviet Accord* (Princeton University Press 1973)

Klaus Knorr, *Power and Wealth: The Political Economy of International Power* (Basic Books 1973)

Library of Congress Cataloging in Publication Data

Morse, Edward L.
   Foreign policy and interdependence in Gaullist France.

   "Written under the auspices of the Center of International Studies,
Princeton University."
   Includes bibliographical references.
     1. France—Foreign relations—1945–   2. France—Politics and
government—1958–   I. Title.
DC412.M588   327.44   72–5391
ISBN 0–691–05209–3